# AS SAFE AS IN
# NEW YORK HARBOR . . .

The *Norness* was en route from New York to Halifax with a load of fuel oil when, sixty miles off Montauk, a torpedo struck without warning.

The captain was asleep at the time, but awoke immediately. "Nobody was expecting a submarine so close in American waters. I thought we were as safe there as in New York Harbor." By 0137, the captain had revised his opinion. He rushed onto the deck and directed the lowering of all lifeboats, motorboats, and rafts.

The youngest member of the crew, seventeen years old, was blown off the deck when a second torpedo slammed into the starboard side; another man fell into the frigid sea when a lifeboat capsized. These two men claimed the dubious honor of becoming the first victims of the U-boat war that would take the lives of hundreds.

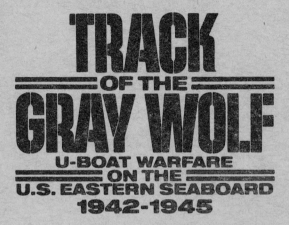

# TRACK
## OF THE
# GRAY WOLF
## U-BOAT WARFARE
## ON THE
## U.S. EASTERN SEABOARD
## 1942-1945

# GARY GENTILE

AVON BOOKS  NEW YORK

The author would like to acknowledge John Vandereedt of the National Archives, and (in alphabetical order) Gina Akers, Bernard Cavalcante, Kathy Lloyd, and Mike Walker, all of the Naval Historical Center, for their expert research assistance.

Except where noted, all photographs appearing in the insert are courtesy of the National Archives.

TRACK OF THE GRAY WOLF is an original publication of Avon Books. This work has never before appeared in book form.

# CONTENTS

# Dedication

"Victims of a relentless and unremitting submarine campaign in the waters of the North Atlantic, who can point to any whose sacrifice has been greater—in order that this nation might triumph over its foes?

"No stripes or bars to show that war was their profession. It was not. Yet war came to them in its most tragic form as they followed their chosen work—the sea . . .

"We who have sailed with these officers, we who knew them ashore, know that in their passing we have lost some of our closest friends, and our hearts are heavy with that loss. Yet we are cheered, and we know their loved ones are comforted, in the knowledge that they have left behind a memory that will ripen into a hallowed tradition."

—from "That This Nation Might Live," published in the Jersey Standard Tanker Officers Association *Review* for February–March 1942

# INTRODUCTION

"It is submitted that should enemy submarines operate off this coast, this command has no forces available to take adequate action against them, either offensive or defensive."
Commander North Atlantic
Naval Coastal Frontier
December 22, 1941

For only the second time since the War of 1812, the line of battle was brought to the coast of the contiguous United States. On January 15, 1942, headlines across the nation proclaimed the sinking of an unarmed merchantman only sixty miles off Long Island, New York. The Panamanian freighter *Norness* was sunk by a torpedo whose blast was heard across the country.

The American military was caught by a jab that was closer to home than expected. To civilians, the attack was as shocking as the bombing of Pearl Harbor. Defense experts had expected it, but their admonitions fell on deaf ears. After all, as soon as the U.S. entered the First World War, Germany sent submarines to the East Coast in order to sink ships, cause disruption, and lower morale. They succeeded admirably. Germany gained from the experience. America did not: she still believed in insularity, and defense by distance.

Modern German *untersee boots* were not intimidated by the long crossing of the Atlantic Ocean any more than their forebears had been. A generation of technology created a new underwater fleet with greater cruising range and more powerful armament. When Hardegen fired his

1

first torpedo from the *U-123*, it was a harbinger of death and destruction that would plunge the U.S. East Coast into a virtual blackout. For the next six months, people living along the shore got used to seeing flames on the horizon, aiding shipwrecked sailors, and watching blimps and planes and vessels of all descriptions fighting the submarine menace.

These gray wolves of the sea seldom left a wake, but their tracks were as distinct as the tracks of their namesake.

Over a hundred steel merchantmen were sunk in an area from Maine to Georgia designated as the Eastern Sea Frontier. At first, the undersea raiders fired torpedoes indiscriminately as they reached the East Coast and worked their murderous way south. They sank ships unopposed by U.S. Naval forces who were not yet versed in the ways of war. Gradually, as coastal defense became an American priority, weapons were brought to bear against enemy submarines. Planes and ships dropped bombs and depth charges; ships ran in convoy.

By mid-July 1942, the ESF was so well-protected that Vizeadmiral Karl Doenitz shifted his U-boat operations to the safer and more productive Caribbean front. Coastal U-boat activity dropped to practically nothing. During the next three years only a handful of ships were attacked. Retribution was severe. Once the Navy was mobilized, East Coast commerce became relatively safe. Eventually, coastal shipping reverted to unescorted, independently running vessels.

*Track of the Gray Wolf* covers this intensely dramatic era when U-boats were the scourge of the merchant marine. Over forty enemy submarines were involved in attacks on more than one hundred seventy merchantmen. Some of these freighters and tankers survived, others were sunk but later salvaged. But most of them never resurfaced.

The story is a distinctly human one. Survivors' reports tell the tale from the merchant marine's point of view: of the horrible explosions that maimed and killed, of miraculous escapes, of frigid days at sea in open lifeboats, of the dropping off or freezing to death of the weak, of oil-soaked sailors burned to death in the crude slicks, of daring rescues.

The focus is on the men who lived through these terrible ordeals. There are no fictional, dreamed-up author's thoughts put into the minds of survivors. I have relied throughout on primary source material. Whenever available, I used actual testimony of the survivors and participants and quoted from interviews and sworn statements: there is no better way to capture the flavor of personal experience than through the words of those who were there.

As must be expected when researching any historic episode, much information is unavailable, misplaced, or destroyed. Direct testimony is not always possible, especially in cases where the seamen in question were foreign nationals and spoke no English. In some cases I had to interpret or interpolate occurrences from conflicting and contradictory reports. All this will introduce some minor errors of detail, consistent with the sometimes limited resources available for record keeping when there were lives to be saved and a war to be fought.

In any case, the purpose of this narrative is not to give every detail of every action in the North Atlantic, but to offer an overview of the trepidations of the merchant marine: to show their continued courage despite the adversity of their plight.

There is also the story of the daring submariners: the bombing and depth charging of their boats, the loss of their craft, their individual humanity, cowardice, or belligerence. The men who fought in U-boats were not necessarily Nazis or criminals, but merely soldiers. Of the ten U-boats sunk in the ESF, six were lost with all hands. From the survivors picked up from the other four, we learn that their story is just as tragic, and as historic, as that of the civilians and sailors, men, women, and children whom they sentenced to a watery grave. In order to preserve the German flavor of their story, all German Naval ranks are given in their own language. A Table of Comparative Ranks is included in the appendix.

Although the narrative is complicated, with many incidents running parallel, I have chosen to tell it in chronological approximation, except that the story of each ship is completed without reference to other calamities occurring simultaneously.

Occasionally, times and dates may be unprecise. In the exigencies of war, strict record keeping is not a prime directive. Errors creep in on the German side because U-boat logs (*Kriegstagebucher*, or KTBs) were kept in Central European Time, but action reports might have later been described in local time where the distinction between daylight and nighttime attacks is made.

The merchant marine generally followed local time, sometimes computed from Greenwich Mean Time when crossing time zones frequently. This leads to temporal confusion. A 1 A.M. SOS sent from two hundred miles off the coast might have been received by a shore installation at 11 P.M. the previous night; the action report therefore reflects an obvious contradiction. Besides, in the nightmare haste of abandoning a quickly sinking ship, the perception of time tends to become distorted.

In addition, German attack places and times may not coincide with the point of the ship's demise. This should be taken into consideration, especially when using the appendices. Because of the artificial midnight date changeover, a ship torpedoed at 11:30 on the night of the twentieth may have sunk an hour later—on the twenty-first. By the same token, two ships sunk an hour apart may be listed as having gone down on different days; or, two ships sunk twenty-three hours apart may be listed as having sunk the same day. (For simplicity's sake, except in quotation, I have used the less confusing twenty-four-hour clock.)

Even locations may be widely divergent. One could assume that a U-boat commander making a calm, controlled attack should have more accurate positional data. Yet, by the very nature of his clandestine operation, it might have been many hours, or even days, since his last accurate star or sun sighting. Merchant marine captains were in the habit of computing their positions continually; yet, there is a certain amount of dead reckoning between navigational fixes due to wind, current, and engine speed fluctuation. When a ship is

# Introduction

abandoned in the heat of battle, there is no time to pull out a sextant, chronometer, and a table of logarithms.

In most cases, the only recorded position of a beleaguered vessel is that taken by the attacking U-boat. The ship in question may not have sunk for hours, or days, and may have drifted quite far, so that her final resting place can be many miles from where she was torpedoed. Since I have dived to more than thirty of these sunken wrecks, and to three of the U-boats, located now by the sophisticated electronics of onboard Long Range Navigation (LORAN), I can attest to the disparity of the figures.

With the Japanese threatening one side of the country, and the Germans assaulting the other, the U.S. was beset by belligerent activity that put a strain on her protective resources while she was still pursuing the war aggressively on foreign shores. The only way to carry the line of battle to the enemy front was by ship. Production tonnage had to exceed losses. But ships were useless without the personnel to man them. In one sense, then, it can safely be said that the war was won by the civilian sailors who manned those ships. They took great risks against harsh odds.

The story of the East Coast U-boat war against the merchant marine has never been told in full. In fact, many Americans today are unaware that U-boats torpedoed and sank ships within three miles of shore, or laid mines off bays and harbors, or deposited spies on some lonely strand. The coastal war was one fought bitterly by those not trained in the ways of fighting, who received no compensation for their struggles, and who died horribly without recognition.

This book will set the record straight.

# 1942

# JANUARY

"TANKER TORPEDOED 60 MILES OFF LONG
ISLAND; NAVY PICKS UP SURVIVORS; WARNS
ALL SHIPPING"
            The New York Times
            Thursday, January 15, 1942

For the cost of three cents, anxious readers of the late
city edition of the *Times* received the frightening news
that war was once again coming to American shores.
This time it was not the distant island of Hawaii that was
under attack, but the mainland island adjacent to the most
densely populated territory of the United States—practically within hailing distance of the seat of federal
government.

After the surprise attack on Pearl Harbor, the Japanese
withdrew the Imperial Fleet and prepared for the next
assault against American Naval might. The West Coast
states of Washington, Oregon, and California geared up
for defense against the ships and planes from the land of
the rising sun, but, except for a few isolated incidents,
the expected invasion never occurred.

Weeks after the U.S. declared war against Japan and
her allies, Germany took the initiative and dispatched the
vanguard of a flotilla of solitary undersea raiders that was
to plague the American East Coast for more than six
months. Hitler's purpose was to reduce the number of
lend-lease cargoes reaching European Allied shores from
American ports.

To a certain extent, U.S. military authorities anticipated the possibility of a U-boat onslaught. Starting in

early 1941, the keels were laid for a large fleet of fast submarine chasers, equipped with depth charges and three-inch guns. None was yet in commission by the opening of hostilities; although a few were launched as early as the spring of 1942, they did not become operational in quantity until 1943. Congress authorized the construction of a host of helium-filled, non-rigid airships (better known as blimps) for patrolling the coastal waters. These, too, were unavailable at the onset of war. Considering the vast amount of damage suffered at Ford Island, and the exigencies of defensive and offensive measures against the aggressive Japanese in the Pacific theater, the U.S. Navy's Atlantic forces were understandably stretched thin.

Recognizing their unpreparedness and the imminence of U-boat incursion, the Navy issued a formal statement on December 20, 1941, explaining that local weather forecasts were being curtailed because they might provide valuable information to the enemy at sea. They theorized that weather movements as far inland as the Dakotas could provide accurate predictions to submarines operating in the North Atlantic.

In early January 1942, the Navy placed a defensive minefield off the approaches to New York Harbor. Meanwhile, Coast Guard vessels were impressed into Naval service, private yachts were purchased and converted into patrol boats, tugs and trawlers were armed for combat, and spotter planes ranged along the seashore searching for telltale wakes and unfamiliar conning towers. The Navy mobilized the ships and personnel at its command, and awaited the inevitable coming of the U-boats.

The wait was not very long.

Admiral Karl Doenitz, commander of Germany's U-boat arm, selected Kapitanleutnant Reinhard Hardegen as the first gray wolf to carry the war to American waters. After slipping through the British blockade, Hardegen took the *U-123* westward on a three thousand mile Atlantic voyage that proved uneventful until just before reaching his assigned area of operations. On January 12, some two hundred miles south-southeast of

Cape Sable, Hardegen spotted a target he could not ignore: the British liner *Cyclops*. He torpedoed and sank the aging steamship, with the loss of ninety-four passengers and crew, then quickly withdrew before Canadian patrol craft arrived on the scene to rescue survivors. Eighty-seven men, women, and children spent twenty hours in lifeboats, suffering from exposure and frostbite, until they were found.

Two days later, on the fourteenth, Hardegen crossed the boundary of the Eastern Sea Frontier and entered the realm of American history. The first ship he encountered was a modern, four hundred eighty-nine-foot-long tanker.

The *Norness* was a ship full of contradictions. Built in 1939 by the Deutsche Werft A.G., of Hamburg, Germany, for the Tanker Corporation, a Norwegian company, she was registered Panamanian. After Germany invaded Norway, the company moved its offices to New York and continued to operate on the side of the Allies. The *Norness* was en route from New York to Halifax with a load of fuel oil when, sixty miles off Montauk, a torpedo struck without warning against her port side.

Captain Hansen was asleep at the time but awoke immediately and pulled an overcoat over his pajamas. "Nobody was expecting a submarine so close in American waters. I think we are just as safe there as in New York Harbor." Hansen revised his opinion at 0137. He rushed onto deck and directed the lowering of all lifeboats, motorboats, and rafts. The decks and tackle were slippery with splattered fuel oil.

The youngest member of the crew, seventeen-year-old Egge Bremseth, was blown off the deck when a second torpedo slammed into the starboard side. Karre Reinertsen fell into the frigid sea when a lifeboat capsized during launching. These two men claimed the dubious honor of becoming the first victims of the U-boat war in the ESF.

Sverre Sandandnes was at the helm when the first torpedo exploded. As the ship started sinking, he scrambled into a lifeboat and was dumped into the water along with Reinertsen. Waves slammed him against the steel hull, but he managed to hold onto the rope falls until he was dragged up on deck. "Was damn cold!"

# TRACK OF THE GRAY WOLF

The ship was settling so quickly that when Anton Slettebarg woke up, he only had time to grab a life jacket, his slippers, and a prized gold watch before making good his escape.

Paul Georgsen was sleeping in the messroom when the torpedo struck. He scrambled in the darkness searching for his pet puppy, Pete, but could not find him. When he missed the first lifeboat and fell into the water, he climbed back on deck by himself and returned to the messroom. He found the dog, then ran outside and jumped onto a life raft. Waves washed freezing water in continuous streams over the low sides, drenching all aboard. The puppy whimpered unmercifully, and shivered so hard that Georgsen knew it could not survive. "So I said 'good-bye' to him, then brained him on the deck."

Einar Anderson, the second officer, along with five others, got away on a raft after the second torpedo hit. "Then we saw the submarine. It was about seventy-five yards away when it fired five or six shots at us—one for each man on the raft, I guess. We all lay as flat as we could. You know, being on a raft is like being in the water. We swallowed plenty, and we got plenty wet."

The circling U-boat fired a third torpedo into the abandoned ship before leaving the area. The *Norness* sank by the stern. As she came to rest on the sandy bottom, forty feet of the bow protruded out of the water at an awkward angle. Captain Hansen rallied his men to remain in the vicinity of the wreckage. This was impossible for those in rafts, since they had no power or sails, and they slowly drifted off with the current. Cold and wet, thirty-eight officers and men suffered the abuse of the open sea, awaiting rescue.

Not until that afternoon did a patrol plane notice the still-floating bow, surrounded by lifeboats, and radio for help. The Navy blimp *K-6* quickly flew to the disaster site. The airmen first spotted four men in a raft some twenty-five miles north of the derelict, then saw a lifeboat with another dozen survivors, and later sighted another raft with six more men. They dropped food and restoratives, and hovered over the latter raft as an aerial buoy until the arrival of rescue craft. The Coast Guard cutter

*Argo*, the destroyer *Elyson*, and a Navy minesweeper picked up all the men and took them to Newport, Rhode Island, and New Bedford, Massachusetts, where they were hospitalized for exposure.

Meanwhile, Hardegen did not let any barnacles grow on his hull. The *U-123* lurked nearby. On the morning of the fifteenth, before the American public had the opportunity to read about his exploits with the *Norness*, he torpedoed the British tanker *Coimbra*.

Less is known about this calamity since most of the crew perished in flames. Leaking fuel oil ignited the vessel; instead of sinking right away, the ship became a floating funeral pyre. Captain J.P. Barnard and thirty-five men were consumed in the blaze, leaving only six to escape. Already military authorities adopted the tactic of reticence and refused to give out information to the public.

Again, first word arrived over the airwaves when a patrol plane spotted the *Coimbra*'s survivors in a dory, south of Shinnecock Inlet. An intensive search and rescue effort was hampered by high winds, whipping seas, and bitter cold. As with the *Norness* incident, a Navy blimp located the wreck floating bow out of the water, dropped supplies to the sorely exposed seamen, and hovered as a marker until the U.S. destroyers *Mayrant* and *Grayson* arrived on the scene to pick up the freezing survivors.

On the seventeenth, a collision off Atlantic City, New Jersey, between the *San Jose* and the *Santa Elisa* resulted in the sinking of the United Fruit Line passenger-freighter *San Jose*. An SOS brought a small flotilla of rescue ships: the *A.L. Kent*, the freighter *Wellington*, and the freighter *Charles L. O'Connor*. Between them, they picked up all the men from the *San Jose*. The *Santa Elisa* remained afloat, although a fire started by the collision raged on in her bow for several hours. People ashore, nearly twenty miles away, reported seeing flames, or the beams of searchlights, on the horizon. No casualties occurred on either vessel. The Third Naval District reported that both vessels were showing running lights at the time of the collision, and that it was an ordinary marine accident and not the result of enemy action.

Yet, in the German records, Hardegen is given credit for torpedoing the *San Jose*. Discrepancies must necessarily occur during battle, and it is often historians with the vision of hindsight and overview who settle disputes of testimony. It is known positively that the collision took place. It is *not* known exactly when the abandoned vessel went down. It is possible that Hardegen happened upon the scene after the collision, saw a blacked-out ship, either did or did not recognize that she was in distress, and launched a torpedo into her hull that hastened, or brought about, her sinking. On the other hand, perhaps German propaganda claimed the sinking for morale purposes. Possibly, Hardegen falsified his log in order to increase his already impressive tonnage credit. There is not enough evidence on which to base a conclusion. The issue remains open to conjecture.

While Hardegen was working his way south, another U-boat entered the arena: the *U-66*, Korvettenkapitan Richard Zapp. He found his first target on January eighteenth: the tanker *Allan Jackson*, of the Standard Oil Company of New Jersey, bound from Cartagena, Colombia, to New York. The ship's master, Captain Felix Kretchmer, tells the story best:

"The vessel was following a course of about 354° true, so as to raise Winter Quarter Lightship, and was about sixty miles E.N.E. from Diamond Shoals. The weather was fine. I was in my bed resting when at 1:35 A.M. the ship was suddenly struck without warning by two torpedoes, amidships on the starboard side, resulting in two consecutive explosions. The first explosion was comparatively mild, but the second, which occurred almost immediately afterward, was very severe and threw me against the walls of my cabin. It broke the vessel apart and set her afire.

"After the second explosion I found myself on the bathroom floor. Flames were coming into the bedroom through the portholes and doors. My only means of escape was the porthole in the bathroom. This I was able to get through and I landed on the port side of the boat deck, which was the lee side of the ship.

"Seeing no sign of the crew, I started up the ladder

leading to the bridge. The decks and ladders were breaking up and the sea was rushing aboard. As the vessel sank amidships, the suction carried me away from the bridge ladder.

"After a struggle I came to the surface, on which oil was afire a short distance away. I never saw any member of the crew or any lifeboat afloat at any time, but later I distinctly saw a large submarine emerge, some distance away.

"With the help of a couple of small boards, I was able to keep afloat until I was picked up, about seven hours later, by the destroyer USS *Roe*. I was almost completely exhausted and hardly regained consciousness until I was landed at Norfolk and placed in the Marine Hospital, where I remained until January 31."

Twenty-two crew members were not so lucky and went down with the ship along with 72,870 barrels of Colombian crude oil. An affidavit signed by three of the thirteen survivors (Kretchmer, Third Mate Boris Voronsoff, and Chief Engineer Thomas Hutchins) stated, "After the vessel was struck, it was engulfed in flames and the oil on the water spread over an area about one-half mile around the ship and was aflame."

Ordinary Seamen Onis May stated that the *Allan Jackson* sank five minutes after the second torpedo struck. Able Bodied Seamen Ross Terrell said, "The ship was ablaze from stem to stern immediately, and all the surrounding water for about three hundred feet in all directions caught fire. Flames leaped at least one hundred feet in the air."

In his own report, Voronsoff stated, "As soon as I heard and felt the first torpedo hit the ship, I rushed out on deck. With some of the other officers, I tried to launch No. 2 lifeboat, but before we could do this the flames from the fire started by the torpedo came so close we had to leap off the ship into the sea. We jumped from the port side.

"After swimming for a short time, I found a strongback from one of the lifeboats and held on to it about four hours until picked up by the destroyer. . . . Francis M. Bacon, junior third mate, joined me some time afterward and clung to the same piece of wreckage I was using. Second Mate Rand, who had also found some wreckage, joined Bacon and me. Mr. Bacon started to get cramps and lashed himself to one end of the strongback. About two hours later he died.''

Boatswain Rolf Clausen, interviewed on June 29, 1945, went into great detail of his travails. ''The first torpedo hit the forward tank on the starboard side. There was an empty cargo hold above this tank and the effect of the explosion was not serious, judging from the hole I saw later when I was in the lifeboat.

''The second torpedo exploded in way of Nos. 2 and 3 starboard tanks and broke the ship in two—about twenty-five to thirty feet forward of the midship house and nearly in line with the foremast. Two men were killed by either the first or second explosion—Able Seaman Nox and Ordinary Seamen Brown.

''The three mates with some members of the crew who were amidships, started to launch No. 1 boat, but found it was a total wreck. I saw it afterward, when we were pulling away from the ship in No. 3, the only lifeboat that was launched. The outboard side of No. 1 lifeboat was torn away by the explosion so that I could see the inside of it. The davits were smashed.

''Then the mates and the men with them, including the radio operator, tried to launch No. 2 lifeboat, but found it impossible. They could not get it out of the chocks. The force of the explosion had bent the handle of the reel and they could not swing the boat out. They tried to heave and roll it off, but the lifeboat was leaning toward them and there were too few men to exert the necessary strength. To escape the closely approaching flames on deck, they jumped overboard.

''When the torpedoes struck the ship, I was in the messroom on the port side aft, playing cards with several members of the crew. We rushed out on deck and made for the nearest lifeboat, No. 4, but we couldn't launch it because the wind was carrying the flames in that direction. With men who joined us, we all went over to the starboard lifeboat, No. 3, which we immediately started to launch. I jumped into the boat with seven other men, including the chief engineer.

"When the boat was in the water and held in position by the painter we were three to four feet from the ship's side. Around us, with a short distance, were the flames of crude oil burning on the surface of the sea. What saved us was the strong discharge from the condenser pump. The outlet happened to be just ahead of the lifeboat. The force of the stream of water, combined with the motion of the ship, pushed the burning oil away to a few yards outboard of the boat.

"I unhooked the falls and cut the painter. At that time, the broken-off bow of the *Allan Jackson* was listing to port and the main part of the vessel was listing to starboard, over our lifeboat. After cutting the painter, I found that in the excitement no one had unlashed the oars. By the time I cut the lashings and the oars were manned, the boat was being sucked toward the propeller. The propeller blades hit the boat a number of times before we succeeded in clearing it by shoving with oars against the ship.

"Again we were saved from the surrounding fire because by that time we were in the backwash of the propellor, which made a clear lane through the flames. Not a man in that boat would have lived except for two elements of luck—the condenser discharge and the propellor's backwash. We rowed after until clear of danger from the fire.

"Our luck held in other respects. The sea was comparatively calm, with a moderate northeasterly wind. We were in the Gulf Stream and it was an exceptionally mild night. The air temperature was about 40°, not dangerously cold even though we were hardly well clothed, having been below where the portholes were screened for blackouts and there was little circulation of air. The men who jumped overboard and survived were also lucky to be in the Gulf Stream, as the water temperature was about 65°.

"We did all we could to find survivors. In the darkness we heard several calls and about fifteen minutes after leaving the ship we picked up the radio operator, Stephen Verbonich.''

After two and a half hours in the open sea, the men of lifeboat No. 3 were picked up by the *Roe*. The destroyer then cruised through the flotsam and scooped others out of the water. Five men, including the captain, were seriously injured, and were hospitalized.

With two U-boats now operating in the Eastern Sea Frontier, the war against the merchant marine was heating up. They did not attack in tandem, or in a pack, but as lone wolves worrying their prey. This had two immediate effects: it threw a good scare into the men of the merchant marine, and it forced shipping to concentrate along the coast closer to Naval and Army Air Force protection. The merchant marine prepared for the worst scenario.

Confusion reigned throughout the ESF as Hardegen ripped into coastal shipping in the vicinity of the Diamond Shoals, North Carolina. He had a field day on the nineteenth as he attacked the *City of Atlanta* at 0207, the *Malay* at 0230, and the *Ciltvaira* at 0500.

The *City of Atlanta* was a freighter headed south from New York to Savannah with a general cargo. Second Officer George Tavelle was one of only three survivors; his testimony taken in the hospital is the keenest insight into the calamity. ''There was no moon. It was a starlit night; smooth sea. . . . Our lights were dimmed on Navy Department instructions.'' He was on watch when ''the ship was struck on the port side, a little abaft of the engine room bulkhead in No. 3 hold. There was a great flare of flame on the explosion, and there was debris in the air, and a very heavy concussion. The concussion blew in the pilot house windows, shattering them. Fragments of glass struck me on the forehead, inflicting a cut over the right eye. I didn't get a chance to see what other damage was done aft of the pilot house, but Mr. Fennell has told me that the explosion blew in the house along the port side. A piece of the wreckage on which I floated until picked up was the frame of the port dining salon door.''

The *City of Atlanta* took an immediate port list. A

minute later, Tavelle had to kick his way through the jammed pilot house door. "The men were already gathering on the deck when I came out on the starboard side, and with considerable difficulty, because of the rapid listing of the ship to port, we managed to get Nos. 1 and 3 boats swung out, but by the time the davits were swung out the ship had listed to port so sharply that the boats rested on the starboard side and we could not release the grips. . . . Within ten minutes—not more—after the explosion the ship turned over. She first lay on her port side for a moment or two and then turned keel up.

"While I was on the starboard side getting boats out, and I should say between four and five minutes after the impact, the submarine came around our stern and up on our starboard quarter and stood off perhaps seventy-five feet from where we were in the boats, but close under the stern. She played a small searchlight over us and it was still on us when the ship was turning over and I got into the water. . . . For sometime after the ship had turned over and we were in the water, the submarine remained in the near vicinity completely surfaced. She then showed running lights and a foremast light which she had not shown when I saw her immediately after the impact and when we were still aboard the ship. Though there were a number of men around the submarine in close proximity calling for help, I saw nothing to indicate that any effort was put out to save any of the crew.

"Just before the ship turned on its side I was standing on the rail trying to release the jammed falls. One of them slipped and broke my hold, and I fell into the water on the starboard side in the space between the two life boats. I managed to get out from between the boats and swam away from the ship, and presently I picked up a piece of wreckage on which I floated until I was picked up. I was picked up by the *Seatrain Texas* shortly before nine o'clock Monday morning, January 19th. I figure that I was in the water between six and seven hours."

Robert Fennell, an oiler, was asleep when the torpedo struck and burst open his locker, spewing out his clothing and personal belongings. He hastily donned a pair of trousers and a sheepskin coat, then clambered on deck to his lifeboat station on the port side. As the ship rolled over, waves washed over the steeply canted deck. With the lifeboat stuck, he jumped free, but the belt of his coat caught in something and he was dragged underwater as the freighter sank. Fennell held his breath and struggled, finally breaking free and bobbing to the surface. He reported that the ship went down without any suction. He held onto a skylight at first, then transferred to a bench from the crew's dining room.

Also rescued by the passing steamer was Able Bodied Seaman Earl Dowdy. Forty-four men lost their lives, either in the initial explosion or by drowning. Tavelle recalls seeing at least eighteen men clinging to wreckage, slowly weakening, slipping off one by one into the sea to lie face down, embracing death.

Hardegen wasted no time on the *City of Atlanta*. Having observed the ship going under, he left the survivors to their fates and pressed a surface attack on the tanker *Malay*.

Chambliss Holston, able bodied seaman, said, "The first sign of the attack was a crash of glass, and I thought that one of the skylights on deck had fallen and been shattered." The shell struck the bridge, inflicting injuries on those inside, damaged a lifeboat and set it on fire. The second shell carried away the port bridge wing.

Captain John Dodge ordered evasive action and full speed ahead. The *Malay* veered away from the U-boat. The short engagement left one man with a broken back, one with a broken collarbone, and several others with broken arms, legs, and fingers. A few minor fires were quickly doused. The *Malay* made off in the darkness. All other ships in the area heeded the radio warning by turning off their lights.

Hardegen pursued the stricken tanker. Forty-five minutes later, three more shells hit the *Malay* aft. In addition to setting the stern partly ablaze, one shell crashed through a bulkhead over the bunk of Adams Hay, cook. He was killed instantly by the blast. Only because the *Malay* was traveling without cargo was the ship saved from being engulfed in flames like the previous tankers.

# January 1942

Three men scrambled into a lifeboat, taking the man with the broken back. The forward lines fouled, the lifeboat capsized, and all were drowned.

Hardegen was persistent and launched a torpedo which struck amidships, flooding No. 7 tank. The *Malay* slowed but kept her course. Captain Dodge fired flares so that Coast Guard vessels, alerted by radio and already on their way, could locate his ship. Hardegen broke off the attack. The Coast Guard removed three seriously injured men, and Hay's body, and raced toward Norfolk. The *Malay* limped along behind under escort and eventually reached Newport News, Virginia under her own power. She went to sea again after $170,000 in repairs.

At 0500, Hardegen torpedoed the Latvian freighter *Ciltvaira*, traveling southbound fully lighted from New York to Savannah. Coal passer Friederich Lusis came out on deck for a breath of air that saved his life. At his station below, two firemen, Rolf Semelin and Carl Gustaefssen, were killed instantly by the blast.

Nick Creteu related his story: "All of a sudden something happened. The whole night was filled with fire. Some kind of a noise happened. I don't know how to say it. I was knocked straight up off my feet, about two feet in the air. But it didn't knock me out."

Rudolf Musts, the radio operator, was locked in his room by torqued bulkheads. "The door was jammed. Everything was black out and everywhere was hot steam. I managed, somehow, to force open the door and that way I got to a lifeboat."

Able Bodied Seaman Leon Lusis (no relation to Friederich) was woken by the tremendous explosion: "I ran on deck, tried to get in a port lifeboat, but found that our ship had been hit right amidships and that the lifeboat was no good. The crew entered a large starboard lifeboat, which was launched before the captain and the officers of the ship followed in a smaller boat. Before leaving they got the log and the ship's manifest."

Of the thirty-two man crew, thirty got away, plus a cat and a dog. The two lifeboats floated nearby the still-floating *Ciltvaira* for three hours until they were spotted by the Standard Oil tanker *Socony Vacuum*, which picked up the men. Captain Skarlis Kerbergs saw that his ship was not settling any further and rallied a boatload of volunteers to return to the vessel.

The only crew member who spoke fluent English (among a crew of Finns, Danes, Estonians, Dutch, Swedes, Latvians, and a Rumanian) was twenty-year-old Leon Da Salva, a mess boy from British Guiana. In an interview, he said, "After we left the ship, we saw she wasn't going down right away. So one of the boats went back at about seven o'clock to see the damage. We also took out the passports and the ship's papers. We hoisted a signal flag—SOS—and went back to the boat again. We looked back and saw now the ship was broken in the middle with a big hole. She was filling fast with water."

Captain Julio Soares, master of the *Bury*, heard the broadcast from fifteen miles away. "The *Ciltvaira* was still floating when I found her. . . . I sent four of my crew to the *Ciltvaira*, in charge of that ship's first officer, in order to pass the cables. It was not until 7 P.M. when all was set for us to tow. Then we started slowly toward Norfolk. We were using three manila and one steel cable. The cables broke at 9 P.M. because of the rough seas.

"There were no lights whatever on the unfortunate vessel because all of her machinery was out of order, so we waited until 11 P.M. Then a heavy fog descended. There was nothing to do but leave her and advise other ships and radio stations of the position of the derelict."

Added Leon Lusis: "The ship was then practically sinking under us. We had to take out our boat again and we were picked up by the Brazilian freighter *Bury*."

Almost completely submerged, the *Ciltvaira* continued to drift. According to reports, she did not settle completely to the bottom until the twenty-first.

Meanwhile, two hundred miles to the east, Zapp found the southbound *Lady Hawkins* in his periscope sights. The Canadian National Steamship Company liner was carrying two hundred twelve passengers and one hundred nine crew, under the command of Captain Huntley Giffin. At 0105, a torpedo fired by the *U-66* hit the *Lady Hawkins* directly under the bridge.

The terrific explosion blew the ship over sharply,

knocking most of those on deck at the time into the sea. The mainmast snapped off and crashed among the rest. Before the ship could recover from her list, a second torpedo exploded against the engine room and destroyed two lifeboats. This ship was plunged into total darkness as the electricity failed.

Down below, stunned passengers struggled out of their staterooms onto the steeply canted decks to grope along pitch-black corridors. Unfamiliar with the layout, many were trapped below and drowned as the vessel slipped beneath the waves.

Mr. and Mrs. Albert Johnson jumped from the sinking ship, Albert with their two-and-a-half-year-old daughter, Janet, in his arms. Together they swam toward a lifeboat and were hauled aboard. The seventy-six people were so crowded that most had to stand.

Mrs. Johnson praised the efforts of Chief Officer Kelly, in charge of their lifeboat: "We owe our lives to the chief officer, whose courage and tact kept our spirits up." Kelly rigged a sail and took over the navigation. What followed was a five-day ordeal that must have been terrifying to those who had no idea when, or if, they would be rescued. Because of the immediate electrical failure on the *Lady Hawkins*, no SOS was transmitted. No one except the crew of the *U-66* knew the liner had been sunk, or that several hundred people were plying the sea in open boats.

William Burton, the ship's carpenter, related how the U-boat checked out their lifeboat: "It was a great big one and it came up about one hundred yards from us and just lay off there with two white lights on us." Then it submerged, and left the survivors on their own.

After the first day, the lifeboats were scattered by the wind. Kelly issued their meager water and food supplies sparingly: he allowed a daily ration of one biscuit, a tablespoon of canned milk, and two ounces of water per person.

Mrs. Marian Parkinson, a Canadian missionary on the way to Trinidad, was separated from her husband during the hasty escape; she encouraged her fellow passengers to sing hymns. She also accepted the sad task of saying prayers over those who had not the strength to stay alive during the harrowing days that followed. Five times she prayed for the departed as their bodies, stripped of their clothing to keep the underdressed survivors warm, were consigned to the sea.

Kelly later told the story to reporters in San Juan, Puerto Rico. "The story of the sinking of the *Lady Hawkins*, as I look back on it, is one of bravery and discipline, tears and laughter, alternate hope and despair, and, above all, a tale of real human courage.

"We had our heroes and our heroines, young and old. One of the real heroines was little Janet Johnson who, with her father and mother, were in our boat. She set an example for all of us and took the whole experience as a picnic. A cute, chubby little girl, two years and eight months old, she was soaked for five days, but we heard hardly a whimper from her.

"That child was wonderful. She spent all her time in her mother's arms and got a thrill out of every waking minute. One night she had a little fever and we gave her a spoonful of brandy. It pulled her through, but for a time made her laugh so much that the whole boat laughed with her and we were all immensely bucked up.

"Everybody helped in some way all the time we were in the boat. Some bailed out water and joked with each other about who was the fastest. We were crowded and sleeping was a problem, but we made out. Everybody kept cheerful and everybody helped everybody else.

"Five persons died in the boat of exposure and were buried at sea. That was our worst time. It was awful to see them go. I might have helped some of them hold out a little longer, as I had one bottle of brandy, but I knew I must keep that to use where it would do the most good—especially for the children. They still had long lives ahead of them and I wanted them to get their chance.

"The spray and the water were bad. We never were entirely dry all the five days we were in the boat. At times I was worried about ever getting out of the trouble. We were in waters, much of the time, where, I knew, there was not much chance of sighting a ship. Twice I saw wisps of smoke, but the ships from which they came were far, far away. I just had to sit and watch the smoke disappear.''

Near midnight of their fifth day at sea, the American liner *Coamo* passed within two hundred yards of the drifting lifeboat. "I cannot tell you how we felt when we saw the *Coamo*," Mrs. Johnson said. Kelly fired flares that alerted the steamer's watch of their presence. Soon, the seventy-one weakened survivors were helped aboard.

The tribulations of the passengers and crew on this lifeboat illustrate what must have happened to the people on the other two boats. We can only imagine their suffering, however, because they were never seen again. Captain Giffin was gone with his ship, and the stalwart Mrs. Parkinson never found her husband. Two hundred fifty men, women, and children lost their lives from the torpedoing of the *Lady Hawkins*. (On December 2, 1942, the *Coamo* disappeared with all one hundred thirty-three hands, apparently torpedoed by the *U-604*, Kapitanleutnant Horst Holtring, off Bermuda.)

Although the story of the *Lady Hawkins* did not come to light until five days after her sinking, Hardegen's three concerted attacks within a three-hour period threw coastal shipping into a uproar. In order to make themselves less visible to marauding U-boats, the Navy ordered that vessels running along the East Coast operate without lights.

While the strategy behind this thinking was sound, it increased the odds of collision. At 2128 that night, off the coast of South Carolina, the American freighter *Brazos* was rammed by the HMS *Archer*. Both vessels were blacked out. Each spotted the other just moments before the crash, not in time to avoid the collision.

Abled Bodied Seamen Reinier Reina reached the deck of the *Brazos* just as the British warship smashed into the side of the freighter. The after cargo boom toppled under the impact, but hit no one. "The skipper thought the ship might be saved if the cargo was shifted in the hold. He asked for volunteers to go below and do the work. Water was pouring in down there, but everybody volunteered."

Water surged into No. 2 hold, which was filled with

rum and sugar. The men stuffed bags of sugar into the jagged hole, but the encroaching sea melted it as fast as they could stack the bags. The hold sloshed with the sticky mess. Eventually, according the Captain Charles Stone, the ocean around the vessel looked like "a big load of syrup."

Finally, Captain Stone ordered abandon ship. The lifeboats were lowered without haste, and every man climbed aboard. They bobbed in the swells alongside their vessel until she slowly settled out of sight. Thirty minutes later the men were picked up by the *Archer*.

When asked if he would go back to sea, Reina said, "Yes, I expect to go back. I'm not afraid. I'll go back any time they want me."

Again, despite the facts, German records credit Hardegen with the sinking. While it is a fact that the pandemonium in the shipping lanes was attributable to the *U-123*, it is decidedly untrue that he made any kind of attack against the *Brazos*. Unlike the *San Jose*, in this case the men stayed right by the side of their foundering ship until she slipped beneath the waves. They would have known if a torpedo had struck to hasten her sinking.

The night of the twenty-second saw the expiration of many lives, but whatever sad misadventures occurred about the *Norvana* and the *Olympic* must go untold: both were lost without a trace.

The American freighter *Norvana* left Neuvitas, Cuba, on the fourteenth, but her cargo never reached Philadelphia. German records credit Zapp of the *U-66* with the kill. The Panamanian tanker *Olympic* left Curacao on the thirteenth, for Baltimore. She is given to Korvettenkapitan Ernst Kals, of the *U-130*.

During the night of the twenty-third, with the *U-66* stalking close to shore, Zapp added two more notches to his gun. The first was the northbound British tanker *Empire Gem*, at 1945. The torpedo that ripped into her hull ignited the cargo of oil with such violence that the ship was instantly turned into a cauldron of flames leaping hundreds of feet into the air.

This was observed from the bridge of the *Venore*, which had been overtaken by the faster tanker at 1800.

26

The *Venore* was carrying 22,250 tons of iron ore from Vera Cruz, Chile, via the Panama Canal, for Sparrows Point, Maryland. Captain Fritz Duurloo was working his vessel north along the coast on a zigzag course and showed only dimmed sidelights. He heard the explosion, then saw the tanker burst into flames.

Duurloo ordered hard left rudder and switched off all lights. As the *Venore* slipped past the raging *Empire Gem*, the captain saw in the flickering yellow glow the sleek hull of a German submarine. It passed astern of the tanker and raced toward the *Venore* at high speed. The *Venore* headed toward shore until she was out of the light of the burning tanker, then veered northward in the darkness.

But Zapp caught up with the freighter at 2025, about fifteen miles from the *Empire Gem*, and fired a torpedo into her port side. The detonation at No. 9 ballast tank belched smoke, flame, and water high into the air. The *Venore* rose upward from the force of the explosion. When she settled back down she was listing so far that her hatches were underwater.

Peter Karlson, the quartermaster, was at the helm at the time. "The captain was cool as a cucumber."

Captain Duurloo, maintaining his station on the bridge, ordered abandon ship. The men swarmed into three lifeboats as another torpedo slammed into the hull and the vessel rolled over under them. They saw the freighter on her beam ends. When she disappeared beneath the waves, she took her brave captain with her.

Coast Guard motor lifeboats from the Ocracoke Station raced toward the scene of the double disaster. Since the *Empire Gem* was closer (twelve miles south of the Diamond Shoals) and still burning furiously and therefore highly visible, rescue craft were attracted to the tanker. The rescuers maneuvered their motorboat as close to the flames as they dared. Only three men were found still aboard. They jumped into the water and swam toward the rescue craft. High seas swept Radio Operator Ernest McGraw back into the flames. The two who made it were Captain Francis Broad, master of the *Empire*

*Gem*, and the second radio operator, Thomas Orrell. Fifty-five others died that night.

The two lucky survivors were transferred to the motorboat from the Hatteras Station and taken ashore for medical aid. A search was undertaken for possible survivors from the *Venore*, but none were found in the darkness and in the uncertainty of her sinking location.

Meanwhile, another tragedy was taking place among the ore carrier's lifeboats. The men of one boat saw one of the other boats swamped by heavy seas. Unable to lend assistance because theirs was already overloaded and shipping water, they could only listen to the cries of men in the water before they drowned. The third boat drifted off and was never seen again.

The lone boat, packed with twenty-one men, spent the rest of the night, all of the next day, and all of the following night floating in the Gulf Stream before finally being picked up by the tanker *Tennessee*.

The night of the twenty-fourth, a fifth U-boat arrived in the ESF. On his way south to the hunting grounds of the Caribbean and South America, Kapitanleutnant Ulrich Folkers stopped his *U-125* long enough to fire a torpedo at the tanker *Olney*. His log records a detonation, but the *Olney*, although she reported a torpedo attack, managed to avoid the deadly missile.

That same night, Kals in the *U-130* was more accurate. Prowling off the New Jersey coast, he fired three torpedoes at the Norwegian tanker *Varanger* and hit her with all three.

With a cargo of oil picked up partly in Africa and partly in Curacao, the *Varanger* was proceeding toward New York when, at about 0300, a tremendous explosion rent her amidships on the port side, knocking overboard the radio room and a four-inch gun. The detonation was so violent that it rattled windows and awakened residents of Sea Isle City, twenty-eight miles away.

The vessel listed sharply. A spokesman for the Fourth Naval District in Philadelphia added, "Seven minutes later the ship was struck by a second torpedo. Five minutes later a third torpedo struck. The ship sank immediately after the third torpedo," which broached the engine room.

Captain Karl Horne acted promptly by ordering abandon ship. Since most of the crew were asleep at the time of the attack, they scrambled on deck in various states of undress. Against all odds, all forty got away in two lifeboats before the tanker succumbed to flooding. One boat was motorized, the other equipped with sail. Lashed together, they plodded westward. Even then many might have died from exposure had not the flash of the explosion been spotted by a fishing boat captain out for an early morning catch.

Captain Monchetti of the *San Gennaro* heard the shipwrecked sailors shouting for help as he approached. Monchetti said, "They were so smeared up with oil that on some of them all I could see was the whites of their eyes." He quickly forgot about trawling for fish and took the lifeboats in tow.

On the way in he came across another fisherman, Captain Dominick Constantino of the *Eileen*, and passed the line of one lifeboat to him. With increased speed, the two diesel-powered fishing vessels towed the lifeboats to the Townsend Inlet Lifeboat Station. Dr. Alexander Stuart, a local physician, was called to treat the men. Some were injured, and all but two were suffering from toxemia from inhaling and swallowing fuel oil.

Coast Guardsmen put out a call for warm clothes and shoes for the bedraggled and nearly frozen men. The local Red Cross collected clothing from area residents. The St. Joseph Roman Catholic Church put up cots for the forty survivors in the basement of the church. For this crew, at least, there was humanity and a happy ending.

Kals struck again two nights later. Despite overcast conditions and visibility of less than a mile, he spotted the blacked-out American tanker *Francis E. Powell* steaming for Providence, Rhode Island, with 80,000 barrels of gasoline and furnace oil she had loaded in Port Arthur, Texas.

At 0245 on the twenty-seventh, off the coast of Virginia, a single torpedo hit the *Francis E. Powell* amidships and exploded with incredible force. The tanker's back was broken. She took an immediate port list and settled so much in the middle that the bow and stern rose up out of the water. A deposition signed by four of the survivors tells the story from there:

"At the time of the disaster the said vessel was proceeding without lights; she was being steered by her automatic steering device; her said second mate was in charge of her navigation, and was in the pilot house on the bridge; and a quartermaster and an ordinary seaman were stationed as lookouts on the wings of the bridge. The officers and crew of said vessel comprised thirty-two men, twenty-eight of whom left said vessel in a sinking condition, in two lifeboats, and while pulling away from said vessel observed a conning tower and superstructure of a submarine close at hand. The master of the vessel, Thomas J. Harrington, while endeavoring to enter a lifeboat which was being lowered on the starboard side of the vessel, was crushed between the lifeboat and the side of said vessel, and in consequence thereof fell into the sea and disappeared, when the lifeboat, which he was about to enter, was carried back upon the deck of the vessel, through a heavy swell, and there capsized; that the first mate of said vessel, Willard S. King, was picked up out of the seas by the occupants of a lifeboat which had been lowered from the port quarter of said vessel."

No SOS went out because when the radio operator ran to his post he found no power and a broken radio antenna. The midship section of the vessel sank in less than five minutes. Had the escaping gasoline and furnace oil ignited, the casualties would have been much greater.

The seventeen men in No. 3 lifeboat floated with the current for nine hours, alongside the remains of their ship, until they were picked up by tanker *W.C. Fairbanks*. This was the first official knowledge of the loss of the *Francis E. Powell*. A distress message sent over the airwaves stated: "*Francis E. Powell* broken in two at 1140. Bow pointed skyward at approximate position, latitude 37-25, longitude 75-10. Drifting two hundred degrees true about one knot. Stern drifting two hundred degrees true at three knots. Position approximately, latitude 37-19, longitude 75-12. Wind, gale force. Seas, rough. Visibility, one-half mile. Request instructions.''

No 2. lifeboat got away with only five men, but they managed to take on six of the men from the overturned No. 1 boat. Fearful of the spreading oil, they rowed to windward to escape the slick. At dawn they raised a sail. The slight breeze helped only a little. It was not until 1900, after sixteen hours in the open boat, that they were rescued by a motor lifeboat sent out by the Assateague Island Coast Guard Station.

Meanwhile, the *Francis E. Powell* was still afloat. The Navy tug *Sciota* tried to tow her in, along with help from the Coast Guard cutters *Woodbury* and *Bayonne*. The attempted salvage was unsuccessful, and the badly buckled ship sank on the way in.

A few hours later, Kals shelled and slightly damaged the *Halo* off the Diamond Shoals, but the steamship soon outdistanced the U-boat. After this, the ESF was quiet for three days. If anyone thought this presaged a slackening in German aggressiveness, he was sadly mistaken. On the thirtieth, for the first time in the U-boat war off the East Coast, an attack was pressed home in broad daylight.

The American tanker *Rochester* was southbound in ballast from New York for Corpus Christi, Texas, enjoying clear weather and excellent visibility, and zigzagging at six minute intervals through moderate seas. Despite three lookouts (on the bridge, atop the wheelhouse, and on the forecastle) no one saw the torpedo streaking toward the ship.

The torpedo exploded on the port side, blowing in the engine room bulkhead and destroying the condensers. Three men were killed instantly. Captain A.L. Clark gave the order to swing out the lifeboats and prepare to abandon ship. On his way to the radio shack, he sighted the enemy submarine fully surfaced only a half-mile to port. Before he could send out an SOS, Charles McDonald, the radio operator, had to replace some of the transmitter's vacuum tubes. The call for help did not go out until fourteen minutes after the initial attack. Then, the surviving crew shoved off in two lifeboats.

As the U-boat closed on the stricken tanker, men of the *Rochester* were able to distinguish what appeared to be a blue porpoise painted on the conning tower. They described the armament consisting of three guns: a four- or five-incher forward with a shorter barrel than the standard U.S. Navy three-inch gun, a lighter gun aft, and a machine gun on the conning tower. They did not see a net cutter.

As the U-boat's gun crew prepared for action, the men in the lifeboats were afraid of being strafed. But not only did the German gun crew wait until the lifeboats were out of the line of fire, someone even waved them aside before opening fire. When the lifeboats were clearly out of range the shelling commenced. From a range of five-hundred yards the *U-106* pumped thirteen shells into the motionless tanker, penetrating the hull from bow to stern and demolishing the wheelhouse.

Oberleutnant zur See Herman Rasch then fired a second torpedo, hitting the *Rochester* amidships. The tanker listed to starboard and sank after fifteen minutes. The *U-106* retreated, still running brashly on the surface.

A half hour later, Navy patrol planes, responding to the SOS, appeared overhead. The *Rochester*'s survivors seemed more interested in seeing the planes pursue the U-boat than in being rescued; they waved in the direction of the retreating submarine, and the planes took up the search. They found nothing, and returned later to drop smoke signals near the lifeboats. The destroyer USS *Roe* picked up the men at 1500, three hours after the first attack.

What did not come to light until after the war, with the examination of captured German records, was the fate of the *Tacoma Star*. She sent out a distress call a day after leaving Newport News, Virginia on her way to England with a general cargo. When rescue craft arrived at her transmitted position, though they scoured the sea, they found nothing. Kapitanleutnant Heinrich Bleichrodt, *U-109*, had taken credit for the freighter and her crew of ninety-two.

Adolf Hitler was so bold as to announce not only the names and tonnages of vessels known to have been torpedoed off the East Coast; he went as far as to mention by name Hardegen and Kals in praise of their successes.

In defense, U.S. authorities shrugged off the sinkings as minuscule when compared to the amount of ship movement. By slewing the statistics so that a loss was equivocated to the number of ships entering and leaving East Coast ports from Maine to Florida, they could show that only 6.5 vessels were sunk out of one thousand ports of call: .065 percent.

This may have sounded good on paper, but it did not alleviate the four hundred forty-four known fatalities, plus the entire crews of the *Norvana*, the *Olympic*, and the *Tacoma Star*, whose fates were as yet unknown.

If anyone understood the increased risks to merchant shipping, it was the insurance companies. It was announced that the North Atlantic sea lanes were considered more hazardous than those in the South Pacific, preyed upon by the Japanese Imperial Fleet. Only two weeks in the East Coast U-boat war, insurance rates doubled. Whereas the previous rate had been set on the ratio of two hundred to one (one half of one percent), the new rate was one hundred to one. They were no longer gambling that if only one ship out of two hundred was sunk, they could still earn a profit. They were expecting one sinking out of every one hundred vessels.

In addition, the entire civilian community was gearing for invasion. On February 3, Philadelphia became the first eastern city to experience total blackout as an emergency precaution against aerial bombardment. Unfortunately, this was not taken too seriously. Coastal resort areas refused to comply with this dictum of safety and continued to let their streetlights burn. U-boats sat offshore and watched for the silhouettes of freighters and tankers as they passed the brightly illuminated shore towns.

The United States was not used to the idea of invasion, and it was slowly, some say sluggishly, that the nation accepted the idea of attack. To most people, merchant ships sunk in the ocean may as well have gone down on the other side of the Atlantic.

This attitude would soon change.

# FEBRUARY

The *Amerikaland* was on her way from Baltimore to Chile in ballast, there to pick up a load of ore. The 15,355 ton diesel-powered freighter was not only the largest ship lost within the boundaries of the ESF, she was also one of the largest cargo vessels in the world. She had been zigzagging throughout a moonless night and stormy seas until a few hours before midnight on the first, when Captain Ragnar Schultz steadied his course. Twenty minutes later, a torpedo exploded under the bridge at the waterline. The giant vessel took on an immediate starboard list.

Kjell Norin was asleep at the time; he was thrown

completely out of his bunk by the force of the blast. In addition to being third mate, he was also the radio operator. He wasted no time in racing to the radio shack and sending out a distress call with the ship's approximate position.

Captain Schultz ordered abandon ship. The crew was still lowering the boats when a second torpedo struck the engine room. While great plumes of black smoke poured out of the machinery spaces, the men got away in two lifeboats. At first they stayed in the lee of the shattered hull. Then they were joined by a third lifeboat which Norin commanded; he had hung back and continued transmitting an SOS. The three boats then drifted away as not one, but two U-boats surfaced and circled the sinking freighter. The men heard two more explosions aboard the *Amerikaland*. The ship was still afloat when they last saw her. Credit for the kill went to Rasch and the *U-106*.

Strong winds soon separated the lifeboats. Each suffered its own travails. Norin's lifeboat, with nine men, drifted for four days before being discovered by the Dutch freighter *Castoria*, which took the survivors to Curacao. By then, three men had perished from exposure. Captain Schultz's lifeboat was equipped with a sail. These twelve men worked their boat into the Gulf Stream. Five days after the torpedoing, with one man dead from injuries, they were picked up by the British ship *Port Halifax* and landed at New York. The men of the third lifeboat turned up in Brazil with one of their number dead from exposure.

The temperate climate was a tremendous aid to survival for the men of the *Amerikaland*. The story of the next sinking is much more tragic, and the casualty statistics reversed in favor of death.

The culprit was the *U-103*, Kapitanleutnant Werner Winter, who sank four merchant ships in a seventy-two hour period. His first target was the American tanker *W.L. Steed*.

The first official portent of calamity came in a brief and hastily transmitted radio message: "Going down fast," and an approximate position. The Coast Guard sent out the cutter *Nike*, two picket boats, and a flying boat, but the first to reach the area was a Navy blimp which radioed back to base: "*K-5* searching area for submarine and survivors. Visibility reduced because of snow." The cold and horrendous weather conditions were to prove to be a worse enemy than the carnage wreaked by the U-boat.

The *W.L. Steed* left Cartagena on January 23 with 65,936 barrels of Colombian crude. She was routed through Key West under Navy orders before continuing on to an undisclosed destination. Right from the beginning of the voyage she braved the tribulations of war. Second Mate Sydney Wayland described one incident: "On January 30, in the early afternoon, while I was on watch, the lookout reported a ship on the port bow. This ship appeared to be a fishing craft, but after a good look at her I notified Captain McAvenia, who came up at once and decided she was a submarine. He ordered the general alarm sounded, with all hands standing by for orders as the ship's course was changed. As the submarine disappeared in the distance, the captain put the ship back on her original course and the crew were dismissed from their stations."

Captain Harold G. McAvenia was a cautious man who took no chances in U-boat infested waters. A joint report made by Boatswain Joaquin R. Brea, Able Seaman Louis Hartz, and Able Seaman Ralph Mazzucco, adds detail: "The captain ordered the rest of the crew to their respective boat stations, except the engineroom crew, who stayed below on duty. All lifeboats were made ready for launching, and life preservers were donned in readiness for any emergency. A radio message was sent by the captain and about an hour later a plane was observed overhead, presumably in answer to our wireless message."

Working her way north, the *W.L. Steed* ran into foul weather and shipped heavy seas that caused deck damage. On the evening of February 1, another suspicious light was sighted, and again the captain ordered the usual safety precautions and a change of course.

Wayland continues: "On February 2, at about 12:45

P.M., I was on watch pacing the bridge, with Able Seaman Jose C. Arroyo at the wheel, Able Seaman Louis Hartz on lookout, and Ordinary Seaman James Erdos looking abaft.

"Without warning of any kind the ship was suddenly struck by a torpedo on her starboard side, forward of the bridge, at her No. 3 tank, setting the oil contained in that tank afire.

"At that time the vessel was proceeding generally in a northeasterly direction, about eighty to ninety miles off the Delaware Capes. The sea was bad, with a strong northeasterly wind, and we had been unable to take a sun position at 8 A.M. or at noon, due to the overcast. It was snowing hard, making the visibility two miles at best.

"The *W.L. Steed* was running under sealed orders, and the master was the only one on the ship who had full information as to the ship's position. From my own observations, however, the vessel was about eighty-five miles off shore.

"The next thing I heard was the engine being stopped by the captain in the pilot house and the general alarm sounded. I immediately reported to the captain, whom I met coming out of the pilot house with the ship's position, which he was taking to the radio operator. I later found out that this message was duly sent and picked up by an Imperial Oil tanker that went down one day thereafter.

"The master ordered me to get the two amidship boats ready for lowering. I carried out these orders by first clearing the starboard boat. Then the captain came along carrying a briefcase and ordered me to proceed to the portside boat, which I also lowered away and launched with the assistance of a fireman. The captain came back again and instructed me to go down the fall, which I did, with the fireman. Then we both helped the following men to slide down a rope into the lifeboat: Radio Operator Francis E. Siltz, Chief Engineer Walter M. Christiansen, Extra Chief Engineer Ernest G. Bornheimer, First Assistant Engineer William R. Burrell, Steward George Zenos, Pumpman Walter A. Tulane, Able Seaman Jose C. Arroyo, Ordinary Seaman James Erdos, Captain Harold

G. McAvenia, Chief Mate Einar A. Nilsson, Wiper David A. Field, Fireman Ralph A. Bone, and two men from below deck whose names I do not recall—making fifteen men altogether, including myself.

"All four lifeboats were launched. My boat, No. 2, was the last to leave the ship and everyone on the ship managed to get into a lifeboat. No one went down with the ship, but after the night of February 2, I never saw any of the other lifeboats.

"We pulled clear of the ship, heading northwest into the sea and wind. I saw two other boats at a distance pulling clear of the stern of the vessel. This all happened within about ten minutes from the time the torpedo struck the vessel.

"At that time a periscope was sighted about three lengths away off the starboard side of our lifeboat. The submarine came to the surface on our port side after going around our bow. Two men came out on the conning tower to look us over as the U-boat proceeded toward the stern of the ship without interfering with us.

"I also distinctly saw another submarine on the surface proceeding from the port quarter to the starboard quarter of the *W.L. Steed*. This submarine started to shell the tanker's after part, but at that time all boats were well clear. The vessel soon caught fire and was burning fiercely on the poop deck until she finally blew up, about forty minutes after being struck by the torpedo.

"Weather conditions were fierce, with a snowstorm and dangerous northwest seas running. Everybody in the boat was suffering from the cold, due mostly to lack of clothes. The men in lifeboat No. 2 died one after another until February 5, when Chief Mate Nilsson and myself were the only ones alive in the boat.

"On the morning of February 6, Nilsson showed signs of weakness and extreme fatigue. At about 9:30 A.M. I sighted a steamer coming close to us and I made every effort, waving and hailing, to get her attention, as she seemed to go past, but finally she hove around, headed for us, and picked us up at about 10:30 A.M.

"When we arrived alongside this vessel, the SS *Hartlepool*, her second mate, and a couple of able bodied seamen came into our lifeboat and examined it. Mr. Nilsson and I were taken aboard the *Hartlepool* with the aid of ropes tied around our waists. The boat was then cast adrift because the captain was concerned with the safety of his ship.

"The *Hartlepool* landed us at Halifax on February 9 and both Chief Mate Nilsson and I were sent to the hospital, where Mr. Nilsson died the following day. I left the hospital on February 28, after recovering from the pains and suffering experienced."

Testifying before the Preliminary Investigation Board in New York, Boatswain Joaquin Brea said, "The temperature was near zero, below zero," when he climbed into No. 3 lifeboat, and that he was wearing only "regular working clothes." As to safety, he stated that they were running a zigzag course, and that the lifeboats were carried swung out and ready to lower.

Able Seaman Ralph Mazzucco also got away in No. 3 lifeboat. "All boats were lowered and, as far as we know, all hands in Nos. 1, 2, and 4 boats got safely away. We went under the stern of the *W.L. Steed*. As we came over the port side of the ship, we saw three lifeboats close by. The four boats then proceeded together to head into the wind in a northwest direction, but we were unable to keep up with the others.

"Just then a large submarine, estimated at about 2,000 tons, painted a light grey, and from what we could see, about one hundred seventy-five to two hundred feet in length, with two guns—one forward and one aft of her conning tower—and with no identification number or symbol, appeared on the port side of the *Steed*. Men came out of the conning tower and immediately manned the guns; the forward one appeared to be a four-inch and the aft one a trifle smaller. They started shelling the *W.L. Steed* throughout.

We counted seventeen shots in all. In about three quarters of an hour we saw the vessel settle by the head and then disappear. Thereafter the submarine shaped her course towards our boats, but soon veered off and proceeded in a southwesterly direction.

"Finding it impossible to catch up with the other

lifeboats, we started to put out our sea anchor. The canvas carried away and we hauled in the frame. At this time we noticed that our water keg was empty. When the boat was suspended slantwise, the water keg got loose and rolled down to the bow, breaking the spigot and letting the water out. We made a sea anchor out of the water keg, first chopping a hole on the top and a hole on each side near the top. We had about six feet of two-inch Manila line which we passed through the two holes on the sides of the keg and secured with a square knot. We then made the line for the sea anchor fast to the bight of the two-inch Manila line.

"It was getting darker and we couldn't see any of the other lifeboats. The sea was running heavier and the weather was getting intensely cold. We stretched our lifeboat cover over the two center thwarts to protect us from the wind. After it grew dark we lighted some of our distress flares in the hope of being rescued. We saw that one of the other boats shot a pistol flare. As we started to row in that direction a big sea came over our boat and washed overboard all but three of our oars, also carrying away our rudder, tiller, sails, and boat hooks, and filling the boat half full of water. Using our buckets and scoop and even drinking cups, we proceeded to bail the boat out. By this time we were all wet to the skin.

"After struggling a couple of hours we had the boat bailed out and then went under the canvas boat cover for protection from the heavy spray and strong wind. We kept talking and joking through the night in a sustained effort to keep up our morale. Finally, Chandler lay down on a life preserver and fell asleep. The next morning, about eight o'clock, I tried to wake him up and realized that he was dead. We carried him to the forward end of the boat. The same morning Burkholder became delirious. Shortly after noon he died and was also carried forward.

"It was so bitterly cold that we decided to start a fire. The lamp in the boat being broken, we poured oil from it on some wood we had chopped up and placed in the water bucket. The fire burned steadily and helped to dry our wet clothes and thaw us out to some extent. Perhaps it saved our lives. By cutting up the thwarts, stern sheets, forward sheets, bottom board, and one of the oars, we managed to keep the fire going the rest of the day and during the night, until we were picked up by a Canadian auxiliary cruiser, HMCS *Alcantara*.

"The morning we were picked up I came from under the boat cover to go to the fore sheets, to see if I could chop any more wood for the fire. When I stood up I sighted the Canadian ship! Quickly I grabbed a hand flare and lighted it. The bos'n gave me another and I waved both flares wildly in the air to attract attention. We were thankful when the cruiser turned around and came slowly toward us, cautious for fear of possible submarine attack. They made a complete circle around us and then stopped about two hundred feet away. I'll never forget that scene. The bluejackets on the cruiser were lined up along the deck with heaving lines, ready to throw them to us. We managed to pull alongside the ship and caught two of the lines; I made one line fast to the forward thwart, then took the other, secured it around the bos'n, and sent him up the scramble net. The next heaving line I fastened to Hartz, who was hauled up. Taking the papers of the dead seamen, I climbed up myself and was assisted on board.

"We were carried to the sick bay, undressed, and put to bed. The doctor examined us and said our hands and feet were pretty well frozen. The captain of the *Alcantara* questioned us about the submarine and the rest of the crew members. He had already sent a message to Halifax to notify them we would be landed there. We arrived at Halifax on February 7 and were questioned by the naval authorities and the consul. Then we were placed in the custody of the Standard Oil agent, who arranged our transportation. We arrived in New York on February 11."

Fully ten days after the sinking another lifeboat was sighted, this one by the British ship *Raby Castle*. The War Shipping Administration transmitted the intelligence: "Captain H. V. Wightman reported that he sighted on February 12 a lifeboat belonging to the *W.L. Steed*, Standard Oil tanker. There were four men in the lifeboat and the location was thirty-seven degrees thirty-eight minutes north, sixty-eight degrees thirty-three minutes west. Of the four men only one was alive, Elmer E. Maihiot, Jr. This seaman died on February 15 and was buried at sea. The other three were not identified."

Another lifeboat was sighted by a South American steamship in the approximate location of the reported sinking. It contained "a number of bodies clad in dungarees." But, "the steamer was lowering a boat to make an investigation when the periscope of a submarine suddenly appeared above the surface. The steamship immediately got under way and reported the situation to the Navy."

After all their hardships, even though every man got away from the sinking tanker, only four men lived to tell their horrible tale of survival. The other thirty-four did not just die—they died a lingering, freezing death.

Both the *Liverstad* and the *Sinclair Superflame* reported near misses on the night of the fourth, off the coast of South Carolina, but the real action was taking place off Delaware and Maryland, where Winter in the *U-103* continued his successes.

"Position, latitude 38°05′ north, longitude 74°40′ west, torpedoed; sinking fast; can't receive." Messages like this were becoming commonplace. The Coast Guard was quick to respond. The cutter *Nike*, on standby status, headed directly for the location of the troubled freighter *San Gil*.

The United Fruit Line steamship was carrying a cargo of bananas from Santa Marta, Colombia, to Philadelphia. She was completely blacked-out, and her radio was sealed to prevent unauthorized transmissions. The torpedo that struck her on the port side just forward of the engine room bulkhead not only destroyed the port lifeboats, but brought down the antenna as well. The ship heeled sharply to starboard and stayed that way. The time was 2350.

Captain Walter Koch supervised the evacuation. "I ordered all lifeboats lowered, but No. 4 was smashed with the force of the explosion. No. 1, in which I was in charge, and No. 3, commanded by the second mate, were only ones that got away."

Meanwhile, Radioman Robert Thorp rigged up a substitute antenna for the emergency radio transmitter and tapped off the three distress signals that eventually brought the Coast Guard.

The first lifeboat got away ten minutes after the attack, the second ten minutes later. Two men who were in the engine room when the torpedo hit were killed instantly and went down with the ship.

Said the captain, "We had just pulled clear when the submarine began to shell the vessel from a range of about one thousand feet. We lay there while the sub fired fifteen shells. Four missed, but the other eleven made a wreck of her. It was just about 12:50, almost an hour after the torpedo struck, that she maneuvered into position on the other side of the ship and launched another torpedo.

"We just sat there and watched it all, hoping against hope they wouldn't shell us. I owe my thanks to whoever was in command of that submarine, that they waited to shell our boat until every one had made a lifeboat. They gave us a break, that's all a man can ask."

The *San Gil* appeared to break in two, then settle stern first. Afterwards, the U-boat took off at high speed. The Ocean City Station motor lifeboat arrived first at the scene and took the two boats from the *San Gil* in tow. The *Nike* arrived seven hours after the attack, attracted to the lifeboats by flares. She removed all thirty-eight crewmen and the lone passenger, and took them to Lewes, Delaware.

Not so fortunate was the crew of the Socony-Vacuum Oil Company tanker *India Arrow*, bound for New York from Corpus Christi, Texas. With two ships already to her credit, the *U-103* continued to lurk in what was a promising area. The next night, at 1900, Winter launched a torpedo that caught the blacked-out ship unawares.

Captain Carl Johnson was on the bridge at the time. "There was a loud report, and the torpedo slammed into the starboard side, to the fore of the engines. The ship caught fire and started sinking in about five minutes. Oil from No. 10 cargo tank, which was punctured, leaked onto the water and caught fire, too."

Edward Shear, the radio operator, in his bunk at the time, rushed for the radio room when he heard the detonation. He immediately sent out a distress signal, but the dynamo failed before he could give their position.

Captain Johnson maintained his station on the bridge, shouting out the latitude and longitude to Shear. The tanker listed sharply. A moment later, the U-boat commenced firing its deck gun. The *India Arrow* suffered fourteen shell hits. One well placed shot blew up the bridge, knocking the captain overboard. Miraculously, he was "washed into a lifeboat" occupied by two crewmen.

A fire started by the explosion was quickly doused by inrushing water. The ship went down so fast that the two stern lifeboats were carried under. Lifeboat No. 2 got away from amidships. No sooner had it hit the water than the *India Arrow* lurched suddenly to port. The boat was caught under the bridge, and was taken down along with half those aboard. Those who struggled free swam away in the frigid water and climbed onto floating debris and hatch covers, until they were picked up by the captain in No. 1. lifeboat.

Edward Shear stood by his station until the last possible second. Even though he could not make out the positions the captain was shouting, he tried to crank up the hand auxiliary radio. A short circuit prevented its operation. As the ship capsized, he leaped overboard and kicked away from the awful suction. He located a hatch cover and clung to it desperately until he was picked up by the captain's lifeboat.

When the count was in, twelve shivering survivors were packed aboard the solitary lifeboat.

The tanker's bow protruded from the water at an awkward angle. The U-boat closed to within three hundred yards, and pumped five or six shells into it. The shelling ignited the giant oil slick fed from below by the leaking tanks.

Said Shear, "The blaze lit up the scene, and we could see the conning tower by the burning boat. We were afraid to do anything—to show our lights, to set sail or start rowing or even to bail out the water that had shipped into the lifeboat—because we thought the sub might start shelling us.''

After the U-boat left the scene, Captain Johnson ordered the sails set and the men to rowing. Two hours later, they could still see the oil blazing. During the night the men spotted two approaching vessels. Both times they lighted emergency flares. So many stories were circulating about U-boats disguising themselves as lightships and lighted buoys that on both occasions the merchant ships changed course and took off at high speed.

Most of the men were barefoot, and all were soaked with oil. They huddled together for the only warmth available: that of each other's bodies. The lifeboat's drinking water was tainted with oil, and undrinkable; the biscuits were likewise coated.

All that day and the following night they pulled toward shore while the ocean current dragged them northward. It was not until 0630, after thirty-five hours in the open lifeboat, that they spotted a fishing trawler off Atlantic City. The men waved flashlights until Frank Marshall, skipper of the *Gitana*, noticed them. He wasted no time in taking them aboard and rushing them to the Coast Guard station at Atlantic City, where they received first aid, hot food, and new clothes.

The smoke had hardly cleared from the blazing *India Arrow* when Winter launched a brazen daylight attack on her sister ship, the *China Arrow*. Her tanks were filled with petroleum bound from Beaumont, Texas, to New York.

Since it was daylight, she was running a zigzag course that repeated the formula 6° right, 15° right, 21° right, 30° right, 36° right, and 45° right, then reverse for 90°, ten minutes on each course. She was also blacked out and on radio silence for the entire voyage, with all the receiving sets locked in one cabin.

Before a ''C'' Marine Investigation Board, Captain Paul Browne testified, ''We was zigzagging according to Navy instructions and lookouts were posted at the crows nest. The third mate was on watch and I was in the chart room getting ready to take radio bearings when about 11:12, we were struck by two torpedoes at the 8, 9, and

10 tanks on the starboard side. These penetrated the ship and exploded throwing the fuel oil about one hundred twenty-five feet up in the air and aft towards the stack and forward over the bridge, and a general alarm was sounded. At the time of the explosion, the telegraph and the telephone went out of commission; the vessel went to the right and the engines went dead and the lifeboats No. 1 and 2 were swung out. Lifeboat No. 4 was swung out and I immediately gave the radio operator our position according to Navy instructions and we hooked up to the DF antenna. That gave us the direction on the bow.

"I went back to the chart room to destroy the papers, rechecked the telephone in the engine room and there was no answer. At 11:40, I sighted the submarine showing his tower above the water. The fire had been reduced somewhat due to the fact that the chief engineer had gone back aft and turned on the smoldering line shortly after we were hit. I seen the submarine surface himself and I ordered the crew to abandon ship."

Captain Browne and the radio operator, Kenneth Maynard, stayed aboard and tried to repair the radio set. "The mate's house was full of smoke and we saw it coming out of the decks." Tanks 8 and 9 were flaming. "I saw the submarine crew coming out on the tower."

One boat came back and picked them up. They pulled away from the fuming tanker until they were well clear. Because of the uneven distribution of personnel (three had been plucked out of the water by No. 1 boat) the captain had them lashed together so they could distribute the load. "The second assistant engineer swallowed a lot of fuel oil. I gave him a pint of rum and he vomited."

Winter then shelled the hulk for thirty minutes, until she finally gave in and sank beneath the waves. The time was 1230.

"We lay away from the ship about a mile, the three boats, after we divided the crew up and about forty minutes later, two Army bombers came over and they flew over the wreckage, and I shot up a parachute flare. I figured maybe it would attract one of them. One of them finally came over and swooped down over us and circled three times and he dropped a message.''

Night fell, but still no rescue craft had come their way. The three boats set up watches and dropped sea anchors to slow their drift. Sails draped over the boats kept them fairly comfortable. ''We decided we might get some heat out of the oil lamp. Those that weren't on watch gathered around in a circle, and we kept the oil lamp burning. We laid there the whole night.

''The next day the day broke and it was beautiful and warm with a smooth sea and a slight swell. We had issued crackers and water and the boys exercised and massaged each others' arms and legs, and I rowed the crew for an hour to the westward.''

They heard engines around 1100. The noise persisted for a couple hours, but they saw nothing. They kept rowing toward the setting sun. A breeze kicked up around 1500, so they rigged the sails. At dark, because the boats were separated due to different-sized canvas, Captain Browne had the boats tied in a line. They continued ever westward. At midnight the painter parted, so the captain sailed back and regrouped with the errant lifeboats. That night they were pummeled by freezing rain.

Their second morning adrift broke with overcast skies and seas running to ten feet. At 1100 they spotted a Catalina flying boat coming toward them. A flare attracted its attention. It could not land because of the huge waves, so it continued to circle them all afternoon. Another plane came by at 1400; it, too, circled. Finally, at 1640, both planes headed for home, and the hapless sailors settled in for another night in the open ocean. Captain Browne set watches. ''I made the boys row once in a while so they wouldn't get stiff.''

Search boats had been out continuously ever since the sinking, but were unable to locate the drifting lifeboats. *Eagle 56* reported a submarine some thirty-five miles east of Five Fathom Bank, and dropped depth charges on it. The USS *Tourmaline* came across the wreck of the *India Arrow*, still partly out of the water.

A 0700 the following morning, the *China Arrow*'s third mate sighted a searchlight. After fifty-six hours at sea, they were picked up by the indefatigable Coast Guard cutter *Nike*. Some of the engineers were treated for burns. Two men were hospitalized for injured ankles, one for a broken pelvis. But all thirty-seven pulled through.

The *Ocean Venture* was a brand new Liberty ship out on her maiden voyage. She was built in Richmond, California, and was one of a fleet of thirty built that year for the British government. She carried a cargo of lumber, foodstuffs, airplanes, munitions, and 1,800 tons of pig lead, with a complement of forty-five officers and men, all British. She passed through the Panama Canal, then headed north.

Because of the recently laid defensive minefield, she was proceeding slowly into the approaches of the Chesapeake Bay, awaiting routing instructions so she could refuel in Norfolk before beginning her transatlantic crossing. A clear moon was just rising early in the morning of February 8 when a torpedo slammed into the port side abaft the engine room.

The tremendous explosion killed some of the engine room crew, and knocked out the engines and the generator. The ship was plunged into darkness. She took an immediate list of seven or eight degrees. Momentum continued to move the ship slowly forward. The radio operator sent out an SOS on emergency power, but got no reply.

About twenty minutes later another torpedo hit the *Ocean Venture* on the starboard side, destroying one of the lifeboats. With water flooding into the hull from the opposite side, the freighter rolled back to a fairly even keel. She was dead in the water. The gun crew raced to battle positions. They searched desperately for a target as the ship settled beneath them.

Captain Reginald Craston ordered abandon ship. Those who had survived the two explosions got away in three lifeboats as the ship settled by the stern.

It was then that the *U-108*, Kapitanleutnant Klaus Scholtz, appeared on the surface. In order to ensure the sinking of his first target in the ESF, Scholtz fired a third torpedo at the helpless Liberty ship. This one hit on the starboard bow between No. 1 and No. 2 holds. Scholtz remained on the surface for ten minutes, until the *Ocean Venture* sank completely. Then he submerged and went on his way, leaving in his wake three lifeboats bobbing gently in the ocean swells.

Unfortunately, the broadcast for help had not been received, and no one was aware of the *Ocean Venture*'s misfortune. Dawn came. The boats drifted aimlessly all during the day, gradually separating until they were out of sight of each other. From Captain Craston's boat, a plane was spotted at 0900. He ordered a flare fired, but the pilot did not see their distress call. Shortly afterwards, they saw another plane. Again, flares were fired; again, they went unseen. By 1700 they had counted seven planes flying by, two or three directly over their boat. None responded to their pleas for help. Craston thought they were flying too high to see a lonely lifeboat in the vast ocean.

With darkness came high seas. A sea anchor was fashioned out of an oar and a mast. This did not stop the cold spray from dousing the huddled crewmen, but it held the bow into the waves and prevented the boat from swamping. All night long, the fourteen men fought the elements and tried to keep warm. The cold was so unbearable that one man died during the night.

Another dawn came. Captain Craston issued food and water sparingly. No one knew when, or if, they would be rescued. Finally, in the afternoon, they saw another plane in the blue sky. They fired a flare, and the pilot waved his wings in recognition. He also radioed the lifeboat's position to a nearby destroyer. At 1600, after thirty-six hours adrift in an open boat, the USS *Roe* picked them up.

They were taken to Norfolk, where nine of the thirteen survivors were hospitalized for exposure and frostbitten feet. Eleven days after the attack, one of the other lifeboats was discovered far out at sea. It was waterlogged, and empty. What horrors its occupants suffered before being swept out of their boat can only be imagined.

With the war of the Atlantic now in full swing, and

with U-boat depradations growing more rampant every day, the need to ship war materials to the European and Pacific fronts became ever more important. It was obvious to military authorities that cooperation between Allied nations and a consolidation of resources was needed.

Therefore, on February 9, President Franklin Roosevelt established the War Shipping Administration. The WSA was designed to "control the operation, purchase, charter, requisition and use of all ocean vessels under the flag or control of the United States," to allocate those vessels for use by the "Army, Navy, other Federal departments and agencies, and the governments of the United Nation," and to "provide marine insurance and reinsurance against loss or damage by the risks of war."

This sweeping reform would not only place every U.S. vessel under charter to the government "in order to secure the most effective utilization of shipping in the prosecution of the war," it would reimburse the operators of those vessels should they fall prey to the bite of the gray wolves.

Once the merchant marine fleet became wards of the government, further steps were taken to protect the lives of the mariners. Solid core rafts were installed on breakaway stanchions. In case a ship went down so quickly that there was not time to launch lifeboats, these huge rafts could be quickly unchocked so they could float free on their own. Inquiries were set up and survivors interviewed in order to learn how to better provide for the safety of the crew in the event of a sinking. Deck guns were installed on tankers and freighters, usually on the fantail, and U.S. Navy gun crews were shipped aboard to man them.

Thus began the era of the armed merchant ship.

Vessels of foreign registry had long been armed with deck guns and gun crews. Thus it was on the *Niobe*, sailing under the Panamanian flag. She carried a four-inch gun aft, and two thirty-caliber machine guns. She did not yet have a U.S. Navy armed guard aboard, but four of her Danish crew had trained at the Hoffman Island gunnery school of the United States Maritime Commission.

Captain Jorgen Jorgensen related one incident that occurred within the boundaries of the ESF: "We were approaching Hatteras when we sighted a periscope and fired about twenty rounds at it. In response to our radio message, five planes came out from shore. One of them, a Catalina bomber, dropped several depth charges."

They may not have hit the enemy submarine, but the efficacy of quick and efficient gun action had the desired effect: it forced the U-boat to submerge, where it could only creep along on battery power, while the *Niobe* steamed off at high speed. Had the *Malay* been armed at the time of her uneven encounter with the *U-123*, she might have done more than run away like a wounded pup.

On the tenth, the Chilean steamship *Imperial* spotted a lifeboat full of bodies at 36-11/75-55W. She slowly steamed around to recover them when she sighted a periscope. She made off at high speed. Had the U-boat been lying in wait, using the drifting lifeboat as a grim decoy to attract merchant ships? In war, any trick is valid.

The night of the eleventh saw two more attacks in the ESF. The American tanker *Hagan* was torpedoed right off Ocean City, Maryland, but managed to avoid the deadly missile. She was not so lucky four months later, however, when Korvettenkapitan Wolf Henne of the *U-157* found her off the coast of Cuba. On June 11, Henne's torpedoes sent the *Hagan* to the bottom along with six of her crew and 90,000 gallons of molasses.

The Norwegian freighter *Blink* ran afoul of the still lurking Scholtz far off the coast of North Carolina. She was loaded down with 3,600 tons of phosphate. The wind was blowing a full gale when the first torpedo bounced off the steel hull abaft No. 2 hold: it was a dud. Within sixty seconds, two more exploded against the engine room, killing three duty personnel. The boilers burst, filling the room with scalding steam. The hot vapors rose through the decking into Chief Officer Briger Lunde's room.

# February 1942

The concussion twisted the steel plates and jammed Lunde's door shut. He had to beat his way out of the steam bath with a fire axe. By the time he got on deck, Captain Sigurd Ulvestad was already giving orders to abandon ship.

Lunde found the port lifeboat smashed by the explosions. With the ship going down fast, twenty-three men scrambled aboard the starboard lifeboat and got away. Four other men were seen clinging to a life raft. Fifteen minutes after the attack, the *Blink* joined the growing list of casualties at the bottom of the sea.

Said Lunde, "We dragged a sea anchor all night waiting to see if there were any men in the water. When we found none we tried to start the motor but it wouldn't go. It was full of water. Then we tried to raise the sail, and the boat capsized. Everybody went into the heavy sea. We lost our food, our water, our oars, our sail. One man was lost. The rest of us clung to the keel and righted the boat."

Two men rolled over the gunwale, and tried to bail out the boat. As fast as they bailed, the waves poured in. Too tired to hang on, the rest of the crew climbed in as well. There they sat, waist deep in the icy water, shivering, suffering. Huge waves continually washed them out of the boat. Twice during the day the boat capsized, dunking the half-frozen survivors into the frigid sea. Each time the boat was righted, their numbers were fewer.

Lunde described their suffering: "One by one the men went mad. They would talk of a comfortable bed or a cup of coffee. Captain Ulvestad talked of his family just before he died. We tried to catch a few drops of rain on our tongues. Several men tried to jump overboard, but we kept them inside.

"Frequently we had numerous encounters with sharks. We shouted, we made noises, we did whatever we could to scare them off because we had nothing to fight them with, not even oars. Our lips were swollen and cracked from lack of water. On two occasions we saw ships, but they were too far off. We couldn't get their attention."

By the time they were found by the steamship *Monroe*,

after sixty-six hours adrift, the survivors had dwindled to six. Those six had watched the slow death of their seventeen companions. The men on the raft were never seen again.

Scholtz then headed for Bermuda, and home, sinking the *Ramapo* and the *Somme* on the way.

As other U-boats filtered through East Coast shipping and moved into the rich, southern waters of the Caribbean, the *U-432*, Kapitanleutnant Heinz-Otto Schultze, filled in the gap. For eleven days his was the only U-boat doing any damage in the ESF. His first notch was etched on the hull of the Brazilian passenger-freighter *Buarque*.

The *Buarque* was bound from Rio de Janeiro to New York, with stops at Belem, La Guaira, and Curacao. In her cargo holds were lumber, castor seed, coffee, cotton, wax, sheepskins, and bauxite; on her decks were rubber, aluminum ore, beryllium, drums of oil, and tanks of oxyacetylene.

Although she had broken diplomatic relations with Germany on January 28, Brazil was so far a neutral country in the war. There was no reason for Captain Joao Joaquim de Moura to fear a U-boat attack as long as his ship was unarmed and fully lighted. In addition, Brazilian flags were painted on the *Buarque*'s sides, and the national ensign flew from the stern, brilliantly illuminated by floodlights.

Two American passengers, Walter Shivers and John Dunn, did not feel quite so confident in the German distinction of non-belligerents. As the *Buarque* passed along the Florida coast and reached South Carolina, they cornered the captain in his stateroom and tried to convince him to black out his ship. Captain de Moura listened to them, but refused to acquiesce to their demands. He maintained that a vessel of a peaceful nation should not show aggression or act with subterfuge.

The captain's philosophy of the need to distinguish a warring nation from one at peace was logical and, for a while, well founded. An hour before midnight on the fourteenth, an unidentified submarine surfaced alongside the *Buarque* and matched speed. It paralleled the freighter's course for a few minutes, at a distance of only two hundred yards. Then it surged ahead on the surface and soon passed out of sight. Seventy-four crew members and eleven passengers breathed a collective sigh of relief. Many went to bed more at ease. Their rest was soon broken.

At 0300, just off the Virginia-North Carolina border, a torpedo exploded into the *Buarque*'s port side between No. 1 and No. 2 holds. The blast knocked out all the lights. "The entire ship shook like a terrier would shake a rat," Shivers recalled.

Dunn, his roommate, said, "I put on my shirt and pants and ran on deck." The crew was in total confusion, shouldering aside passengers in their haste to get away in the lifeboats. "We never received an order to abandon ship." Flashlights cast a dim, flickering glow on the pandemonium. "I saw Mrs. Ferreira and Freddie in a lifeboat. She told me she had left their cabin without lifebelts." He ran to her cabin, and returned with lifebelts and blankets.

By this time the first three lifeboats were gone, and only No. 4 remained: half launched, and bow down by the water line. Dunn tossed his load down to the boat, where Adrian Ferriera and her five-year-old son received them gladly. Then he and Shivers climbed down the Jacob's ladder and into the lifeboat. Heavy swells smashed the frail wooden craft against the steel hull of the freighter, threatening to break the lifeboat apart and sink it. The Brazilian crew appeared not to know what to do, so the two Americans took over. They spoke no Portuguese, but communicated by gestures. They got the boat free from its falls, shipped the oars, and started rowing.

They were only a hundred yards away when a second torpedo struck amidships, letting cold seawater into the boiler room. Said Dunn, "There was a terrific screaming sound as the water rushed into the ship's open spaces. I think she was ripped in half by the explosion."

Shivers declared, "A young tidal wave which followed the explosion almost swamped our lifeboat. The screaming of that sinking ship was almost human. It was the most eerie sound I've ever heard. It made my blood run cold.''

Dunn added, ''The ship started down by the bow. The boilers exploded and she sank within thirty seconds.'' Only ten minutes had elapsed from the first detonation to the *Buarque*'s last gasp.

No. 4 lifeboat moved away slowly. The Brazilian sailors did not know how to rig the sail, so it was up to Shivers to do it. Dunn said, ''Freddie became seasick; he was cold, wet, and cramped. But he didn't complain and he smiled when anyone spoke to him.''

At 0700 a land plane swooped low overhead, and circled the tacking lifeboat. Rescue seemed imminent, but another ten hours passed, during which time several other planes were sighted, before the Coast Guard cutter *Calypso* hove to and took aboard the nineteen occupants. A little later, the *Calypso* located a second lifeboat, and took on another twenty-four people.

The other two lifeboats were not found until two days later, on the seventeenth. At 1030, the Socony-Vacuum Oil Company steamship *Eagle* picked up one boatload carrying twenty-seven passengers and crew. One passenger had already succumbed to the icy winds and freezing temperatures, and other seamen were suffering from shock, frostbite, and exposure.

At 1530 that afternoon, after sixty-three hours in the open sea, the destroyer USS *Jacob Jones* located the last lifeboat from the *Buarque*. The sixteen crewmen aboard seemed in reasonably good health, and all were able to scramble up the cargo net on their own. They were all dressed well, except for two who had no shoes.

In deference to the opinion of the two Americans, Shiver and Dunn, none of the other passengers had any complaints about the Brazilian crew.

When the total count was in, out of the original eighty-five on board the *Buarque*, only one had died. Statistically, at least, it had been a fortuitous sinking.

The government of Brazil, on the other hand, did not care for the fortunes of war. It was appalled at this overt transgression of the neutrality laws. But cool heads were in charge. Fearing that their constituency might be incensed to riot, especially in light of the national carnival then taking place, they withheld public announcement of the torpedoing until the singing, dancing, and frenzy of the carnival was over. They wanted no mob destruction of German-held property, such as had occurred during the previous war when the sinking of Brazilian ships was partly responsible for opening the conflict between Germany and Brazil. By the time the newspapers were again being printed and the public apprised of Germany's transgression, the pre-Lenten celebration had ended.

In addition, there was consternation among all South American countries over U-boat depredations against ships in the Caribbean, and against land installations. Oil storage facilities on Aruba had been shelled by one German submarine in a daring nighttime attack. Chile and Argentina were the only two South American republics still maintaining diplomatic relations with Germany, Japan, and Italy.

Something had to be done. The Brazilian government was intent on its purpose of delivering strategic materials to the U.S., so they decided that in the future their vessels would be convoyed for added protection. The U.S. agreed to supply warships, as well as land-based planes that could operate from the various Caribbean islands, to keep open the supply routes between Brazil and the U.S.

At the same time, it was thought that action might have to be taken against the Vichy governments of Guadeloupe and Martinique. Many believed that since those countries were controlled by the Vichy French, they might be supplying marauding U-boats with fuel and munitions.

While all this was going on, Schultze aggravated the situation by sinking a second Brazilian ship, the *Olinda*, on the eighteenth.

The *Olinda* was steaming toward New York with a cargo of cocoa beans, coffee, and vegetable oil. Because of radio silence, there was no way for the captain or crew to know about the *Buarque*'s demise, or the rescues only recently completed. When dawn arrived, the large

Brazilian flags painted on the freighter's hull were clearly visible, and the ship's neutrality loudly proclaimed. The ship was two weeks out of Rio de Janeiro, with ports of call along the way, and the crew was looking forward to landing in New York the next day.

Some two hours later, off Parramore Island, a desolate strip of sand near the south end of the Delmarva Peninsula, Schultze fired his deck gun at the northbound freighter. The first three shells fell short. If Captain Jacob Benemond, master of the *Olinda*, thought they were warning shots, the next three shells quickly changed his mind. One carried away the wireless antenna; the next two slammed into the superstructure. The Brazilian ensign was raised, but it had no effect.

Since his ship was unarmed, Captain Benemond could do nothing but order the engine stopped and abandon ship. As soon as the ship's forward momentum ceased, all the time under constant shelling, both lifeboats were lowered. All forty-six crewmen pulled away.

The U-boat then came alongside one of the boats and took off the radio operator, Francisco Nogueira. Inside the pressure hull he was photographed and asked about the *Olinda*'s routing and cargo. Afterwards, he was returned to his lifeboat.

Next, the U-boat approached the other lifeboat. Captain Benemond was taken aboard the submarine and interrogated. When asked to produce the ship's papers, he explained they were still on the *Olinda*. He said the U-boat commander spoke only German; none of the U-boat men spoke Spanish, although some spoke a little English. Captain Benemond was duly released.

Schultze gave his gun crew further practice. He closed to within three hundred yards of the freighter and let them pummel it with some twenty shells. This caused secondary fires, but the aged vessel refused to sink. Schultze finally had to pump a torpedo into her hull to send her to her grave.

Just about that time a plane swooped into the fracas. The U-boat submerged and was not seen again. The plane was soon joined by several others, which circled the lifeboats and dropped a lifebelt inscribed "HELP

COMING.'' Another ship appeared on the horizon. Some of the planes signaled for her to veer toward the lifeboats, but their signals were not understood. One plane hung around until dark, then left for shore.

Help did not come soon. The *Olinda*'s crew were forced to spend the night at sea in their open boats. They became separated. Fortunately, the weather stayed calm and the temperatures mild. The destroyer USS *Dallas* hove into view at 0730, picked up the first boatload of survivors, and an hour later located the second. There were no casualties, and only a few minor injuries.

If the government of Brazil was appalled at the sinking of the *Buarque*, it was outraged by this second flagrant abuse of neutrality. Its response was immediate: it ordered all shipping companies to paint their vessels dark gray, it started arming its merchant ships, it increased air and naval patrols along its coast, it instituted the draft of all men between the ages of twenty-one to thirty-two years, it shortened officer training periods from three years to two, it started the seizure of German assets in Brazil, and it charged for economic reprisals for damages done to the country's shipping. Through the Portuguese Government, which had been representing Brazil with respect to the Axis powers since the breaking of diplomatic relations, a formal protest was made.

Extra newspaper editions printed bold headlines: "Acts of war against Brazil by Axis." The press referred to the sinkings as "piratical acts," and went on to state, "Germany is committing aggression against us by sinking our ships. The purpose is to make us pay for the crime of having a conscience and respecting our international agreements." Despite the fact that not a single Brazilian life had been lost (the one fatality, Manuel Rodriguez Gomez, a passenger, was not Brazilian), the fervor caused by the lack of humanitarianism on the part of the U-boat commander was heated. Killing the soldiers of an aggressive nation was one thing, but assaulting innocent women and children was quite another. The country was in an uproar.

By this time, the war was so hot in the Caribbean that torpedoes were the most common fish seen on the surface of the sea, and ships were being sunk nightly. One torpedo missed its intended target and, like a scene right out of "Operation Petticoat," ran right up onto the beach in Aruba. It did not sink a truck, but it did kill the four men who tried to disarm it.

Between the two Brazilian calamities there occurred an incident on the sixteenth with no apparent explanation. The *E.H. Blum* was a brand new tanker just out of the shipyard. She received secret routing instructions from the Port Director of the Fourth Naval District, and steamed out of Philadelphia on the fifteenth on her maiden voyage, bound for Port Atreco, Texas, in ballast. In maritime jargon she was "stout, staunch, and strong; was well masted, manned, tackled, victualed, apparelled and appointed, and was in every respect fit for sea."

The next day, at about 1430, she encountered fog off the Virginia coast. It became increasingly dense during the afternoon. The first leg of the journey was to take her to Hampton Roads. Captain William Evans steered the *E.H. Bum* for the Junction Buoy, some four miles east of Cape Henry at the entrance to the Chesapeake Bay, in order to communicate with the Navy's examination vessel for identification and to pick up a pilot. Through the fog, he observed the masthead lights of two vessels. Four blasts of his horn signaled for the pilot. Because he received no response, and was not allowed to proceed without authorization westward of 74°50′ west, he let his vessel drift.

An hour and a half later, still with no response to the continuing wail of his foghorn, Captain Evans put his engines slow ahead and headed back for the Junction Buoy. At 0832, the lookout on the forecastle head reported a light dead ahead. The rudder was swung hard to starboard, but before the ship could respond a loud explosion occurred on the port side of the ship, just aft of the midship house. Captain Evans immediately sent out a distress signal and ordered the lifeboats swung out. However, a cursory inspection revealed that the ship was in no danger of sinking.

Again, the *E.H. Blum* went slow ahead. At 0849, another explosion rent through the port hull between Nos.

8 and 9 tanks, and disabled the tanker's engines. The ship's lights were knocked out, and the crew left in darkness. With a sharp list to port and the ship settling rapidly, Captain Evans ordered abandon ship. At 0915, as the last lifeboat was being lowered into the water, a third explosion ripped open the port aft.

The Coast Guard cutter *Woodbury* was operating in the area at the time when her radio operator picked up the SOS. She got underway and shaped course for the stricken tanker. She then heard the last two detonations and veered through the fog for the sound. They soon located one of the *E.H. Blum*'s lifeboats, and took aboard the survivors. Within thirty minutes they found the other three lifeboats. The entire crew of forty was picked up, without injury, and the incident for them was over.

But the odyssey of the *E.H. Blum* was just beginning. It was at first determined that the tanker had blundered into the recently sown protective minefield. The testimony of Ernest Thomas, on lookout at the time of the first explosion, contradicts that.

"I saw a light, which I took to be the mast light of another ship, about seventy-five yards off the starboard bow. I reported this light to the bridge and about fifteen seconds later the captain ordered full speed ahead and hard right. Then there was an explosion and the bow came up five or six feet. I thought we had rammed a submarine. The tanker listed to port.

"The captain gave the order to stand by the lifeboats but not to lower away. Fifteen minutes later there was a second explosion and the skipper gave the order to abandon ship. After the second blast the ship stopped dead. That is why I believe the third explosion, which took place after my lifeboat had left the tanker, must have been from a torpedo, because a motionless ship could not run into a mine."

Radio Operator W. Hammer agreed: "I have never been torpedoed before, but the ship was stopped dead still after the first hit. When the second and third hits came her motors were dead. Although she wallowed in a choppy sea there was no forward motion."

On the other hand, other crew members felt that mines were responsible for the explosions.

Notwithstanding these observations, German records do not credit any U-boat with the kill, either from the laying of mines or firing of torpedoes. Indeed, it seems unlikely that in a fog as dense as that described, a U-boat could have spotted the drifting tanker even if it dared to venture that close to the coast under such dangerous conditions.

Even with all the evidence in, the cause of the *E.H. Blum*'s explosion is open to conjecture. The most likely scenario appears to be mines accidentally cast adrift from the American minefield. But this is far from the end of the story.

The next day, after the fog had lifted, the hulk was found broken in half at No. 5 hatch, but still afloat. Each half was towed separately into drydock at the Newport News Shipbuilding and Drydock Company. Unlike Humpty Dumpty, a massive four-month operation put the *E.H. Blum* back together again. Newly welded, she sailed off under her own power in July to ply her trade carrying petroleum products for the Atlantic Refining Company.

The next phase of her life lasted only until December 29, 1942. Navigation was hampered by storm and fog when the *E.H. Blum* ran aground on Fenwick Island Shoal off the coast of Maryland—a mere hundred miles from the location of her first casualty. With the midships stranded on a sand bar and the bow and stern afloat in deeper water, the pounding waves beat against the recently reconstructed hull for two days until the ill-fated tanker split in two. The bow jackknifed, coming to rest parallel with the stern. All thirty-nine crewmen were taken off by the tug *Samson*. The two parts were later refloated and towed to the place of her birth, in Philadelphia. Once again she was reassembled. Somehow, the *E.H. Blum* survived the war.

On the nineteenth, the *Oklahoma* transmitted an SSS: submarine sighted but did not attack (as opposed to SOS, which was reserved as a call for emergency aid.) Vessels were encouraged to transmit such announcements unless under strict radio silence, in order to aid U-boat plotting intelligence. Then the *Oklahoma* radioed "torpedo crossed bow." She altered course, put on a full head of steam, and went on unmolested.

On the twentieth, Kapitanleutnant Heinrich Lehmann-Willenbrock in the *U-96* torpedoed the freighter *Lake Osweya* off the coast of Massachusetts. There were no transmissions, no reports, no survivors.

On the twenty-first, Schultze got the *Azalea City*. The freighter left Buenos Aires, Argentina, in January, loaded more cargo in Trinidad, and left that port on February 12, commanded by Captain George Self. Neither the ship nor her crew were ever seen again, except through the lens of a German periscope.

After a three-day lull, Schultze caught the *Norlavore* en route from Baltimore to Puerto la Cruz. He torpedoed the freighter on the night of the twenty-fifth, and sent her to the bottom with all hands. No knowledge of her fate was known to Allied authorities until captured German records were evaluated after the war.

Schultze shot his bolt after midnight, the twenty-sixth, when he found the *Marore* (sister ship to the previously sunk *Venore*) steaming north from Chile to Baltimore with a load of iron ore.

Captain Charles Nash, master: "We had no warning. The torpedo struck amidships on the port side. I gave the order immediately to abandon ship. Although all the crew but nine were in their bunks, the concussion had an alarm effect. All members were on deck almost instantly. They went to their respective lifeboats without confusion. In ten minutes the ship was abandoned."

Well that they wasted no time, for Schultze decided to leave the ESF not with a bang, but with a lot of little pops. He peppered the *Marore*, dead in the water, by circling around her and firing at her from all sides like a wolf worrying a wounded caribou. So energetically did the *U-432* besiege the helpless freighter that the merchant mariners thought there must have been at least three U-boats involved in the attack.

"They must have fired 100 rounds or more. All three intermittently fired tracers. They hit the water, bounced like crazy tennis balls and lit up the whole area, giving the gunners a perfect target. They had good marksmanship, too. Looked like ninety per cent of the shells hit.''

Probably, Schultze had no more torpedoes, and was intent on adding one last ship to his total tonnage score. Whether or not three U-boats operated in concert is a matter of testimony.

Praise was given to Third Assistant Engineer E. B. Stahl who, ''though knocked off his feet when the torpedo hit, had sufficient presence of mind to grope through the darkness and shut off the ship's motor. This made it easier for the crew to launch the lifeboats and leave the ship.''

The three lifeboats drifted away with the *Marore*'s full compliment. The next morning, two boats were found by the tanker *John D. Gill*. Under Captain Nash's command, the fourteen men in the third lifeboat had rigged sail and tacked westward. They were found that afternoon by a motor surfboat from the Big Kinnakeet Lifeboat Station, North Carolina. Taking seven men at a time, the surfboat made two trips through the surf and landed the men safely on the beach.

That same night, after the *U-432* made its last kill in the ESF, the *U-578*, Korvettenkapitan Ernst-August Rehwinkel, made its first.

The *R.P. Resor* was bound from Houston, Texas, to Fall River, Massachusetts, with 78,729 barrels of fuel oil. Along with a compliment of forty-one officers and men, an armed guard consisting of an ensign and eight Navy gunners manned a four-inch deck gun carried on the fantail. Captain Fred Marcus ran his ship blacked out and on a zigzag course as he worked his way north. In addition to lookout watches maintained by his crew, the armed guard posted one man at the gun and one on the monkey bridge.

Able Bodied Seaman John Forsdal, one of the helmsmen on the night of the twenty-sixth, tells his story: ''The evening was fine and clear. There was a light northwesterly breeze, small ripples on the water, and a long, moderate, lazy easterly swell. It was a brilliantly lighted moonlight night, there being a little better than half a moon showing. The sky was cloudless and the night was so clear I could easily distinguish the individual lights on the New Jersey shore. The evening was cold and it was necessary to wear heavy clothing and ear muffs.''

Forsdal yielded the wheel at 2200. For the next hour he was on standby duty. At 2300, he "proceeded to the foc'sle head and relieved Ordinary Seaman Hogard. The *Resor* would soon be about twenty miles east of Manasquan Inlet, New Jersey.

"Just before seven bells, I was standing slightly to port of the stem. Suddenly I sighted a dark object lying low in the water about two points on the port bow. Although not far distant from the vessel, it was indistinct. I did not hear any engine or a motor exhaust, possibly due to the sound of the *Resor*'s bow waves. I immediately turned and walked aft along the port side toward the bell, to report the craft. A few seconds after I sighted the vessel, which I thought might be a small fishing boat, she turned on her navigating lights. I could see that her white light was about five feet above her green and red side lights. The lights were then about two hundred to three hundred yards away and were heading for a point midway between the stem of the *Resor* and the break of the foc'sle head.

"A second or so after the strange vessel showed her navigating lights, I rang two strokes on the bell and then reported by voice to the bridge: 'Small vessel about two points on your port bow, sir!' The bridge answered: 'Aye! Aye!' From the time I first observed the craft until I reported it, only ten to fifteen seconds had elapsed.

"As I turned to walk forward, I saw that the lights were about three points on the port bow. They were too dim to show any part of her hull and after a few seconds she switched them off. Thinking that she was a fishing boat because of her small outline and not realizing that a submarine would venture so close to shore, I resumed my lookout without giving further thought to the vessel, which had disappeared in the darkness. At this time, as I recall, the moon was either aft or on our starboard quarter.

"I had continued my lookout for a minute or two,

when all of a sudden I felt and heard a violent explosion on our port side. Within what seemed a fraction of a second the *Resor* was aflame from her bridge aft and debris was hurled high into the air. I was thrown to the deck and lay there momentarily in a dazed condition. Then to protect myself from falling fragments I crawled under a platform on the foc'sle head which had been constructed for a gun.

"When it seemed safe, I got up and went down to the fore deck. In the light of the flames, the submarine was now clearly visible, about four points on our port bow and four hundred to five hundred yards distant. The enemy vessel, without lights, appeared to be on her way to the Jersey shore and I could hear the noise of a heavy diesel exhaust. Then she disappeared from view.

"Removing my lifebelt and heavy overcoat, I put the lifebelt on again and proceeded to the foremast rigging on the port side, where I tried to size up the situation to see whether I could go aft. I decided that the fire was too severe. Then I released the portside life raft, found a line hanging over the side and lowered myself into the water, which was icy cold.

"When about fifty yards from the ship, as I kept on swimming in heavy oil, I heard a second violent explosion. Looking over my shoulder I saw that the oil floating on the water in the vicinity of the ship was afire. I had to swim out to sea at least twenty minutes to get away from the burning oil.

"About this time I heard a voice and paddled toward it, shouting. A moment later I heard another man calling nearer by. It was Radio Operator Clarence Armstrong and I swam in his direction. Sparks shouted to me and to the other man in the water, whom I could not identify: 'Come over here so we can be together.' He also told us he had a life raft. The *Resor* was then between us and the Jersey shore and I could see the mass of flames growing steadily worse.

"Covered with more and more oil, I struggled hard to reach Armstrong, answering him each time he shouted. In the light of the flaming *Resor*, after a period of time I cannot estimate, I arrived at the raft, which was about half a mile distant from the ship. Hooking my arms around the lifelines I rested for ten minutes or so in a state of exhaustion. Sparks was hanging to a lifeline on the other side of the raft.

"I was heavily weighted down with cold and clinging oil; the exertion of climbing up on the raft taxed my strength so seriously that I was unable to do anything but lie down. The cold and the heavy oil seemed to be paralyzing my body.

"While lying on the raft I observed what I took to be a Coast Guard patrol boat. I told Sparks to keep his chin up, that help was coming. At the same time I was shouting toward the boat so they could locate us. When she passed us she turned around and put a searchlight on the raft. Then a lifebuoy was thrown, attached to a line. I managed to get my arms through the ring but as the vessel went ahead I was hauled off the raft into the sea. Then the patrol boat's headway pulled the life ring from my grasp. I managed to return slowly to the raft, but as I felt warmer in the water, I did not attempt to climb aboard it. Armstrong was still hanging on, but did not reply when I talked to him.

"A small boat came over to me and a rope was put under my arms. Soon afterward a picket boat came along and the line secured to my body was passed to it. I cannot remember what happened after that until I found myself on board the boat, which landed me on the New Jersey coast. Another man had been hauled out of the water by the picket boat before they rescued me. He was a member of the Navy armed guard named Hey." Armstrong was never seen again.

Coxswain Daniel Hey was the gunner Forsdal referred to. He was asleep when the torpedo struck. He leaped out of his bunk, rushed onto deck, and found the ship engulfed in flames. He and three others tried to launch the port lifeboat, but they were driven back by the spreading fire. They were driven overboard by the heat, and swam "for an opening in the ring of fire." He was the only one to get through. He fought the icy sea for an hour and a half before being picked up, and was on board when Forsdal was found.

Hey declared that he saw the starboard lifeboat lowered away. Its normal capacity was thirty-two, but when it shoved off it was "loaded to the gunwale."

The rescuers tell their story as well. It was a lookout from the Shark River Lifeboat Station who first noticed what appeared to be flames on the horizon. Motor boats were dispatched immediately from that station and from the Manasquan station, and shortly airplanes, Coast Guard cutters, and a blimp were on their way to the disaster site.

Rescue craft found the sea thick with oil. One boat surged through the coagulated oil toward two emergency rafts, but was forcibly stopped when oil on the propeller blades became so heavy that the motor stalled. When the crew determined that no survivors were on the rafts, they worked the boat out of the slick, staying just ahead of the flames.

Another boat heard cries for help. Said a Third Naval District report, "We found a man completely covered with oil. Efforts to pull him aboard were unsuccessful, but we managed to get a line around his waist and towed him away from the intense heat coming from the white hot sides of the ship. Already so near the fire that the paint of the picket boat was blistered, we could proceed no further with the man caked with oil and weighing three times his normal weight being towed under. He was yelling that we were drowning him so we moved him from amidships to cockpit aft and four of the crew managed to pull him aboard.

"Cruising nearer the ship we found another man hanging to a raft. Two Navy men from *PC-507* were trying unsuccessfully to get him on board a rowboat. We went alongside and ordered Thomas J. Evans and Oswalk M. Etheridge, coxswain (Pro), to go on raft and pull the man out of the water. These two crew men were exceedingly brave, took many chances of being burned or falling overboard, but managed to pull the man from the water and he was hauled aboard the picket boat. The two survivors were stripped, wrapped in blankets and secured in cabin aft where there was a hot fire and coffee."

The oil covering the ocean burned itself out after four

hours, but smoke and broiling flames poured into the crisp, early morning sky. Thousands of residents of Asbury Park and neighboring resort towns witnessed the spectacular display. The Standard Oil tanker continued to burn all day.

As the *R.P. Resor* drifted slowly northward, the search for survivors and the missing lifeboat went on. Searchers from the Shark River Lifeboat Station came across the body of man wearing a cork life preserver. They recovered it with great difficulty: so much oil had accumulated on the hapless sailor that he weighed an estimated three hundred fifty pounds.

During the course of the week, five more bodies were discovered floating in the slick. Forsdal and Hey remained the only survivors out of a compliment of fifty stalwart men. The missing lifeboat was never found; it very likely burned up with all the men in it.

The tanker finally burned itself out. The intense heat buckled the steel hull plates amidships, breaking the ship's back. The bow and stern rose out of the water until the blackened derelict resembled a flattened V. The hulk was taken in tow by the Navy tug USS *Sagamore* on the twenty-eighth. They were making for shallow water when the stern submerged under the weight of the steam turbines. With the vessel grounded, the *Sagamore* cut free and stood by. Finally, at 2112, after a valiant forty-five hour battle, the *R.P. Resor* gave up the ghost.

In order to protect its merchant fleet, the U.S. Navy began regular coastal patrols with whatever craft were available. With the larger ships of the battle fleet destroyed at Pearl Harbor or cruising the Pacific Ocean, only the lesser and older ships were assigned to the East Coast. Private yachts were taken over, and their graceful teak decks hidden under gunmounts and depth charge racks. Even fishing trawlers were being armed.

The USS *Jacob Jones* was a World War One leftover, one of two hundred seventy-four flush deck, four stack destroyers known affectionately as the "four pipers." During the years since the Great War nearly a hundred were disposed of in accord with the London Treaty. Some, such as the seven lost on the rocks at Honda,

California, met harsher fates. With the outbreak of hostilities in Europe, fifty were given to England as part of the great lend-lease program. A few underwent conversion for other duties. DD-130 was one of seventy-one retaining U.S. destroyer status at the outbreak of war.

On the morning of February 27, the *Jacob Jones* quit her berth at the Brooklyn Navy Yard and headed south along the New Jersey coast. At a speed of fifteen knots she soon reached the site of the *R.P. Resor*, which was still burning furiously. The destroyer spent two hours circling the tanker in search for survivors. None was sighted.

By mid afternoon, the *Jacob Jones* terminated the search and continued south on a regular submarine patrol mission. After nightfall she ran completely blacked-out, with no port lights showing and no running or navigational lights lit. By the glow of a dull moon, lookouts scanned the horizon with binoculars. Westward lay the Delaware coast.

Dawn was just breaking at 0500 when two torpedoes in rapid succession slammed into the destroyer's port side. The first hit forward and detonated the magazine, which blew off the bridge and charthouse and separated the bow. The second hit aft and not only stopped the engines, but carried away the entire stern above the propeller shafts.

The concussion immediately knocked out all the ship's fuses: the destroyer went dark. The odor of carbide gas wafted across what little remained of the deck. Machinist Louis Hollenbeck, from his watch station in the crow's nest, ducked debris that was tossed high in the air. Shrapnel rattled through the superstructure like hail through tinsel. Small fires blazed everywhere.

When Hollenbeck next opened his eyes, nothing remained forward of No. 2 boiler. Gone were the captain's cabin, the officers' quarters, the forward crew's quarters—and all the officers, including Lieutenant Commander Hugh Black, the ship's captain. Aft of the engine room the whole fantail, including the deck gun, was missing, and the crew's quarters there as well.

Hollenbeck was sitting high above a floating midship section. In a span of seconds, more than half the *Jacob Jones'* three hundred fourteen-foot length had been neatly excised. Of the one hundred forty-five-man crew, less than thirty were still alive—mostly those fortunate enough to have been on duty in the engine room and after boiler rooms.

Radioman Albert Oberg woke up when the blast ripped through the aft bulkhead between the firemen's quarters. The violence of the explosion tossed him out of his bunk. He climbed over the debris, found a massive hole in the hull, climbed out onto the port side of the ship, and walked forward along the smashed outer skin.

Hollenbeck climbed down to the slippery, oil-covered deck, where dazed survivors were gathering. He tried to free a brand new life raft just shipped aboard in Brooklyn, but the debris was piled on it so heavily he could not move it. He ran into the only officer who had survived the attack; Ensign Smith, an assistant engineer, was incoherent, and unable to issue orders. Yet despite the lack of command, discipline was good, and the able-bodied seamen went about the task of abandoning ship as best they could.

Fireman Joseph Tidwell left the engine room at 0455. "I had just gone up to the galley to get some sugar for some coffee we had made when there was a terrible explosion forward and the ship seemed to bog down. Pots and pans in the galley began to rain down over our heads. Then another explosion. I ran up to see what to do and found some of the boys cutting rafts away." The stunned survivors remained calm as they prepared to leave the sinking destroyer. "We were a very orderly bunch. We had good sailors on the 'Jakie'."

Machinist Thomas Moody grabbed his coat and life jacket as he scrambled out of the engine room. Topside, he tried to launch a lifeboat, but found that the launching gear had been shattered by the explosion. He headed amidships. "I wasn't going to go out in that cold water without getting something warm in my stomach." He guzzled hot coffee from a soup ladle. He and Fireman George Pantall ransacked the locker room for heavy underwear; each donned three pairs as protection against the ordeal they knew they must soon face.

At this point, most of the *Jacob Jones* had already sunk. The severely truncated machinery space was all that was left, and as water gushed in through bent and twisted watertight bulkheads, it too began to settle. Two lifeboats were lodged in their cradles, but there were not sufficient uninjured personnel to dig them out from under the oily debris, swing them out, and lower them. Forty-five minutes after the attack, the midship section was awash.

Tidwell: "I jumped in the water and climbed on one raft with Struthers and Dors. . . . There was fuel oil in the water all around, but it did not catch on fire." He also thought he saw the offending U-boat: "It was outlined in the darkness about one hundred yards off the port side."

The raft was unstable in the rough seas, and kept banging into debris. The three men decided that the tiny raft was fit only for two. Dors volunteered to swim back to the *Jacob Jones*. Tidwell described Dors' experience: "The front end of what was left of the ship was sunk under by that time and Dors climbed back up on the middle section to see if he could cut another raft loose and maybe help some of the other fellows off the boat."

Dors was unable to dig out another raft. "When my feet got wet I jumped in the water again and swam for a while. When I reached another raft with some other fellows on it I grabbed a hold, then looked around and saw the last of the 'Jakie' go down."

Moody cut loose three life rafts and threw them over the side to men struggling in the frigid water. These rafts had no floors; they were simply five by nine foot rings of flotation material with loops of rope for handholds. Then came the final tragedy. "I jumped over the side and swam around until I found a raft. Just as I grabbed hold, an explosion went off in the ship. I was blown clear of the water. I finally got back on the raft. I was the thirteenth man to get on it. After I got on it we pulled Pantall over the side."

Pantall stayed on deck until the water was lapping at

his ankles. Then he jumped overboard and swam for the raft. "The explosion knocked me away from the raft and the water went over my head. But I got hold of the raft again and held on to it for about an hour before they found room on it and pulled me aboard."

Dors also made it to this raft. "I was still holding on when a big explosion shot up from out of the water. The explosion knocked some of the fellows off of their rafts and almost blew me out of the water, but I held on. The water was plenty cold, about thirty-eight degrees."

The torpedo hits had apparently knocked some of the depth charges out of the safe position. As the tortured wreckage crashed to the sandy bottom, the armed explosives detonated. The concussion hammered the men in the water. Those nearest the ship were killed outright; those farther away suffered internal injuries to which most succumbed. The fatally injured men slipped off one by one. The fourteen sailors on one raft dwindled until only Moody, Pantall, Hollenbeck, and Dors were left. Ensign Smith was one of those who disappeared.

Several hours later, in a calm but deadly sea, the lingering survivors were spotted by an air patrol. Since no SOS had been sent, this was the first the Navy knew of the attack on the *Jacob Jones*. At 0930, the *Eagle 56* steamed into the area and picked up the nearly frozen men clinging to the three rafts. Of the total ship's compliment, only twelve ratings were left. Yet another died on the way to Cape May.

Rehwinkel left the ESF after sinking the *Jacob Jones*. The *U-578* moved south into the Caribbean Sea Frontier, where it continued its rampage by sinking the *Ingerto* on March 12, before returning home.

The death toll for February was four hundred three, of whom nearly a third were killed on the *Jacob Jones*, for a running total of almost a thousand. This included citizens of a dozen different nations, as well as civilians, merchant marines, and naval personnel.

Hitler was making the best of the propaganda, boasting that the *U-123*, which had sunk the *Norness*, had not only entered New York harbor, but had been so bold as to torpedo and sink a moored tanker. German reporter Hans Krels purported to have been aboard at the time:

"We have seen New York and the turmoil of traffic in the port and at the piers of Long Island. The climax of our cruise was the entry of New York Harbor. There was a big tank ship of 10,000 tons which did not suspect anything and sailed along. Our torpedoes hit the engine room and bunker and set fire to the whole cargo, which developed into a huge sheet of flames four hundred yards high. It was a fantastic sight for us and without doubt a terrifying sight for the Yankees. The tanker sank gradually."

While this may evoke the imagery of the audacious Gunther Prien, who in 1939 slipped the *U-47* into Scapa Flow under the very noses of the British and sank the battleship *Royal Oak*, somehow the five million inhabitants of New York City failed to notice the event. Even in that city of hustle and bustle, tongues of fire a quarter mile high were bound to elicit *some* comment.

Despite this Bunyanesque exaggeration, increased shipping losses were having their effect on the American economy. Rubber was becoming a rare commodity, and automobile tires were strictly rationed. Even retreading was limited to truck tires whose owners had to meet certifiable requirements. But the big shortage was in petroleum products.

Atlantic seaboard stores of kerosene, No. 2 heating oil, and bunker C and No. 6 fuel oil were on the wane. The country was warned that the sinking of tankers was drastically reducing existing supplies. Inland refineries, including those that normally exported through the Gulf of Mexico, were asked to phase in tank car deliveries by truck and train. The first oil crisis had hit the states.

At the same time, with the American shipbuilding program not yet in full swing, cargoes bound for overseas battlefronts were piling up on the wharves due to the shortage of ships. Washington and London were cooperating in establishing a joint Anglo-American shipping board which would oversee the pooling of merchant ships so that the flow of war materials could be expedited. They might concede that one reason for the backlog was the immense distances involved in reaching the world's far-flung war zones, but they could not ignore the effect of the U-boat campaign.

The worst was yet to come.

# MARCH

"These men are doing their duty to the nation in a splendid way. They are facing daily hazards and loss of life, but they do not falter. It is to be expected that every able-bodied man will do his job for the nation wherever his talents best may fit him. We count on our merchant seamen and they will not let us down."

Jesse Jones, Secretary of Commerce
February 12, 1942

The month started out misleadingly slowly. While the nation was recovering from the grave loss of so many young sailors on the *Jacob Jones*, the U-boats were changing the guard. Nothing happened the first week, but once the torpedoes started skimming across the blue Atlantic waters it seemed as if they would never stop. During the second week of March, six U-boats arrived in the ESF.

Brazil got a double dose of the action. In midafternoon on the seventh, Kapitanleutnant Adolf Piening, *U-155*, caught the *Arabutan* off the Virginia coast. The freighter had just taken on a cargo of coke and coal at Newport News, Virginia, and was southward bound, for Trinidad. The blast of the single torpedo killed Manuel Goimbra in his bunk.

Third Officer Jose Madeiros was on the bridge with the captain when the deadly missile struck. "The captain notified all aborad to stand by the lifeboats. We stood there for about five minutes and then he gave the order to abandon ship. We were loaded in four lifeboats. We pulled away from the ship and waited until she sank, which was about twenty minutes after we abandoned ship.''

The U-boat surfaced and circled the lifeboats. Madeiros counted four men in the conning tower. ''They were small of stature, of swarthy complexion and all appeared to have black hair. This led us to believe they were Italian.''

Radio Rome had been broadcasting for weeks that Italy had sent submarines into the Western Atlantic to work in unison with the German wolf packs, and claimed that some of the East Coast shipping losses were attributed to the Italian undersea fleet. The story, although untrue, was readily believed at the time.

The Brazilian crewmen were understandably concerned about their lot as the U-boat approached. But two U.S. Navy patrol planes roared overhead, causing the German submarine to crash dive. One plane dropped a buoy in the *Arabutan*'s flotsam. The men in the lifeboats relaxed and, expecting immediate help, waited to be picked up. High waves beat against the boats hour after hour. Night came, and no rescue craft arrived.

The next morning they spotted a ship on the horizon, but were unable to attract her attention. They drifted together all day until they were again found, this time by a searching Coast Guard plane. The Coast Guard cutter *Calypso* had spent the entire night following the current, stabbing the darkness with searchlights, scanning for any sign of bobbing lifeboats. As soon as she received the plane's signals, she turned and raced for the transmitted location.

All the survivors were duly taken aboard. Among them was Elyseu Nascimento, who had only three weeks before survived the sinking of the *Buarque*.

Because of the delay in locating the survivors and determining what ship had been sunk, another Brazilian vessel was sent to her last port of call before word of the *Arabutan*'s fate reached the outside world. Oberleutnant zur See Otto Ites, *U-94*, was responsible.

The *Cayru* was northbound, completely blacked out, carrying goatskins, sheepskins, cotton linters, coffee, cashews, castor seeds, assorted nuts, and beryllium ore from Rio de Janeiro to New York. Also aboard were eighty-five passengers and crew.

Ites took her down with two torpedoes. The first struck the starboard side amidships, causing the vessel to list as she took on water. The time was 1930. It was dark and cloudy, with no moon and poor visibility. Captain Pequeno wasted no time in swinging out the lifeboats. The *Cayru* was abandoned in orderly fashion.

Otto Jaegers and his wife got away in a twenty-six-foot lifeboat. "Four boats were launched and we pulled away from the ship without much fuss. The water was comparatively calm at this time. It was quite dark and suddenly the submarine came into view on the surface close by. I could see it plainly. Two men seemed to be looking out of the conning tower.

"They called out in broken English with an unmistakable German accent asking the name of the ship and its destination. Practically everybody in the boat answered them. The submarine then went over to boat No. 1, which contained the captain, and asked if everyone was off. After receiving an affirmative answer, they approached the ship and sent a second torpedo amidships, right by the engine room. This blew the ship apart and it sank rapidly.

"The submarine circled our boats, and then disappeared. The sea was calm at first, but very shortly after we were in the boat the wind blew up to gale force. We had rain, hail, thunder, and lightning. The waves were terrible, they washed over the boat continually until we were all completely soaked and terribly cold.

"The bravest of the lot was the fifteen-year-old girl, June de Sousa. She never let a peep out of her, nor complained from the time we were left in the lifeboat until we were rescued.

'The crew started to row and then rigged a sail, but the wind was so strong they had to lower it. As the sea grew rougher, they rigged a sea anchor and finally the men had to take down the boat's mast to keep the tiny craft from capsizing."

The lifeboats became separated in the dark. No. 2,

with the Jaegers, June and her mother, and twenty-two crewmen, were picked up the next day by a northbound steamer and taken to New York. News of the calamity preceded them. The Navy sent out search planes and patrol boats, but it was not until after three terrible days and nights in the tumultuous sea that the second lifeboat was located. By that time, of the twenty-one passengers and crew aboard, fifteen had died horribly of exposure. The six survivors all had frozen feet when they were brought into New London, Connecticut. The two remaining lifeboats, containing thirty-eight souls, were never found.

As these facts came to light, Brazil went into an uproar. The tonnage of the vessels lost amounted to some five percent of the country's total shipping reserves. This was bad enough but, while the commodities could be replaced through reparations, human lives could not.

The Brazilian government held Germany accountable. President Getulio Vargas instituted measures of reprisal against Axis powers. His first act was to amend the Constitution in order to allow the government to suspend guarantees safeguarding property ownership for the national affected. Stated simply, this meant that the government could "seize the possessions of Axis subjects to compensate for losses incurred by the sinking of Brazilian ships." This meant more than confiscating personal property belonging to German, Japanese, and Italian citizens; it meant nationalizing more than five hundred banks and corporations. Axis assets in the Banco de Brazil were frozen, to be held as a guarantee of indemnity. Japanese Imperial Government land holdings in the Amazon Valley were revoked; a concession larger than the states of Connecticut, Delaware, and Rhode Island combined was revoked.

Vargas also ordered the government owned shipping company, Lloyd Brasileiro, to cancel all voyages until a convoy system could be organized. The Brazilian Finance Mission completed lend-lease agreements with the U.S., bringing the two countries closer together. Military escorts would help ensure that South American cargoes reached their North American destinations.

# TRACK OF THE GRAY WOLF

While Vargas may seem to have been executing dictatorial powers (which he had ever since his 1937 coup), in this instance the people completely agreed with him. Headlines such as "Reich Goes on Assassinating Brazilians," and "One More Axis Crime," incensed the populace.

Riots reigned in Rio. Angry mobs destroyed German department stores, a surgical supply store, and a book shop. Books were piled in the street and set afire. "Hitler isn't the only one who can burn books." Other establishments pulled down iron shutters to keep out rioters. But those places were forced to fly the Brazilian flag. A pro-Nazi newspaper was protected by police, and that company wisely raised the national ensign.

The situation was not helped by one German customer who shouted defiantly, "Viva Allemanha!" ("Long live Germany!") More than 2,500 police were called out to quell the riots, but it was a sudden rainstorm more than anything that eventually doused the angry Latins.

The culmination of Brazilian feelings arose in Vargas' decree that "acts of war practiced against the American Continent" would be staunchly defended, and his statement that he had the personal power to declare war. Indiscriminate U-boat warfare was doing more than sinking ships: it was uniting nonbelligerent nations against the Axis aggressors.

Meanwhile, the U.S. fishing industry was having its own problems. It was reported that in several incidents Georgia fishing boats had been stopped by U-boats and hijacked of their oil and gasoline, then left stranded. While this sounds unlikely (a U-boat would undoubtedly expend more fuel stalking and stopping a fishing boat than it could hope to recover), it caused a decline in the working fleet: crews were reluctant to sign on cruises, and boat owners were afraid of losing their expensive trawlers and draggers.

At forty minutes after midnight on the morning of the tenth, Kapitanleutnant Viktor Vogel of the *U-588* came upon the Gulf Oil tanker *Gulftrade* nearing the end of her voyage from Port Arthur, Texas, to New York. The vessel had been traveling blacked out until a lookout spotted other ships in the vicinity. In order to avoid collision, Captain Torger Olsen ordered the masthead and running lights turned on. The *Gulftrade* was then only three and a half miles from Barnegat Light.

Vogel must have aligned the blank spot between the lights on the crosshairs of his periscope. Minutes later, "the torpedo struck between the mainmast and the birdge-house, cutting the ship in two. Oil was sprayed over the entire vessel, and flamed spectacularly, but within a minute was extinguished by the high seas breaking over the deck."

Captain Olsen testified, "As I was sitting at my desk, closing up the payroll, I heard a sound, a whining sound, and I couldn't get into my head what this sound was, and after a moment's notice I said to myself, 'That's a torpedo.' I was going to leave my chair to come up on the bridge, and at that moment the torpedo struck. Everything went dark. The ceiling came down; the doors came in; and the portholes broke and scattered all around. I managed to get out on deck. After I looked down on the after deck the ship was on fire from amidships to poop deck. All the mainmast was burning, right to the top, and the water was breaking over amidships on both sides. Some part of the deck was standing straight up in the air.

"From this scene I left and went on the boat deck to the starboard boat; the starboard boat was stove in. I went to the port boat, amidships, where there was a number of men already engaged to try to launch this boat. I immediately took charge of the launching, and the boat was landed safely by me and one A.B. When the boat hit the water she immediately unhooked the falls and swung around the bow. At that time there was three men in the boat and six remaining on deck. We commenced pulling in the painter of the boat to shorten it up, so this boat could come under the forecastle head. Then we made a line from the forecastle head to the boat and the remaining six men slid down this line into the boat and left the scene."

The Coast Guard cutter *Antietam* happened to be cruising only half a mile to landward. She wasted no time in sounding a general alarm to all ships at sea, and wading into the debris field to search for survivors. No sooner had she arrived at the wrecked tanker when another torpedo passed less than fifty feet from the cutter's bow. Ignoring the danger, she made a lee for the lone lifeboat and soon took aboard the captain, the ship's officers, and the bridge watch.

The two halves of the *Gulftrade* drifted apart. Twenty-five men remained on the stern section. Both aft lifeboats were launched. Eighteen men scampered aboard, but seven elected not to give up the ship. Both boats swamped in the high seas, and all the men were lost.

Chief Engineer Guy Chadwick stayed with the still floating stern. "We could see the bow section drifting off, but we knew there were no men on it. Nobody said much at all. We all just sat around on the deck and smoked. When the rescue boat showed, I never saw anything that looked so good in my life. I hollered as much as the kids."

The *Antietam* charged in close to the *Gulftrade*'s fantail, where the seven survivors huddled. A line from the wreckage fouled her port propellor; due to the wind and the sea, she found it impossible to maneuver on one engine. She backed out, but stayed nearby and waited for help to arrive. Two hours later, the U.S. Navy tender *Larch* arrived and took the men off the stern. They and the nine men from the midships lifeboat were the only survivors.

That night, about 2100, the Norwegian freighter *Hvoslef*, carrying sugar from Sagua, Spain via Cuba to Boston, ran afoul of the *U-94* two miles east of the Fenwick Island Buoy, off the Delaware-Maryland border.

Second Mate Harry Olsen was on watch at the time. With visibility of three miles, he saw an object resembling a submarine only half a mile away. He was reporting the sighting to Captain Arthur Dahl when, according to the official summary of the event, "the first torpedo struck aft on the starboard side at about the No. 3 hatch. The explosion blew away the entire stern. A second torpedo almost simultaneously struck the starboard side amidships. The ship was abandoned and sank within one and a half to two minutes.''

That anyone managed to get away in such a short time is miraculous. Fourteen of the twenty man crew crowded into the open boat. They rowed all night in calm seas. Twelve hours later found them surging through the surf half a mile north of the Fenwick Island Station, where they were sighted by a lookout. They were greeted by lifesaving personnel as they came ashore, and made comfortable in the station.

Later that day, the pilot of a Navy patrol plane noticed a cork raft and a body. The plane circled a nearby fishing boat, the *Karla*, and dropped a message directing it toward the site. Captain Carl Svord was heading home, but turned his boat around and followed the plane offshore. When he got there, he found the body of Captain Dahl entangled in the raft's netting. He brought the body aboard, and turned it over to the Cape May Naval Air Station.

The other five men apparently went down with the ship.

A few hours after the *Hvoslef* was sunk, the *Caribsea* also took her final plunge. This freighter was the first target of Kapitanleutnant Erich Rostin, *U-158*. The chronicle of the calamity is best told by the Congressional testimony of Gerald Thibodeau:

"I was an ordinary seaman on the steamship *Caribsea*, owned by Stockard Steamship Line, when she was torpedoed on March 11, 1942, off the coast of Cape Lookout. We were returning to Baltimore from Santiago, Cuba. The torpedoing took place about 2:01 A.M.; the vessel was hit in No. 2 hatch and a second torpedo hit the vessel in the engine room. The ship began to go down immediately and sunk within two to three minutes after she was struck. There was no time to launch the lifeboats or the life raft. I found myself in the water and I managed to reach a hatchboard to which I clung until a life raft came near and I got aboard that.

"There were five men hanging on to the hatchboard when the life raft came by. Since the life raft had no means of control or propulsion it was just a matter of luck that the wind drifted it near us so that the four of the five men were able to board the raft. One of the men on the board could not make it because the raft had begun to drift away at the time.

"There were altogether on the life raft seven men. I think these were the only ones who survived. I later found out that the life raft had been thrown in the water by the force of the explosion and found by men swimming in the water.

'During the ten hours in the water we saw a convoy of three tankers and a destroyer about three miles away but were not noticed. We also noticed about three planes flying at different times of the morning at fairly low altitudes. One of them came about three miles of us, swooped low, and returned. Yet, there was no report given. . . . We were picked up about 12:30 that day by the steamship *Orlando*, who sighted us about five miles away by a reflection of the sun on a tin cover which we were using as a reflecting mirror.''

Whether the other twenty-one men went down with the ship, or drifted until they drowned or died of exposure, is not known. Their bodies were never found. Thibodeau misunderstood the name of the rescue vessel, however: she was the freighter *Nolindo*, which was herself sunk two months later off the Dry Tortugas.

The night of the eleventh-twelfth was quiet, but starting just before midnight of the twelfth, repeated jackhammer blows against merchant shipping threw the East Coast into a long, bloody turmoil. For the next week and a half, not a day passed that a vessel was not attacked within the boundaries of the ESF. Twenty-three vessels were accosted by four different U-boats reigning terror in the shipping lanes, sea wolves nipping at the rudders of hapless ships.

The *U-158* found a fiery target in the American tanker *John D. Gill*, from Philadelphia, Pennsylvania, to Atreco, Texas. Her paint was fresh and her decks unspotted by rust, for she was on the return leg of her maiden voyage with her first cargo. She was also one of the first of the new armed merchantmen, sporting a five-inch deck gun on her stern. Her crew of fifty was augmented by an armed guard of seven.

The *John D. Gill* was off the coast of North Carolina when a torpedo ripped into her steel hull. Her cargo of refined gasoline and oil erupted in flames with such violence that residents of shore communities fifteen miles away heard the explosions.

Coast watchers saw fire on the horizon and immediately reported the situation to Naval Intelligence at Wilmington, North Carolina. Word went out over the telephone to all adjacent lifeboat stations. Coast Guard patrol boats swarmed to the burning tanker, alit like a gigantic funeral pyre.

Although the *John D. Gill* did not sink right away, the intense heat and the threat of explosion forced surviving crew members to abandon ship. Ensign Robert Hutchins was the gunnery commander: "There was a terrific blast, and I ran from my room to join my gun crew. Everything was dark at first and I ran along the catwalk. When I got to the gun, we looked for the sub, but nothing could be seen or heard." After fifteen minutes of futile searching, the fire roared over the fantail. "Then the flames got on top of us, and we jumped over the side. I saw two of my boys go into those flames, and I heard them scream as they died."

Herbert Gardner was making his first voyage at sea: "We were calm at first, but it wasn't long before everybody got excited. I guess we couldn't help it with that kind of death staring us in the face." He was unable to squeeze onto one overcrowded lifeboat, and the next one he tried to board capsized in the water when the panicked crew rushed the launching. Gardner climbed down the rope and tried to right the heavy lifeboat. He fell into the water. "I saw a buddy of mine about fifty feet away and I began moving over toward him, intending to let him hang on to me if he didn't have a life jacket. He told me to stay away. I guess he thought I was after his jacket, and I don't blame him." Gardner became engulfed by flaming oil that set his hair afire. He was forced to duck underwater as he swam away.

Two seamen were sucked into the still-turning

propellor and chopped up by the immense blades. Quartermaster Edwin Chaney scrambled aboard a life raft. His stentorian voice directed many others toward the temporary refuge. He kept yelling directions so that sailors struggling in the water knew which way to swim. Said one survivor, "We could hear that voice of his above the roaring of the fire."

The raft had oars, but no oarlocks. The men took turns pressing the oars against their bodies so that others could row them away from the flaming sea.

The tanker was still afloat at dawn, but shortly thereafter she broke in half and sank. Although the cutter *Agassiz* was the first to arrive at the scene, it was the Oak Island Lifeboat Station motor boat *#4405* that spotted a signal flare at daybreak, and soon picked up eleven survivors clinging to a tiny raft in the oil-soaked sea. The merchant seamen were transferred to *CGC-186* for fast transport to medical facilities at Southport, North Carolina.

The search continued throughout the day. By the time rescue operations were called off at 0100, fourteen bodies had been recovered by the *#4405*, and another by the Navy tug *Umpqua*. It was not until the boats returned to base that they learned through Naval Intelligence that a passing tanker, the *Robert H. Colley*, had stumbled upon fifteen other survivors in a lifeboat, and had taken them to Charleston, South Carolina. Sixteen men remained missing, and were presumed dead.

Meanwhile, along the New Jersey coast, another disaster was taking place. The *U-404*, Kapitanleutnant Otto von Bulow, entered the fray by sinking the Chilean freighter *Tolten*.

Chile and Argentina were the only two Latin American countries that had not severed diplomatic relations with the Axis powers. As the vessel of a nonbelligerent nation, the *Tolten* traveled fully lighted so that her neutrality could be clearly identified. Her cargo of nitrate was discharged in Baltimore, Maryland, from which the freighter then proceeded in ballast to New York.

In Baltimore, the Navy Patrol Service warned Captain Aquilez Ramirez that for the last leg of his voyage he must run blacked-out after dark. At first he did not comply. He ran fully lighted until he "was stopped about midnight the same day by a patrol boat and received orders to put out the lights in accordance with instructions he had been given to follow." (Official U.S. statement to the Chilean government.)

In the wee hours of the thirteenth, shortly after he had turned off his lights, a torpedo "ripped apart" the *Tolten*. The tortured freighter sank within six minutes. There was no time to launch lifeboats. Of the twenty-eight man crew, only Julio Faust, an electrician, was thrown clear of the wreck. He climbed aboard a loose life raft, and lost consciousness.

Twelve hours later, Faust was found by a Coast Guard patrol boat. He was taken to the Marine Hospital at Stapleton, Staten Island, New York, suffering from shock and exposure.

The U.S. sent a communique to the government of Chile, informing them of the tragedy. Chile's Foreign Minister Juan Bautista Rossetti ordered an extraordinary Cabinet session, and "summoned" German and Italian ambassadors and the Japanese minister to discuss the ramifications of this act of aggression. The Axis powers were losing credibility in South America.

Very quickly a repetition of the Brazilian riots occurred in Chile. Shouting "Down with the Axis," mobs protested the sinking the *Tolten* by smashing the windows of the pro-Axis newspaper *Chileno* and damaging other German establishments. The U.S. acting secretary of state played it up for all it was worth, claiming in a press conference that the Axis powers intended to sink all ships of the American Republics without distinction. His purpose was to widen the gap between the governments of Brazil, Chile, and Argentina and the governments of Germany, Italy, and Japan, and to convert those Latin American nations to the Allied cause.

Continuing to prove nondiscrimination in submarine warfare, at 1135 on the thirteenth Kapitanleutnant Johannes Liebe in the *U-332* sank a Yugoslavian vessel. The *Trepca* was bound for Portland, Maine, with a cargo of bauxite from Mackensie, British Guiana. Because of the recent spate of coastal sinkings, Captain Stanko Narochini steered his ship far offshore.

The *Trepca* was two hundred miles off the North Carolina coast when a torpedo slammed into the starboard side amidships, tearing a forty-foot hole in the hull and ripping up the deck. The starboard side lifeboats were torn to splinters. The radio transmitter was destroyed, and two men were killed outright by the blast.

With his ship going down rapidly by the head, Captain Narochini gave the order to abandon ship. From the port side was launched a twenty-five-foot lifeboat and an eighteen-foot gig. Two men were crushed between wood and steel when waves swept the boats against the *Trepca*'s hull. Others jumped overboard. The hero was Fourth Engineer Albert Toninic, who stayed on deck with the ship sinking from under him; anything floatable he threw into the water, including life rafts, wooden railings, and hatch covers. He succeeded in saving the lives of many men who could not swim.

The U-boat surfaced and cruised the area, taking photographs of the travails of the merchant seamen struggling in the water. The Germans also recovered bits of debris believed to be a lifebuoy with the name of the vessel stenciled on the cork. A portable radio mast was rigged above the U-boat's conning tower, and taken down after ten minutes. Then the submarine submerged and was not seen again.

All the survivors were eventually rounded up and squeezed aboard the two lifeboats. The afternoon dragged on. As darkness intruded, Captain Narochini kept both boats together. Despair over their situation, especially being so far out of the shipping lanes, gripped a Polish fireman that night. He ran amok and stabbed five fellow crewmen before he was restrained with rope. The only food they had was hardtack; their water was livened with a little rum.

Thirty-four lonely men drifted for three days before they were picked up by the Swedish steamship *Sicilia*.

The *U-404* caught the collier *Lemuel Burrows* off Atlantic City, New Jersey, with three torpedoes. The first hit between No. 2 and No. 3 holds on the starboard side.

Captain Grover Clark, master of the *Lemuel Burrows*, was lifted bodily from his chair and thrown to the floor of his cabin. He was in shock from the concussion. When he recovered, he ran out on deck and ordered abandon ship. During launching operations, the U-boat surfaced, passed aft of the freighter, and fired a second torpedo that hit the port side amidships. It hit directly under where Captain Clark was standing, with a concussion that "blew my shoes off my feet and left me standing in my stocking feet."

The starboard boat was smashed, but twenty-six crew members got away in the port lifeboat. The backwash of the explosion capsized the lifeboat; those who were able clambered onto its overturned hull.

The captain and seven others tossed two life rafts over the side, then leaped into the water and swam for them: the captain and four others on one raft, three men on the other. Still circling the badly damaged ship, the U-boat drew close to the captain's raft. Captain Clark was asked the name of his ship, but he refused to answer. The U-boat then backed away and fired the third torpedo into the collier. The ship was lifted out of the water by the force of the explosion. When she fell back down, she went right to the bottom. Satisfied at the destruction, the U-boat took off.

Then began the awful agony of survival. Fighting the effects of the cold, the men clinging to the upturned wooden hull dropped off one by one. After seven hours, the eight who were left were picked up by the steamship *Sewalls Point*. The raft with Captain Clark and four men was found by rescue craft. The other raft was found, but by then only one badly frozen seaman still clung to it. All told, fourteen men survived the sinking of the *Lemuel Burrows*. Six of them were hospitalized for submersion and exposure.

Later, the Coast Guard picked up three bodies found floating in an oil slick. One body washed up on the beach in Wildwood and was discovered by a civilian. Another body was found wedged under the thwarts of the overturned lifeboat after it was towed to the Hereford

Inlet Coast Guard Station. Fifteen others were never found.

Confusion reigned in the early morning hours of the fifteenth, as U-boats bunched up off the South Carolina coast. Two ships were attacked three hours apart and, although merchant seamen reported seeing as many as three submarines at once, the *U-158* was credited with both.

The American tanker *Olean* was the first of the pair. Captain Theodore Bockhoff related that just after midnight three submarines surrounded his vessel. One fired a torpedo that struck the port side of the engine room, disabling the engines. The crew remained calm, but wasted no time preparing the lifeboats for launching. They had to wait for the forward momentum to ease way, in order not to capsize the boats as they touched the water. The men stood by their stations waiting for the captain's order.

Another submarine surfaced and fired a second torpedo from less than three hundred yards. Said Captain Bockhoff, "They knew the lifeboat was being lowered. As the starboard lifeboat hit the water with six men in it the second torpedo came under her, striking the ship and blasting the boat to bits. The boat wasn't seen again, although one of the recue vessels found its air tanks floating near the scene later."

Those remaining on deck launched the port lifeboat. Added Able Bodied Seaman James Sherlock, "Just then a submarine came between our lifeboat and the ship. We could almost touch it. We were trying to row away from it when somebody yelled: 'Take it easy, there's another one.' Then we changed our course and by mistake rowed right between two subs."

At 0330, motor lifeboat *#3827* from the Beaufort Lifeboat Station arrived. The crew noticed a dim glow in the water, and soon found five men on a raft aiming a flashlight at them. Two hours later, the motorboat came across the *Olean*'s lifeboat with twenty men aboard. This was more than they could handle, but by then motor lifeboat *#5184* had arrived to take ten of the survivors. *#3827* then headed directly for shore with four serously injured seamen, and took them to the Morehead City Hospital.

Others, including the captain, were rescued by the USS *Cole*. When Captain Bockhoff saw that the *Olean* was still afloat, he returned with some of the crew, and anchored the ship. The *Olean* was later salvaged.

While this rescue was going on, the American tanker *Ario*, New York to Corpus Christi, came under attack. Second Mate Francis Doudreau was on watch when he saw green and red Very lights fired into the nighttime sky. That the purpose of this pyrotechnic display was to lure unsuspecting ships into the nose of a torpedo by faking the signal of distress, like the Sirens calling Ulysses to his death on the rocks of their island, can be interpreted from the many previous incidents of U-boats showing running lights in order to disguise themselves as fellow merchantmen.

Before Captain Thorolf Hannevig could respond, however, a torpedo exploded under the ship and set her afire. With flames raging out of control, and likely to blow the ship to pieces any moment, some of the crew leaped into the sea. Others ducked the heat long enough to launch one of the lifeboats. Captain Hannevig was still aboard when first one, then another U-boat surfaced on opposite sides of his vessel. Both U-boats began shelling the *Ario*, trapping the ship in a deadly crossfire. Captain Hannevig estimated that "the shelling lasted for ten minutes and that each submarine fired about fifty shots." Five men were killed in the barrage of shell fire.

Suffering from numerous shrapnel wounds, Captain Hannevig and the rest of the crew still left on board launched the second lifeboat. They rowed around the riddled wreckage and plucked a number of crewmen out of the water. At 0800, the U.S. destroyer *Du Pont* arrived at the scene and took aboard those who had survived the onslaught.

But the *Ario*, shredded like confetti and full of holes, had not yet sunk. Captain Hannevig and a select crew reboarded the vessel to see if she could be brought to port under her own power. They found the ship too badly damaged. The fatally wounded tanker lingered on until late afternoon before sinking beneath the calm, blue sea.

Although Admiral Karl Doenitz had long coordinated teams of U-boats against escorted convoys making the long Atlantic crossing, this was the first verified instance of wolf pack tactics off the East Coast.

Along came the American tanker *Australia*, Port Arthur, Texas, to New Haven, Connecticut, with a cargo of crude from the Texas oil fields. The *U-332* caught her in broad daylight on March 16. The single torpedo exploded aft against the engine room, on the starboard side, killing instantly four duty personnel.

Captain Martin Ader ordered abandon ship. This was done in orderly fashion, all thirty-seven survivors getting away in three lifeboats. They were picked up within the hour by the *William J. Salman*.

The *Australia* grounded on the Diamond Shoals, and for a while it looked like she could be saved. But pounding seas and Gulf Stream currents did their damage. The ship slipped off into deep water, a total loss.

Next to enter the East Coast arena was Kapitanleutnant Johann Mohr and the *U-124*. His eight-day reign of terror began on the night of the sixteenth when he sank the small Honduran freighter *Ceiba*.

The torpedo hit the port bow at 2045, ending immediately the *Ceiba*'s voyage from Jamaica to New York. The ship sank within three minutes. Third Mate Timothy O'Brien stated, "After the torpedo had hit I rushed down to No. 2 boat on the port side forward. I tried to get her loose but she was jammed so I went back to the starboard boat No. 1. There was just too much of a list to port to get her off. She would have just hit the side of the hull. I saw a life raft just floating away from the ship. I saw the second cook on it and the boatswain. I yelled and jumped for it."

Second Cook and Baker Vincent Halliburton went into greater detail: "I heard a crash. I went on the main deck and heard the women and children screaming, there were twelve passengers in all: seven men, two ladies, and three children. I found that I couldn't launch the boats on account of the list that the ship had, and therefore it was impossible to launch the ships. While standing there I felt the ship disappear from under my feet. I started to swim and I picked a raft. There was one other person on this raft. While drifting on the raft we picked up two more seamen. We noticed another raft with nine people and we paddled to each other. We tied the two rafts together but found that they continually bumped into each other and so we had to untie them. Before untying the rafts we transferred two people from the other raft onto the raft I was on thus making a total of six people on my raft.''

Ruben Saavedra, a Honduran seaman, was one of the fortunates who left the overcrowded raft and joined that of Halliburton's and O'Brien's. He related how, before he traded rafts, the submarine surfaced and came close. A well-dressed officer who spoke excellent English asked the vessel's name, tonnage, and cargo. After receiving this information, the U-boat hung around for ten or fifteen minutes before submerging and leaving the survivors to their fate.

Halliburton: "On Tuesday morning we took our bearings by the sun and we rigged a sail with a piece of canvas which was in the raft and with two of the paddles. We were making very good headway until we sighted the other raft about one o'clock in the afternoon. We threw out our sea anchor and waited for them and that was the last we ever saw of them. We were picked up on Wednesday evening at 6:30 by a United States destroyer. It was raining and the visibility was very bad and we had to burn flares in order for the ship to see us.

"As far as I know only six people were saved out of a total of fifty people.'' Included among the forty-four dead were three women, two girls, and a small boy. The destroyer was the USS *Hambleton*.

Halliburton's story is told with a simplistic lack of histrionics, glossing over the travails of hunger and thirst they must have endured in two and a half days adrift in the open ocean, not knowing when—or if—rescue would arrive. Those on the other raft may not have been so forgiving in dramatic presentation.

Von Bulow in the *U-404* had been lying low for four

days. Now he found the British tanker *San Demetrio* in the sights of his periscope. The British had long since armed their merchant ships, and the *San Demetrio* was no exception: she carried an old 4.7 inch Japanese after deck gun, a twelve-pounder forward, a Bofors antiaircraft gun, and two machine guns. Her tanks were loaded with 11,700 tons of valuable fuels: 4,000 tons of pure alcohol, 5,000 tons of gasoline, 2,000 tons of kerosene, 600 tons of diesel oil, and 100 tons of boiler fuel. She left Baltimore, Maryland, unescorted and passed the Chesapeake Lightship on her way to Halifax, where she planned to join an eastbound convoy to make the Atlantic crossing to England.

She was zigzagging some eighty miles offshore when the lookout cried, "Submarine one point abaft the starboard beam!" Captain Conrad Vidot ordered hard aport, sounded the alarm, and scrambled the crew to emergency stations. Now came some information which was to cause Naval Intelligence to launch a full-scale investigation: a fully lighted freighter was spotted to the stern, paralleling the tanker's speed and direction.

The submarine disappeared from view. The strange freighter lingered behind by two or three miles, a sitting duck for any but a blind U-boat commander. Captain Vidot had the helmsman change direction. The unknown lighted vessel altered course and followed the *San Demetrio*'s retreat. Several more course changes were matched perfectly.

Captain Vidot did not know what was going on, but he decided to take no chances. He ordered "the aft gun crew to fire at the pursuing surface ship, but twice the old Japanese gun refused to fire; then it was too late, for at 2017, just after the last change of course, the white track of a torpedo was seen on the starboard beam. The torpedo hit the engine room on the starboard side, and, approximately six minutes later, a second torpedo, unseen, blasted into the aft compartment at about No. 2 tank; both hit at the waterline, and the tanker began to sink."

With the engines knocked out by the blast, the friction of water against the great hull gradually slowed the ship's forward motion. Captain Vidot ordered abandon ship, and gave their position to the radio operator to include with the SOS. Before leaving, he crammed all official documents into a weighted bag, carried just for this purpose, and threw it overboard.

Four lifeboats got away. The *San Demetrio* went under about twenty-five minutes after the first torpedo struck. As the boats drifted about in the darkness, the strangely lighted vessel hung around for an hour before taking off at high speed.

The wind was fresh, and the seas moderate. The lifeboats bobbed in the gentle swells all night—and all the next day. Since the radio man had received two replies to his broadcast for help, the best plan of action was to remain in the vicinity of the sinking so search planes and rescue craft could locate them. But they saw no sign of life until 2000 that night when an eerie, dark shape followed by a phosphorescent glow passed directly beneath their boats. A half hour later, in the direction which the dark shape had taken, the beam of a powerful searchlight arced vertically into the starlit sky. "For the next six hours this light appeared about every half-hour, for a duration of fifteen–twenty seconds."

That night the waves became tumultuous. The lifeboats were separated. No. 3 lifeboat capsized, and two men drowned. The others managed to right the boat, bail it out, and recover the bodies; but it was a wet night for all.

Again came daylight, and still there was no sign of rescue. Worse yet, each boat was alone and had no knowledge of the others. It was not until that afternoon, on the eighteenth, that a patrol plane located them and broadcast the sighting. Vessels in the area were alerted. At 1700, the men in lifeboats one and three were picked up by the steamship *Beta*, those in No. 2 by the Coast Guard cutter *Cuyahoga*. No. 4 boat was never found; what horrors those nineteen men must have suffered can only be imagined.

Upon debriefing, the Office of Naval Intelligence learned of the fully lighted vessel seen prior to the attack, and of the searchlight beam in the sky. Corroborating the story was a report from the steamship *Baccus*, which had also sighted a well-lit ship at about the same place and time. ONI concluded that an enemy supply vessel was fueling U-boats off the coast.

Thus began the rumors that U.S. oil companies were rendezvousing with German submarines in order to sell them diesel fuel.

The night of the seventeenth found Mohr in continuous action. He first found the *Acme*, and did her in with a single torpedo. Captain Sigmund Schulz was on the bridge of his ship at the time, and saw the torpedo's track. "The explosion was muffled and made very little noise. I saw the ship was not going to sink immediately, so I gave the order for the men to stand by the lifeboats. Then I saw that at least one-third of the crew were not on deck."

Eleven men had been killed outright by the blast. The only man alive in the engine room was Oiler Leo Bojarski; both his legs were broken. A rescue party sent below found him clinging to a barrel as the sea flooded in through a gaping wound in the ship's side. They pulled him out through a hole in the deck.

As the men lowered both lifeboats into the water, two Navy planes flew overhead. In addition to radioing for help, they dropped depth charges over the spot from which the torpedo had come. Ten minutes later, the Coast Guard cutter *Dione* arrived and took off the survivors.

The *Acme* did not sink. She was towed to Newport News by the *Acushnet*, drydocked, and repaired.

The *Kassandra Louloudis* was carrying a general cargo from New York to Cristobal, Panama, when Mohr found her. Captain Themis Millas saw the deadly track coming, and deftly maneuvered the Greek freighter out of its way. But the second one was unavoidable; it slammed against the hull and tossed salt spray high in the air. The ship took an immediate list, but did not appear to be in imminent danger of sinking.

The radio operator sent out an SOS, while the lifeboats were swung out on their davits. The crew, none of whom had been injured by the blast, stood by until the list became so great that the captain feared for their lives if they did not leave soon. In orderly fashion the crew got away in two lifeboats.

The survivors saw a periscope poke out of the water some two hundred yards off, but the U-boat was cautious enough not to surface. A patrol plane flew by moments later, saw the sinking ship, and radioed for help. Forty-five minutes later, the entire crew was picked up by the *Dione*. There was no loss of life, and no injuries. A little later, the *Kassandra Louloudis* slipped sadly beneath the waves.

Midnight came and went. Thunderclouds rolled up from the south; sheets of rain swept across the surface of the sea, and lightning lit the sky with stroboscopic brilliance. Mohr was still lurking off the Diamond Shoals. At 0135, now the eighteenth, the *E.M. Clark* hove into view. The Esso tanker was bound for New York with 118,725 barrels of heating oil loaded at Baton Rouge, Louisiana. Mohr fired a torpedo that struck the port side amidships. In addition to killing Thomas Larkin, who was asleep in the hospital room, the explosion destroyed No. 2 lifeboat and knocked down the radio antenna.

Captain Hubert Hassell was in his stateroom when the torpedo hit. ''Immediately after the explosion I proceeded to the bridge where I took charge from the second mate, who had already sounded the general alarm and ordered the engines 'Full astern' and then 'Stop.' These orders were promptly complied with. I then went to the Radio Operator's room and assisted him to rig an emergency antenna in order to send an SOS.''

Radio Operator Earl Schlarb was asleep at the time. ''The auto alarm bell in my room was ringing madly when I awoke, finding myself halfway out of my bunk. I hurried into my clothes and snatched up a flashlight. As I opened my door I breathed in the sharp, acrid odor of burnt powder in the companionway. Rushing up to the radio room, I turned on my flashlight and found the whole place in chaos. Parts of the apparatus, the filing cabinet, spare-parts locker, table, and racks were in a tangled heap on the floor. The typewriter had been flung across the operating chair and table and had crashed into the receiver-battery charger. The door leading to the boat deck had been blown off and part of the bulkhead was gone. Feeling lucky to be alive, I pulled the auto alarm switch and stopped the clamor of the bells. Then I heard the captain saying, 'Sparks, get on the air!'

"There was no ship voltage, as the power lines were broken; that was why the alarm bells rang. A battery started them when the line voltage fell below normal. Immediately I threw in the battery switch for the emergency transmitter power supply. It worked! Then I connected the antenna transfer and telegraph key switches and 'sat on the key,' sending and repeating SSSS-SOS. But there was no radiation on the dial."

Feeling his way into the inky darkness outside, Schlarb waded into the wreckage of the deck. As a bolt of lightning illuminated the ship, he saw a great tangle of wires lying about like torn confetti.

"Another flash of lightning revealed the starboard lifeboat being prepared for launching. Some of the men were in it, others on deck. I returned to the radio room, put on my life jacket, and grabbed the coil of spare antenna, tangled by the explosion, but intact. As I backed out on deck, trying to straighten out the wires, it was a matter of great urgency to find a place to attach the emergency antenna. I thought of the small runway atop the radio room, with a ladder leading up to the wing of the monkey bridge. Somehow, I grasped the top of the sheer bulkhead, pulled myself up, and bent one end of the tangled antenna wire around the iron railing.

"Suddenly, off the port side of the ship, distant about three hundred yards, a submarine's yellow searchlight was turned on and played about the *E.M. Clark*, apparently to inspect the damage caused by the torpedo.

"Someone approaching me called out 'Sparks.' I answered with a shout and up came Captain Hassell and Second Mate Ludden. 'The antenna is down,' I said. 'Here is the spare coil of wire. It's badly messed up. Can you give me a hand?' I scaled the bulkhead again and unhooked the wire. All three of us started pulling and twisting. A considerable length came free and I climbed with it up the ladder to the bridge wing. Part of the awning bar was still up. To get the spare antenna as far out from the ship's house as possible, I inched along in the murky dark, holding the rail with one hand, the wire with the other. As if by instinct, I halted where I found the railing gone. At the same instant a bolt of lightning showed that the outer wing of the bridge had been torn off. Black water and wreckage gleamed up from far below. One step farther. . . . I could feel my heart beating as I made one end of the insulator fast to the swaying, broken awning bar. When I went back on deck, the captain told me the lead-in was free. We ignored the rest of the tangle, pulled taut what we had, and hooked up the lead-in to the bulkhead insulator.''

However, before a message could be sent, a second torpedo penetrated the port hull between No. 1 and the dry cargo holds. Oil blown into the air fell like rain, but fortunately did not catch fire. Part of the jury-rigged antenna wire was destroyed. Said Schlarb: ''The ship's whistle jammed and sent forth a steady roar. Broken steam lines hissed loudly.''

Captain Hassell: ''This second explosion caused the ship to settle by the head rapidly. About one minute thereafter I gave the orders to launch the lifeboats and abandon the ship.'' The captain returned to his office and ''collected the ship's documents and secret wartime codes. I took the former along with me, but threw the codes overboard in a weighted canvas bag provided for the purpose.''

Schlarb: ''Captain Hassell, believing all hands were accounted for, was the last man to enter the lifeboat. Although we were on the windward side, the boat was safely launched, but once it was in the water the trouble started, as the wind and waves slammed us against the ship's side with great force. All hands worked hard trying to shove off, using the heavy oars and boat hooks. Finally we got the boat clear and all the oars in the water. Rowing was difficult because of the choppy waves and the rolling of the lifeboat.

''Suddenly a seamen yelled and pointed to a man standing at the ship's rail. Captain Hassell directed us to pull back part way, and shouted for the man to jump.

His orders were muffled by the din of the ship's whistle. The man on deck, Wiper Glen Barnhart, slid down a boat fall and dropped into the sea. He wore a life jacket but weighed about two hundred forty pounds and floated low in the water. A wave picked him up and tossed him within a few yards of the lifeboat. He was soon hauled aboard and covered with a blanket.''

Captain Hassell: ''We then rowed away from the ship in a northeasterly direction and almost immediately we saw the submarine flash a focusing light on the stern of the ship. The stern was raised quite high and she was then going down by the head. It was about 1:34 A.M. when we saw her completely disappear below the surface. The submarine stayed around for about one and one-half hours, continuously displaying her light over the place where the ship had sunk; then the submarine disappeared in a northeasterly direction.''

Schlarb: ''The sea was covered with oil, which kept the waves from breaking over our lifeboat, but the fumes were sickening. Several of the men—I was one of them—became violently ill.'' Captain Hassell took a count; he found fourteen men in his own boat, and twenty-six in No. 4: all accounted for except for Larkin. ''We rowed until the lifeboat was out of the oil slick. The waves were now six to eight feet high and all hands were busy with the oars, keeping the boat's head into the wind.'' The dark hours dragged on. ''The captain then ordered the sea anchor put out to keep the boat from broadsiding to the seas and shipping water. We saw no sign of lifeboat No. 4. Rain started to fall again and those who had not had time to put on warm clothing began to suffer from the cold.''

A new day dawned. ''At about 7 A.M., a destroyer appeared over the horizon. We shot two red flares and she changed course. A few minutes later another flare was fired and before long the destroyer neared us, maneuvering to windward, and carefully came alongside. After five hours in the lifeboat, we were soaking wet with rain and spray and chilled by the cold wind. When we were picked up, it felt mighty good to be safely aboard a United States man-o'-war—the USS *Dickerson*.

"No definite word of No. 4 boat was received for some hours. Finally the *Dickerson* sighted an empty lifeboat containing several pieces of discarded wearing apparel. It was No. 4 boat of the *E.M. Clark*. We later learned that the twenty-six men in this boat had been rescued by a Venezuelan tanker and landed at Norfolk." That tanker was the *Catatumbo*.

Mohr hid out during the day, but that night, at 9:30, he torpedoed the American tanker *Papoose*. Captain Raymond Zalnick's deposition was a masterpiece of understatement: "She was struck by two torpedoes about fifteen miles southwest of Cape Lookout Light. We immediately sent out SOS and abandoned the ship in two life boats. The crew consisted of thirty-four men, including myself. Thirty-two men, including myself, were saved and two were lost. These thirty-two men were picked up by an American destroyer the next morning and brought to Norfolk, Virginia. The last we saw of the *Papoose* was about 10:00 A.M. March 19th, 1942, located about twelve miles south of the position where she was torpedoed. She was adrift and we have not seen nor heard anything from her since that time." (The destroyer was the USS *Stringham*.)

Able Bodied Seaman Frederick Sostack added a tidbit of information, complaining that the ship "was not armed. Had it been, we could probably have sunk the submarine, because after the first torpedo, she rose to the surface and threw its searchlight at the vessel."

The *Papoose* finally sank, taking with her the bodies of both engine room crewmen: Edward Peters and George Kreuger.

The night of the nineteenth was a fiery one. Said Captain Harry Heffelfinger, master of the *Peter Hurll*: "At Hampton Roads we joined the tankers *Gulf of Mexico* (Gulf Oil Corporation) and *Mercury Sun* (Motor Tankship Corporation). The three ships formed up in a single file with the *Mercury Sun* first, the *Gulf of Mexico* second, and the *Peter Hurll* third. On the first night out of Hampton Roads, when we were in the vicinity of Cape Lookout and I was watching for Lookout Shoals Buoy, I saw tracer bullets. The *Gulf of Mexico* was being machine gunned by a submarine. Soon the U-boat sent up star shells and then began to fire on the *Gulf of Mexico* with her heavier guns. The *Peter Hurll* changed course and escaped in the darkness. Both the other ships sent out distress messages but neither was sunk.''

The *Mercury Sun* was sunk two months later in the Gulf of Mexico, by Kapitanleutnant Ulrich Folkers and the *U-125*.

The *W.E. Hutton* and the *Liberator* ran up against more aggressive opponents who were willing to expend their torpedoes instead of risking a gun battle. Mohr took out the *W.E. Hutton*, Liebe the *Liberator*.

The *W.E. Hutton* was carrying 65,000 barrels of Bunker C oil from Smith's Bluff, Texas, to Marcus Hook, Pennsylvania. Her routing instructions were mandated by the U.S. Navy. Captain Carl Flaathen, master, was almost as unemotional as Captain Zalnick:

''At about 10 P.M. without warning or any visible sign or indication of any nature that another vessel was in the vicinity, the SS *W.E. Hutton* was torpedoed on the starboard side almost in the stem of the vessel. The vessel commenced to fill up and went down by the head and her anchors ran out. At the time the torpedo struck, I was on the bridge with the third mate, a lookout sailor was on the other side of the bridge and a lookout sailor was on top of the pilot house. The engineer on watch shut off the fuel oil pumps and the remaining steam of the boilers was consumed by the vessel going slow ahead. Immediately after the torpedo explosion I ordered the SOS and the SSS sent and it was acknowledged by several shore stations. I sounded the general alarm and I personally heard the alarm ring throughout the vessel.

''That about eight to ten minutes after the first torpedo, another torpedo struck the SS *W.E. Hutton* on the port side amidships, in way of No. 3 tank, and her amidships section caught fire, which started to spread quickly.

''That between the striking of the first and second torpedoes I had returned to the bridge with a view to navigating the vessel to shallow water, but when the second torpedo struck I descended to the deck and instructed a seaman to assist me in lowering No. 1 life boat, which we did.

"That I with the wireless operator and the assistance of two seamen, who were the only men in view, arranged for the release of the life rafts fore and aft. I then proceeded to the bottom of the ladder, with the intention of entering No. 1 life boat, but I then found that it had pulled away. I was covered with oil, and the vessel was surrounded with fire and smoke of the burning oil and superstructure.

"That I saw a life raft being launched from the after deck, which contained the wireless operator and the seamen who were assisting me, they advised me that all men were off the boat, so I jumped in the water and swam to the raft.

"That we drifted on the raft and watched the vessel burning. She was down by the head with her stern sticking out of the water. After about forty-five minutes when we were about one-quarter of a mile from the vessel, the fire seemed to be extinguished suddenly, and we lost sight of the vessel in the darkness.

"That we drifted and in due course located one of the vessel's life boats, into which we all entered. Subsequently we searched for survivors and came upon No. 1 life boat with three men, and later upon another raft with four men on board, all of whom we took into our life boat, and made for the shore.

"That in due course we were overtaken by a British steamer, which took us aboard and brought us into Savannah, Georgia." The rescue ship was the *Port Halifax*.

Captain Flaathen neglected to mention that of the thirty-six men aboard the *W.E. Hutton*, only twenty-three escaped with their lives. The others either were killed in the explosions, drowned, or burned to death in the oil-covered water. Walter Clark was actually seen consumed by flames as he plunged through burning oil to reach the lifeboats. Jorgen Bauner, who for a time shared a raft with the Mate, added, "While we were in the life raft, we heard four or five members yelling for help. The life boat was launched O.K. Was trying to locate these members that were yelling for help but none could be located.'' The living could do nothing but listen as the agonized cries of their companions slowly faded.

Technically, Mohr could also be given tonnage credit for sinking the *Suloide*. A year later, on March 26, 1943, the Brazilian freighter ran into the submerged wreckage of the *W.E. Hutton*. The *Suloide*'s stem was ripped out, and she went down near the wreck that had holed her.

With all this action going on, merchant marine crews stood extra sharp lookouts against lurking marauders. Gun crews were itchy. When Frank Camillo, captain of the armed guard aboard the *Liberator*, spotted a suspicious looking "dark object" off the port quarter, he wasted no time in calling his gun crew into action. They fired one well placed shot that hit the "conning tower of the submarine," sending sparks and flames into the air. A minute later they fired again. After this second hit, they saw the U-boat "turn over on its starboard side and go down."

Unfortunately, what the *Liberator* mistook for a U-boat was the U.S. destroyer *Dickerson*. According to the Navy's official report, "a shrapnel shell suddenly struck the starboard side of the *Dickerson*'s bridge, passing through the railing on the wing of the bridge, the chart room, and finally exploding in the radio 'shack.' Three men on the *Dickerson* were killed outright, and seven persons were injured, including Lieutenant Commander J. K. Reybold, Commanding officer, who later died, ten minutes before the ship docked." The destroyer's executive officer assumed command; Lieutenant F. E. Wilson was wise enough to realize that the gunfire came from a friendly vessel, and did not return fire.

A few hours later, as dawn approached, the *Liberator* was struck amidships on the port by a single torpedo that blasted a gaping wound in her side, killed five engine room personnel, demolished the engine, and destroyed No. 4 lifeboat. As the ship slowed to a halt, Captain Albin Johnson ordered abandon ship. The freighter went down in thirty minutes. The survivors, in two lifeboats, were picked up within the hour by the Navy tug *Umpqua* and taken to Morehead City, North Carolina.

On the evening of the twentieth, Kapitanleutnant Walter Flachsenberg, *U-71*, shelled the *Oakmar* with deadly accuracy: the first shot hit the bridge wing, the second blew up the chart room, and the third exploded on deck. Since his ship was unarmed and unable to defend herself, Captain Nolan Fleming ordered abandon ship. Thirty officers and crew men launched a lifeboat in horrendous seas with fifteen-foot waves. Captain Fleming and five others did not make good their escape.

For the next fifteen minutes, shells continued to pour into the freighter "tossing like a cork." The survivors pulled away, and did not see the vessel go down. They then fought the mountainous seas for fifty-four hours, until they were rescued by the Greek freighter *Stavros*.

On the twenty-first, Mohr was operating off Cape Fear, and succeeded in torpedoing two tankers in rapid succession. The first was the *Esso Nashville*. The Standard Oil tanker was on a northbound voyage from Port Arthur, Texas, to New Haven, Connecticut, with 78,000 barrels of fuel oil. She was unarmed, and unescorted.

Captain Edward Peters remembered: "At 12:20 A.M., as I was resting in my room, I heard a thud against the ship's hull as if it had brushed against a buoy or some wreckage. I immediately got up and went to the bridge to inquire about the cause of this shock.

"As I reached the bridge a terrific crash occurred on the starboard side abaft the midship house, raising the vessel up bodily and throwing her to starboard and then keeling her to port so violently that I feared she was going to turn over. The entire ship was flooded with oil which spouted as high as the foremast; dense smoke and sparks emanated from the explosion of the torpedo.

"All communications with the engineroom were disrupted at once, but in accordance with previous instructions the engine was stopped."

Third Assistant Engineer Henry Garig also heard the dud torpedo, but said it sounded much louder below decks. He described the evacuation: "All the lights on the ship were out, but fortunately I always carried a flashlight. On the way to my room I found many of the crew in the outside passageway, standing in water and oil up to their knees. I held my flashlight to assist them and they all followed me to my room and waited while I put on my rubber suit. Then they followed me to No. 4 lifeboat. They were very orderly and there was no panic. By Captain Peters' orders all the lifeboats were kept swung out.''

Captain Peters: "Second Mate Boje sounded the general alarm, all hands rushed to their station, and the lifeboats were made ready for launching. Both the ship's bow and stern were raised high out of the water and as she was settling amidships where the torpedo struck, I gave the order to abandon ship. As the four lifeboats were being lowered I tried to go to my room to fetch the ship's secret documents and papers, but I was unable to reach my room because of the smoke and gas.

"I went to boat No. 2, which was then lowered in the water, but as I stepped down the pilot's ladder I fell into the water between the ship's side and the lifeboat. By that time the ship had changed position to windward and the crew members in No. 2 were experiencing great difficulties in handling their boat and keeping it away from the ship's side. Seeing this and fearing trouble for them in case the ship sank, I shouted to them to get away and pick me up later if they could.''

Chief Mate Hansen was in charge of No. 2. "When the boat was lowered we all proceeded into it but Captain Peters, who fell into the sea. Second Mate Boje and Steward Frank Sories grabbed him and tried to assist him into the boat, but the sea threw the lifeboat against the side of the ship and they lost their grips. The captain called to us and we hollered back to him that we were coming as soon as we could get clear from the ship rail and the rigging into which the lifeboat had been thrown. After about four or five minutes we had the boat clear and we yelled for Captain Peters, but there was no response.

"When able to man the oars of the lifeboat, we rowed to a point off the stern of the vessel. We kept rowing all night until we were about three or four miles from the ship.''

Both this lifeboat and No. 1 were picked up nine hours

after the torpedoing by the U.S. destroyer *McKean*, which took them to Norfolk. There they told newspaper reporters of the unfortunate circumstances surrounding the loss of their ship and her gallant captain.

Garig continues with the escape of No. 4: "Electrician Christie and I got into the boat and I held the light so that the other men could slide down the falls. We cast the falls loose, but as we were on the windward side the waves were banging the boat against the side of the ship. With twenty-one of us in the lifeboat the men at the oars had too little space to row. I therefore called for the six other men wearing life suits to follow me into the water. We were then able to clear the ship."

Garig went on to comment on the silent heroism of Oiler Leonard Mills in a narrative which characterizes the men of the merchant marine better than any other. "A man fifty-six years of age, Mills was in the Navy in the First World War and had since then served many years in the Fire Department of Akron, Ohio, until retired on a pension. Feeling it was a patriotic duty regardless of age to go to sea in time of war, he signed as an oiler on the *Esso Nashville* March 4, 1942, the day before we sailed from the New York on this voyage.

"When the men were getting into No. 4 boat, Mills appeared in a life jacket but on that cold night with the drenching rain he was clad only in his trunks. When one of the younger men standing nearby yelled for a life preserver, Mills took his off and gave it to him. I at once told Mills to take his life jacket back, but he told me he could swim better than the younger man. Later, when I asked the men wearing rubber suits to get into the water, Mills jumped in before we did and he stayed with us, hanging on in the cold water for three or four hours. When we got back into the boat he was suffering from the cold and I offered him my rubber suit. Refusing it, he wrapped himself in a blanket and took one of the oars."

That morning, they were picked up by the Coast Guard cutter *Tallapoosa*. She remained on patrol, so it was not until three days later that the rescued seamen were landed at Savannah, Georgia. Four months later, Leonard Mills was serving aboard the tanker *R.W. Gallagher* when that vessel was torpedoed and sunk in the Gulf of Mexico by the *U-67*, Oberleutnant zur See Gunther Muller-Stockheim. Eight men were killed out of a crew of fifty-two; Mills was one of them.

The men on No. 3 were taken off by the Coast Guard cutter *Agassiz*. Since the *Esso Nashville* was still afloat, the *Agassiz* proceeded to check out the hulk to see if any assistance could be offered in salvaging the badly broken vessel. Crew and rescuers alike were pleasantly surprised to find a man waving at them from the fantail of the tanker.

Captain Peters certainly had a story to tell. He had broken his leg during his slide down the slippery deck. Because of the oil coagulating on the surface of the ocean, he had been unable to catch up with the departing lifeboat. "After three-quarters of an hour of hopeless efforts, I decided to swim back to the ship, which was still afloat and where it seemed I would stand a better chance of being rescued.

"I boarded her quite easily forward of the mainmast, where her deck was awash, and after considerable effort I got aft to the engineers' quarters. After resting in the second assistant's room and bandaging my leg which had badly swollen, I fastened a white sheet to the rail on the windward side and ran up the ship's ensign upside down on the flag pole on the poop deck. I also tried to put on one of the lifesaving suits, but could not manage to fasten it around my neck and gave up.

"At daybreak, I sighted three U.S. Navy vessels about three miles off the bow, which were apparently picking up the crew from the lifeboats. One of them came off the stern of the *Esso Nashville* as I tried to swim to it and then launched a lifeboat from which a line was thrown to me and I was rescued."

The *Agassiz* then headed for Southport, North Carolina, where the tanker crew were given kerosene baths to remove the oil caked onto their bodies. With the various survivors coming ashore at three different points over the course of three days, it was quite a while before a final head count was in and it was determined that the entire thirty-eight man crew was safe.

But the story is not yet over.

The *Esso Nashville* continued to drift, spewing out her precious cargo of oil, until she grounded on a shoal. The vessel then broke apart. The forward two-thirds sank with the bow out of the water. The after third, containing the engineering spaces and two of the eight tank holds, stayed afloat. Salvage operations got underway immediately. On March 23, the Navy tug *Umpqua* took the stern section in tow. The truncated ship was listing forty degrees, so far over that her starboard bilge keel was high and dry. This unlikely pair was assisted through the channel by the salvage tug *Relief*. What was left of the *Esso Nashville* was towed triumphantly into Morehead City.

The two cargo holds were then emptied of their oil, the engine room was pumped dry, a temporary bulkhead was fabricated across the jagged cut, and the ship was delisted and reballasted. On May 28 the Moran Towing Company undertook the three-day towing job and delivered what remained of the tanker to her original builders in Baltimore, the Bethlehem Steel Company. There the ship was drydocked.

A completely new forward section, including the midship house, was constructed and mated to the salvaged stern. With great engineering skill, the job was completed in less than ten months. When the latest reincarnation of the *Esso Nashville* sailed again to deliver her wartime petroleum products, she was fully armed. Her career continued undaunted by the travails she had undergone at the hands of a wayward German torpedo.

Only three hours after torpedoing the *Esso Nashville*, Mohr torpedoed the *Atlantic Sun*. This tanker fared even better. She was en route from Sun Station, Texas, to Marcus Hook, Pennsylvania, with a cargo of crude. The explosion caused extensive damage and stopped the ship in her wake, but did not sink her. No one was injured by the blast. She was towed to Cape Lookout where she underwent temporary repairs that allowed the ship to proceed under her own steam. After completing her voyage, she laid up at Chester, Pennsylvania, and was repaired.

However, while the *Atlantic Sun* may have escaped total destruction this time, she had less than a year to live. She was torpedoed and sunk in the north Atlantic by Kapitanleutnant Ernst Mengersen, *U-607*, on February 15, 1943.

Mohr accounted for one more vessel in the ESF before retiring home. After the armed British trawler *John Cabot* reported exchanging gunfire with a U-boat, the American tanker *Naeco* met an untimely end.

The tanker was carrying 97,000 barrels of domestic heating oil from Houston, Texas, to Seawarren, New Jersey. Utilityman Walter Swank testified: "We were torpedoed between about 3:00 and 3:30 in the morning. The ship parted immediately and went into flames. Every man had to think for himself and act fast."

He went on to describe the horrors of evacuation in unsatisfyingly meager detail: "The rafts that were on there burned up when they hit the water as soon as the wind swept them into the fire. One boat was launched and got away with two members in it which were later found burned to death in the boat. The other lifeboat, in trying to speed cranking it out and lowering it, capsized. One man was drowned even though he had on an obsolete cork life preserver."

Some men were burned to death in the fiery cauldron, others managed to abandon ship only to fall prey to the oil-covered sea. Lifeboat No. 3, containing Swank and nine others, was picked up by the Coast Guard cutter *Dione*, which also plucked two men found floating in the water. The Navy tug *Osprey* rescued another seaman from the ocean. The boatswain found himself swimming; he returned to the ship and climbed aboard, cowering from the flames, until the Navy tug *Umpqua* drove her hull against that of the *Naeco* and took him off. The rest of the crew perished.

Both halves of the *Naeco* eventually sank about a mile apart.

Thus ended the most intense period to date of the U-boat war in the Eastern Sea Frontier. But the three-day lull that followed was nothing more than the changing of the guard as the pack of U-boats, their torpedoes expended, returned to their bases in France and Germany for refueling and rearming.

In the meantime, another wave of marauders arrived off the East Coast to continue the harassment of merchant shipping. Flachsenberg stayed behind and bridged the gap by sinking the *Dixie Arrow*.

Three torpedoes slammed into the blacked-out tanker, killing eight men instantly and igniting her cargo of crude. Another man was hurled off the deck by the force of the explosion, and slammed into a lifeboat davit; he fell back dead.

Although nearly the whole ship was enveloped by fire, and the wheelhouse was ablaze, Able Seaman Oscar Chappell refused to leave his post. Paul Myers remembered Chappell's heroism: "He was at the wheel. Fire was shooting up all about him. He saw several men trapped by flames that the wind was blowing toward them. He turned the ship hard right, which took the flames off the men on the bow but threw them directly upon himself. He lasted only a few minutes after that. He died at the helm."

Men leaped overboard in desperation, escaping the living flames only to find themselves entrenched in a seething sea. One man died when his life raft drifted into a pool of burning oil. Captain A. M. Johanson was among those cremated by the conflagration, as were all the deck officers.

Two lifeboats were consumed by fire, another fouled its lines. One got away with eight men. The radio shack was destroyed, and with it, the operator. No distress call went out. The U.S. destroyer *Tarbell* was in the area and could not help observing the broiling, black smoke that curled thousands of feet into the air. She charged toward the pyrotechnic display, dropping depth charges as she came. Survivors who clung to life rafts or floated in life jackets were "almost thrown clean out of the water" as the detonations took place, or felt the concussion "like blows in the stomach." Despite all this, twenty-two men survived the holocaust. They were picked up by boats lowered from the *Tarbell*.

The ship burned furiously for an hour before she buckled in the middle and slipped beneath the waves. The Fleet Air Photographic Unit captured the *Dixie Arrow*'s last moments on film.

Up to this point in the narrative it might seem as if the U.S. Navy was doing nothing to defend the American coast. Nothing could be farther from the truth. The Navy was aggressively pursuing antisubmarine warfare with incessant air patrols and a plethora of surface craft. Blimps were now a common sight along coastal communities; they ranged far out to sea and kept a constant vigil for shipwrecked sailors and surfaced U-boats recharging their batteries. Fast submarine chasers, the ''Cinderellas of the fleet,'' were as thick as flies, flitting across the water with their deadly guns and always-ready depth charges. Navy destroyers, Coast Guard cutters, and a host of converted yachts, plied the sea lanes daily. Airplanes carried bombs that could easily crush the skin of an unwary U-boat.

But perhaps the most intriguing of all offensive measures was the Q-ship. This was not a new idea. It was developed by the British during the First World War as a method of luring German submarines to their deaths. The idea was to take a seedy looking tramp freighter and convert it into a heavily armed warship, but in such a way that her armament was concealed behind cleverly disguised trapdoors and false superstructure houses with collapsible sides. When an unsuspecting U-boat came in for the kill, the naval ensign was raised, the facade fell away, and the fully loaded guns were run out and fired.

The British brought the scheme to perfection. Q-ships were designed with fake funnels and masts that could be raised or lowered, in order to change their profiles, and they carried quick-changing name boards. Thus, they could run one day south imitating one ship, the next day north mimicking another; by extension, they could continue to patrol the same area, always presenting a different impersonation. In case they were observed by an astute U-boat commander, the disguises would allay suspicion. The British even went so far as to create the "panic party": a select group of sailors dressed as scared crew and women passengers who lowered a boat and made their escape, while the real gun crews waited quietly behind their counterfeit bulkheads.

More than one German submarine fell to the devices of the British Q-ship. It worked in one war, why not another? And if the British could use them again, so could the Americans. The U.S. Marine Commission acquired an aging freighter built in 1912 as the *Carolyn*, and which still carried that name in the Lloyd's Register. She was converted from freighter to Q-ship at the Portsmouth Navy Yard. Without changing her outward appearance, she was given new boilers that increased her speed, fitted with sounding gear, and armed with four four-inch guns, four fifty-caliber machine guns, and six depth charge throwers, all cleverly concealed behind false bulwarks and deck houses. Her holds were packed with pulpwood for floatability.

In order to maintain merchant ship status, she was still carried in the Lloyd's Register as the *Carolyn*, owned by the A. H. Bull Steamship Company. If hailed by a suspected enemy craft, she was to respond by International Procedure as the *Vill Franca*, of Portuguese registry, and to use the call sign CSBT. She was commissioned into the U.S. Navy, and officially renamed the *Atik*.

Under the command of Lieutenant Commander H. L. Hicks, the *Atik* was still on her shakedown cruise when she encountered the worst possible adversary: the already experienced Kapitanleutnant Reinhard Hardegen of the *U-123*, the man who first brought U-boat warfare to the United States, and who was returning for a second patrol. Hardegen fired a torpedo which struck the Q-ship forward on the port side. Hicks played his part to the hilt. He slowed down the *Atik* as if she were sorely wounded and transmitted "SSS SOS LAT. 36-00 N, LONG. 70-00 W, CAROLYN burning forward, not bad." Two minutes later he broadcast, "Torpedo struck, burning forward; require assistance."

Hardegen was taken in at first. Running on the surface,

he crossed the wake of the *Atik* and brought out his gun crew. He wanted to sink the rusty looking freighter without expending another valuable torpedo.

Hicks steered the Q-ship so as to bring the U-boat on his starboard beam. When the advantage was his, he dropped his merchant disguise and opened fire. His broadside was far more powerful than that of the U-boat. Shells screamed both ways in a high explosive duel. One German was killed during the engagement as shrapnel splattered across the U-boat's wintergarten.

Hardegen pulled out of the unequal battle. He hauled out of range, his boat not seriously damaged, and crash dived. The Q-ship was a dangerous adversary when fought on her own grounds, but once the U-boat submerged the advantage shifted to the undersea raider. The *Atik* now became quarry, and one that could not be left alive to ensnare some other overconfident U-boat commander.

During the next two hours, Hardegen stalked the Q-ship as he waited for the moon to rise. Still submerged, he took his time getting into a favorable firing position. He launched another torpedo at the crippled freighter and hit her squarely in the engine room. The *Atik* started going down fast by the head. As she sank to the level of the bridge, with her single screw out of the water, men began launching lifeboats. Before they could get away, a cataclysmic explosion blew up the Q-ship. Hardegen recorded hearing underwater detonations as he left the scene.

The German High Command grasped the opportunity to demonstrate U-boat prowess and efficacy by broadcasting the particulars of the battle. An April 9 communique from Berlin confirmed the sinking of the Q-ship after a "bitter battle" that was "fought partly on the surface with artillery and partly beneath the water with bombs and torpedoes."

Unfortunately for those valiant sailors serving aboard the *Atik*, this was no mere propaganda. The *Atik*'s sister ship *Asterion*, converted from the *Evelyn*, arrived at the site of destruction in answer to the distress call. She found no wreckage and no survivors. The *Atik*'s six officers and one hundred thirty-five men were either killed in the explosion, or died in the gale that blew up a few hours later.

At the same time, closer to shore, another U-boat entered the ESF. This was the *U-160*, Oberleutnant zur See George Lassen. In a two week period he caused quite a furor, starting with the *Equipoise*.

The Panamanian freighter was carrying 8,000 tons of manganese ore from Rio de Janeiro, Brazil, to Baltimore, Maryland, under Naval routing instructions. She was armed with a four-inch deck gun and four machine guns. Five lookouts scanned the sea for suspicious objects or fast moving buoys—one of the disguises adopted by inventive U-boat captains.

No one saw the torpedo that exploded with such violence between No. 1 and No. 2 holds, starboard. It apparently ripped the bottom right out of the ship, for she went down in the unbelievably short time of two minutes. Of the fifty-three men aboard, thirty-eight were unable to climb out of the tomblike interior before the vessel slipped beneath the waves.

Those lucky enough to be topside were galvanized into action. In that brief span of time, two lifeboats and two rafts were launched, although one lifeboat capsized in the process. Almost in the blink of an eye, fifteen men who had been comfortably ensconced on an oceangoing freighter now floated upon the cool sea in irrevocable loneliness. To make matters worse, the ship sank without getting off a radio distress call—no one even knew they were out there.

Soon afterwards, the ship's carpenter died of injuries. The next morning, Captain John Anderson passed away. The lifeboat nearly swamped in rough seas, and the captain's body was washed out. The men were cold and wet. All that day, not a ship was seen, so the survivors from the *Equipoise* were forced to spend another night on the open sea. It was not until 1630 on the twentieth that the eight men in the lifeboat were picked up by the U.S. destroyer *Greer*. The *Greer* cruised the area, and within an hour located both rafts with an additional five men.

Yet their travails were as nothing compared to those of the *City of New York*'s people. Again it was Lassen who caused so much death and agony.

The *City of New York*, of the American-South African Line, was carrying in addition to forty-seven passengers, eighty-eight crew, and nine gunners, a cargo of sheepskins, wool, and raw furs. Her round trip route took her to ports in the Union of South Africa, with a return stop at Trinidad before proceeding to New York. She was off the coast of North Carolina when, at 1245, a torpedo exploded directly under the bridge, port side.

The blast destroyed No. 2 lifeboat, and the column of water filled lifeboats No. 4 and 6 right up to the gunwales. The radio room was damaged. All lines of communication between the bridge and engine room were severed.

With one hundred forty-four souls depending on him for survival, Captain George Sullivan wasted no time ordering abandon ship. Chief Radio Operator Albert Viada stuck to his post, effecting temporary repairs to his equipment so he could send out a hasty SOS.

According to the Statement of Master submitted to the loss committee, "all undamaged lifeboats were swung out, and when it was noted the vessel's engines were stopped the boats were lowered into the water. Before the Nos. 4 and 6 lifeboats could be entered they had to be cleared of water. . . . The lifeboats had hardly entered the water when the vessel was struck by another torpedo, about three minutes after the first one struck her. This second torpedo struck the vessel on the starboard side apparently in the way of No. 4 hold, and caused the No. 1 lifeboat in charge of the chief officer to capsize. Upon being struck by this second torpedo the vessel began to sink rapidly."

Quartermaster Americo Rodriguez was in the ill-fated lifeboat No. 1: "There were two women and one child in my boat. After the boat capsized they had disappeared. I found a life raft and climbed aboard it. Several persons were in the water nearby, including a woman and a little girl. We helped them aboard the raft."

Dr. L. H. Conly, the ship's doctor, had a near escape,

too. The antenna of the sinking ship caught his boat and "almost dragged it under the water."

During this time, the armed guard scrambled to their fighting stations. They sighted a periscope some two hundred fifty yards off the port side, and immediately opened fire. Captain Sullivan joined the gun crew at the stern platform. The gunnery officer directed shell after shell at the U-boat until it submerged.

After the second torpedo attack, Captain Sullivan counted four undamaged lifeboats and three rafts clear of the ship. The captain and gun crew leaped into the water and swam away furiously. They were able to reach one of the rafts. From there, Captain Sullivan watched his ship go down on an even keel. From the first explosion to the last ripple of water, it had taken only ten minutes to swallow every vestige of the *City of New York*.

The call for help set prearranged mobilization plans in motion. Planes and blimps and boats on standby status were sent to sea like firemen to a fire. Whether the positioning data had been miskeyed, misread, or wrongly transcribed, is impossible to say. It is only known that the plethora of rescue craft was unsuccessful in locating the survivors.

All this was out of Captain Sullivan's hands, but more immediate problems were not. One of his women passengers, twenty-eight-year-old Mrs. Desanka Mohorovicic, was pregnant and near the end of her term. In addition to this, he had people scattered all over the ocean.

Jack Rodriguez, who was crammed on a life raft with seven others, said that they were continuously surrounded by a school of sharks. "We beat them off with our oars."

Viada was on a raft on which ten people huddled. They tried to help aboard Mrs. Richard Wrigley, Jr., whose husband and daughter were in a lifeboat, but "the waves carried her away."

Captain Sullivan took charge. The four lifeboats rowed around and tended to the people on the rafts. There was no room for all of them on the boats, but the women and children were taken aboard and all the emergency blankets were given to those who would have to spend their time out in the open. The captain took a head count and, amazingly, found that everyone had escaped the sinking vessel except for three men who were reported killed by the blast.

For the remainder of the day, tumultuous seas beat against the boats and waves washed across the rafts. Darkness came, and with the loss of the sun came the cold. Most people were still soaked from their hasty retreat. Those on the rafts were constantly showered with salt spray. But the worst problem was Mrs. Mohorovicic: the shock of the experience forced her into labor.

Aware of her condition, Captain Sullivan made sure that she was in the same lifeboat as Dr. Conly. The baby that was not due for several weeks decided at that point to make a premature appearance. The doctor was not in the best of health himself, for he had broken two ribs during his exit from the sinking ship: the lifeboat had dropped to the bottom of a deep trough just as his feet touched a seat and as he let go of the falls, and he had fallen sharply to the floor. Nevertheless, he prepared for the delivery.

A sail was stretched across the stern of the lifeboat, giving a small measure of protection from the elements. Even so, waves frequently slapped against the wooden hull and splashed inside. During Mrs. Mohorovicic's three- to four-hour labor, Dr. Conly crouched beside her in the darkness, fingering the simple instruments contained in the lifeboat's first aid kit.

Mrs. Mohorovicic was already suffering the pain of battered and bruised legs: she had crashed heavily to the deck of the *City of New York* as she was rushing to her lifeboat station with her two-year-old daughter, Visna, in her arms. The young mother held up well to the pain. Dr. Conly praised her as "a brave, lovely woman."

Around midnight, Mrs. Mohorovicic gave a final push and the baby boy, a hefty eight-pounder was born into a lifeboat crowded with twenty-four people—bobbing around in frothy seas and in the wake of death and destruction wrought by the German war machine.

Dr. Conly wrapped the infant in the only swaddling available at the time: "We took a turban from another woman in the boat and wrapped the baby in it.'' Waves splashed over the gunwale, and the baby was quickly doused by the sea. His mother was wringing wet. Water constantly sloshed in the bottom of the boat. ''She kept him inside her lifebelt, which was like a kangaroo's pouch. It was the only place where he could be kept at all warm. After that first night, when she was too weak to move, she sat up and stayed there the rest of the time, holding the almost naked baby against her chest. She is a remarkable woman.''

Indeed, it was remarkable that any of them survived the next three days. It was not until the morning of April 1, after sixty hours adrift, that the ragtag array of lifeboats and rafts was sighted by the U.S. destroyer *Roper*. Unfortunately, during that time and the hours of darkness, one lifeboat had gone out of sight and the rafts were nowhere to be found.

The survivors were taken to Norfolk, Virginia, where most were hospitalized for exposure and injuries. When word of the lifeboat birthing hit the newspapers, even though the *City of New York* was not mentioned by name, a young attaché of the Yugoslav Consulate knew intuitively from the combination of circumstances that the mother must be his wife. Joseph Mohorovicic had arrived in New York only weeks earlier, delayed and hospitalized because the ship he had embarked on was also torpedoed. Now he journeyed to Norfolk to visit his wife and daughter and newborn son. The baby boy was duly named Jesse Roper, after the vessel that had rescued mother and child from the cold Atlantic swells.

On April 11, fully thirteen days after the sinking of the *City of New York*, an Army bomber spotted a lifeboat in the open ocean a hundred miles off Cape May, New Jersey. A Navy blimp was called in to investigate and found the people aboard still alive. The blimp hovered over the spot and led the Coast Guard cutter *#455* to the scene. When the rescuers arrived they found eleven survivors (eight men, two women, and a three-year-old girl, Miriam Etter) and two bodies from that disastrous voyage. Their lifeboat had drifted north some three hundred miles. They had convulsed with hunger and thirst. Indeed, Miriam's mother Sora had died only an hour before they were picked up.

The sad story of the *City of New York* had at last come to an end. No more bodies or survivors were ever found. Of the original one hundred forty-four aboard, one hundred eighteen survived through great hardships, five were known dead, and twenty-one counted as missing, presumed dead. The fatalities could have been worse, but the suffering could not.

The final action of the month was fought by Kapitan-leutnant Johannes Oestermann, *U-754*, who chose to announce his presence in the ESF with an open gun battle.

The tug *Menominee* left Newport News, Virginia, with three barges in tow: the *Allegheny* and the *Barnegat* carried coal, the *Ontario* was piled high with lumber. The tug was manned by a crew of eighteen; three men rode each of the barges. They were headed for Stamford, Connecticut. At 0210, tug and tows were crossing the Parramore Bank, off the desolate northern Virginia coast, when the U-boat ran in on the surface and fired a shot from fifty feet.

The high explosive round burst through a window in the captain's cabin, smashed through the radio equipment and ship-to-shore telephone, and passed out the starboard bulkhead without exploding. The second shell passed through the forecastle from port to starboard; it, too, failed to explode.

Captain Leslie Haynie ordered the barges cast adrift. Without the drag of the tows, the *Menominee* lurched ahead at her full speed of eleven knots. The captain spun the wheel and headed for the open ocean.

Oestermann ran his U-boat down the line of barges, firing into the hulls as he passed by. In order to shield themselves from exploding gun shells, each three man crew was forced to scramble over the cargo to the opposite side of the barge. The odor of burned charcoal wafted across the decks. Oestermann swung left around the last barge and ran up the starboard side, raking the hulls and deck cargo at a leisurely pace like a tin duck shooter at a penny arcade. He cut close around the bow of the *Allegheny* and made a second pass at the port side. The barge crews clambered from side to side of their charges.

With the easy targets well-holed, Oestermann took off after the retreating tug. His gun crew fired eight shells at long range, but all overshot their mark. He soon overtook the *Menominee*.

As the U-boat drew near, Captain Haynie knew the game was up. He ordered the motors stopped, and had both life rafts cut loose. He figured on the U-boat captain having the decency of letting the crew make good their escape. Oestermann, however, had no such preconceptions of honor. He reopened fire at close range, blasting into the tug's superstructure. One well-placed round hit amidships, in the paint locker. The *Menominee* blew up and caught fire. The men were forced to jump for it. Captain Haynie swam through the frigid water until he reached a raft to which five others clung desperately. Only two more men found the raft. The rest of the crew was not seen.

Back at the barges, each crew was having its own difficulties. Those on the *Ontario*, last in line, saw the tug go up in flames. They took to a small lifeboat and rowed for shore, along with the barge's mascot, a puppy named Snowball.

The *Allegheny*, first in line, sank. Its crew rowed back to the *Barnegat*.

After the *Menominee* went under, Oestermann returned to the two still-floating barges. He circled the bow of the *Barnegat* and did another port side run, pumping shells into both barges. At the end of this run, the *U-754* retired to the southeast. The *Barnegat* sank. The six men huddled on its coal covered deck got off just in time. They retired to the abandoned *Ontario* which, because of its cargo of wood, continued to float.

At 0930, a lookout in the tower of the Metomkin Coast Guard Station peered through his spyglass and spotted three men in a lifeboat about a mile and a half offshore. The station's surfboat #4489 was dispatched immediately. As soon as the *Ontario* crewmen were brought ashore, and their story told, motor lifeboat *#4063* was sent out to search for more survivors.

The Coast Guard rescuers found the *Ontario* riding at anchor, with all six men safe. They were taken off. Later, the badly listing barge was towed back to port.

Meanwhile, a patrol plane sighted a raft and put out a call for help. The tanker *Northern Sun* was in the vicinity, and changed course for the radioed location. When she arrived at the site she found a life raft half inundated by large Atlantic swells. Of the eight men who had sought refuge on the emergency raft, six had died of weakness and exposure: five had slipped off, one body remained. Only Captain Haynie and the *Menominee*'s chief engineer lived to tell the story of the savage shelling and subsequent survival.

Several actions occurred during the month of March that related directly to the U-boat campaign against American shipping. First, Secretary of the Navy Frank Knox proclaimed a limited ban on merchant casualty bulletins for media release. With all the publicity offered by the newspapers, it was far too easy for enemy agents to collect intelligence of possible military value simply by picking up the evening edition. His March 11 announcement stipulated that "vessels falling prey to the enemy in Western Hemisphere waters will be identified only as large, medium, and small." The nationality could be designated, but not the name or tonnage of the ship, whether it was a tanker or freighter, or location of the sinking. Canada had taken this tack long before, even to the extent of refusing to acknowledge to which port survivors had been taken.

On March 23, one *New York Times* headline read, "100,000 Cars Go Dry If Tanker Is Sunk." This followed the previous week's order from the American Petroleum Institute rationing gasoline deliveries to filling stations and the suggestion of a coupon rationing system. The API report on stocks of gasoline, distillate fuel oil (heating oil), and residual fuel oil on the East Coast stated that "in the first two and a half months of 1942 East Coast inventories of these principal products dropped 19,000,000 barrels, while in the comparable 1941 period they declined only 5,500,000 barrels.'' The delivery reduction for the week was twenty percent.

Marine underwriters were still concerned about the casualty rate off the East Coast. They now decided to increase the rates for freighters plying waters north of Cape Hatteras. As an innovation in the insurance industry, they advanced the idea of split rates so that freighters paid one rate for that part of their voyage south of the Cape, and an additional rate for that part of the voyage north of the Cape.

But by far the most high-level response was a special Executive Hearing before the House of Representatives. The Committee on the Merchant Marine and Fisheries convened on March 26 in order to listen to testimony concerning safety aboard vessels of the Merchant Marine. Chairman Schuyler Bland opened by avowing that the purpose of the meeting was ''to consider problems of coastal patrol under the Coast Guard or other governmental agencies by fishermen, seamen, or other personnel, civilian, military, or naval, and other means of protecting water-borne commerce, personnel, and vessels.''

The hearing was confidential, and no newspaper reporters were allowed to attend. Many items were discussed, including the arming of merchant ships (and the shortage of guns, or the time to install them), the proper loading of war cargoes (where longshoremen's advice was ignored by Army and Navy personnel in charge), the designation of incoming and outgoing lanes for busy ports (especially since ships now habitually ran without lights), the use of the nation's fishing fleet for national defense, even the lurid accounts of sinkings propounded by the press.

The importance of radio in saving the lives of merchant seaman led to suggestions such as around-the-clock radio service aboard ship (by increasing the number of operators from one to three); the installation of automatic recorders that would put on tape every transmitted dot and dash; emergency antennas; back-up motor-generators; separate locations for main and auxiliary transmission equipment; and bomb-proof radio rooms.

For merchant ship evacuation safety, the committee took testimony from the best witnesses of all: the survivors of actual sinkings. Suggestions by the seamen state the case.

"Would suggest that a more thorough fire and boat drill be done. For instance, a drill in port. Lower a boat and let crew operate same." (Harry W. Burlingame, third assistant, *Malay*)

"Lights were shining through portholes and after passageway and so this ship had lights all over it. As far as the black-out goes, there was none. I feel that we should have things just as good as the Navy has. On some of their ships when you open doors the lights go off; that way we could have a blackout all the time." (H. B. Graham, *Papoose*)

"I believe if the crew were supplied with those lifesaving suits, a larger number would at least have been saved." (Juan Rivera, *Caribsea*)

George Williams, first assistant, *E.H. Blum*: "It is my request that more ways of escape be provided from the engine room and fireroom, so that if there is any ladder that has been carried away, it will be possible to have a means of escape for the personnel endeavoring to reach their lifeboats."

Captain Grover Clark, master of the *Lemuel Burrows*, suggested "that the Jersey coast is a great menace insofar as the neon shore lights are concerned. This should be remedied."

"The lifeboats were not swung out, and it took between fifteen and twenty minutes to get them out. There were no blankets in the boats." (Alexander Robinson, chief cook, *San Jose*)

Arif Mahmut, a fireman on the *Malay*, recommended "that there be a safety-first committee composed of members of the crew to see that everything is in order before ship is ready to sail."

John Larson, of the *Allan Jackson*, mailed his testimony from his hospital bed at the United States Marine Hospital in Norfolk, Virginia: "The turnbuckles were frozen and it took anywhere between five and ten minutes to release the grips." He also mentioned that "there were no life rafts on this vessel."

The crew of the *Rubilene* banded together as their ship was leaving port, and commented wryly, "Life rafts have been specified by the government, but the ones put on this ship might just as well be pictures of life rafts painted on the deck. They cannot be launched from where they are placed. Rafts for instant ready launching should be fixed on the shrouds on the slip carriages. Ours are lashed to the deck or set in walk-ways where they can only serve to bruise shins during blackouts. They wouldn't even float off if the ship sank."

They went on to request a vastly increased shore patrol. "The well-meaning pleasure-boat owners who have turned over their luxury toys to Uncle Sam have done a very commendable deed. We seamen appreciate the sacrifice involved when a man turns his yacht over to his country. But there are too few of them, much better to turn the hundreds and hundreds of small fishing boats over to the service."

They also suggested adequate compensation for "a string of tough little fishing craft armed with ashcans . . . strung out along the coast along our sea lanes. These horny, hardy, seawise, seaworthy fishermen know every bump or wave by first and last name on the Atlantic Ocean and a submarine commander would think thrice before he would come up among them to shell a helpless merchantman or machine-gun a lifeboat. No one has yet solved the submarine menace, but it is our contention that the more armed boats patrolling our coast, the fewer tankers and freighters will be lost."

Ingolf Pettersen, who was on the *Gulftrade*, summed up his suggestions with, "We want to 'Keep 'Em Sailing' but won't be able to if these conditions aren't remedied pronto."

This was not a threat, but a dire prediction.

If the sinkings in the ESF seemed to be on the upswing, they were nothing compared to the amount of action in the Caribbean. The gray wolves were spreading farther afield, seeking out the greatest density of shipping. U-boats were also slipping into the Gulf of

Mexico, the tanker-rich shipping lanes leading from the Texas oil fields.

The U.S. Navy was not sitting idle through all this. While the number of bombs and depth charges dropped on alleged U-boats was little less than phenomenal, their effect was pretty close to zero. U-boats did have to be wary, especially of the swarm of patrol planes that buzzed along the coastline like a cloud of mosquitoes. But despite the commissioning of Coast Guard vessels into the U.S. Navy, there was still a dearth of watercraft available for coastal defense.

Claims for sinking U-boats became an almost daily event. The number of U-boats supposedly sunk in the ESF rivaled the amount in existence in Hitler's fleet worldwide. Practically every pilot who ever dropped a bomb or depth charge or marker buoy on an unidentified object or periscope sighting claimed to have sunk a U-boat. Propaganda works both ways, so it was certainly good for the morale of the country to fill the newspapers with Allied successes.

In February, Donald Mason, an enlisted man, made the headlines with his now-famous laconic message: "Sighted sub; sank same." In March, not only was he credited with another U-boat kill, he received a commission for it. Other flyboys received similar commendations for aggressive and relentless attacks against undersea raiders, and for their claims of victory.

Yet the fact remains that not one U-boat was even so much as damaged, much less sunk, by these aerial attacks. They might have been harried, and forced to crash dive, but that is a long way from total destruction. It seems never to have occurred to anyone that a U-boat disappearing beneath the waves after a bombing or depth charge attack was doing anything other than making the final plunge to its grave. No one seemed to know the difference between "submerging" and "sinking." There was a definite lack of understanding in U-boat defense: it *always* submerged when attacked. That was how submarines escaped. That is why they are called submarines, because they have the ability to get away underwater.

But the reports of U-boat casualties continued to pour in, not just from overexuberant pilots, but from coastal defense craft as well. The loss of paper U-boats made it seem as if the Navy was exacting a heavy toll for the number of merchant ships torpedoed.

Soon, however, such claims would change from paper to steel.

# APRIL

"You people don't know just what it is all about—we do. We feel that it is worth giving our lives to help defeat the Nazis. We know what they have done. We have heard from our families in Norway. We want to get back on a ship as soon as we can."

Unidentified survivor of the *Svenor*

Although the March 27 sinking of the Norwegian tanker *Svenor* took place far enough off the Carolina coast to place it in the Bermuda Area, the survivors were landed in Gloucester, New Jersey. They said that, when their ship did not sink from a torpedo hit, the U-boat surfaced and shelled them unmercifully, killing their captain and seven crewmen in the process. The culprit was the *U-105*, Korvettenkapitan Heinrich Schuch.

An interviewing reporter tagged the sailors heroes. Their humble reply was, "No, we're not heroes. We've got a job to do, and some day you fellows will have a job to do, too."

Even as they were coming ashore, Oestermann was still afoot. Going for bigger game and still clinging to shore, he played an April Fool's joke against the American tanker *Tiger* just after midnight.

The *Tiger* was nearing the end of her voyage from Aruba, an island in the Netherlands Antilles, with 65,000 barrels of Navy fuel oil. She was one of three ships awaiting a pilot to show them the path through the defensive mine field. Captain Rein Schnore signaled the pilot boat, and was maneuvering for the pickup, when the *U-754* surfaced a hundred fifty yards off the starboard quarter.

A bridgewing lookout spotted the U-boat in the moonlight and shouted a warning. Captain Schnore ordered full speed ahead and hard aport. The ship had hardly moved when he saw the torpedo track. The deadly explosive struck just aft of midships as the *Tiger* was turning away. There was no flash since the torpedo blew up well below the waterline. George Gardner, a fireman, was killed by the blast.

The tanker slowly settled by the stern. The U-boat passed by aft, partially submerged, and disappeared into the night. Both the regular and the emergency antennas were down, so no call for help reached shore. The ship was abandoned in an orderly fashion. The captain even had time to save his codes. The forty-one survivors got away in three lifeboats and were picked up two hours later by the USS *YP-52*.

The *Tiger* sat low in the water but was still afloat when the Coast Guard cutter *Jackson* arrived at 0500. She took the tanker in tow and for six hours struggled inland, until the ship took a sharp list and sank by the stern with the bow, bridge, stacks, and masts projecting from the water.

The Navy tug *Relief* tried to tow her in, but found the ship too hard aground to be moved. Since the wreck lay only sixty feet deep, the Navy Salvage Service then attempted to raise the wreck, but ''abandoned operations when condition of the vessel was found to be such that salvage, if successful, would require extensive operations of such length that salvage vessel could not be employed due to other more urgent work.'' The wreck was later destroyed as a hazard to navigation.

Later that day, Lassen torpedoed and sank the British steamship *Rio Blanco*. The British freighter was en route from Freetown, Sierra Leone, West Africa, to Hampton Roads, Virginia, with 6,400 tons of iron ore. At 0920, a lookout on the *Rio Blanco* saw the track of a torpedo porpoising on the surface, and heading directly for the ship. He shouted a warning—too late, for seconds later the deadly device exploded just below the waterline amidships. The detonation was so great that it blew off the hatch covers and collapsed the bridge and radio room. The forehold flooded instantly. It took only two minutes for the freighter to nose under the water and disappear forever.

Two lifeboats and two rafts were launched. Captain Aiden Blacket found himself on a raft with Chief Engineer Thomas Smyth, who had also jumped from the deck of the steeply tilting freighter just moments before she went down. They were soon picked up by No. 1 lifeboat. Both boats rowed around and picked up the survivors, locating in all thirty of the forty men: twelve in No. 1 lifeboat, eighteen in No. 2.

No. 1 had been damaged by the blast. Several planks had sprung; some of the survivors manned the pumps, while others jammed old rags into the leaks. Against the captain's wishes, No. 2 lifeboat pulled away in charge of the second mate. Left to their own devices, the men in No. 1 lifeboat settled down for the long, dark night. Once, a patrol plane passed overhead. Red flares and shouts of despair did not bring the plight of the lonely lifeboat to the attention of the airmen.

The next day, Captain Blacket took stock of their supplies and provisions. The food was stored in water-tight containers under the seats; it had not been contaminated by the previous day's flooding. There was no compass. Nevertheless, they rigged a sail and headed on a dead reckoning course toward shore. Little progress was made against strong westerly winds. Already, contention was building between the six white men and the six West African blacks.

On the second day, they spotted what they later described as a "Navy patrol flying boat." Again, they were unable to attract its attention. Anticipating the worst, Captain Blacket started rationing. Fresh water was at a minimum. Toward the end of the first week, and against the captain's protests, three of the blacks assuaged their thirst with salt water. They died the next day and were buried at sea.

A few days later, a severe storm washed pounding waves over the gunwales, and nearly capsized the lifeboat. The men were drenched. They suffered horribly from sunburn and salt sores. Their feet swelled with fluid.

On April 12, a four-engined Army bomber flew directly overhead at an altitude no higher than eight hundred feet. It could not distinguish the tiny lifeboat among the waves. Toward the end of the second week came the scent and sight of land. Before they could make shore, another storm blew them away. It was not until the morning of the fourteenth day that a speck on the horizon gradually grew into the shape of the British antisubmarine trawler *Hertfordshire*. They were saved.

Lifeboat No. 2 was picked up at sea, and the twelve remaining survivors taken to Halifax.

On the second of April, Hardegen was at it again. This time he viciously shelled the American tanker *Liebre*. Two men were killed outright, and seven were lost during the hurried evacuation under fire. For some reason, Hardegen broke off the attack before the disabled and unmanned ship went for the final plunge. Several hours later the twenty-five survivors, including four seriously injured, rowed back to their darkened, still floating vessel.

The crew reboarded the *Liebre* and effected temporary repairs. That morning, first the British trawler HMS *St. Zeno* then the tug *Resolute* attached hawsers, and together started towing the tanker into port. It was slow hauling, for the ship was low in the water. A day and a half later the two towing vessels steamed triumphantly with their charge into Morehead City. The *Liebre* was later towed to Baltimore, repaired, and returned to service.

Enter a U-boat for its first visit to the ESF: the *U-552*, and the already successful Oberleutnant zur See Erich Topp. In less than a week of high speed activity he would sink six ships. In order to save his valuable torpedoes for larger targets, Topp opened up with his deck gun on the small coastal freighter *David H. Atwater*.

The collier was en route from Norfolk, Virginia, to Fall River, Massachusetts, with 3,800 tons of coal, and was manned by a crew of twenty-seven. For safety she hugged the coastline, never straying more than three miles from the beach. It was 2115 when Able Bodied

Seaman Ernest Cartwright "was awakened by what sounded like a sharp cracking noise. I looked up and the paint was cracked on the wall in my quarters. I rushed on deck as the third crack came, and the ship shook all over."

The watch crew was already launching a lifeboat. Six or eight men got it away before Cartwright could board. He clung to the deck as the U-boat found the range and began blowing the ship to bits. Cartwright saw "balls of fire originating aft, where the engine room was located, indicating that the vessel had been set afire."

Destruction reigned as Captain William Webster and all the engineers were killed by hot, flying shrapnel. Fifteen or twenty rounds fired in rapid succession exploded against the hull and superstructure. Sabino Gomez, fireman, saw two men blown away by one burst.

Cartwright joined forces with Gomez and two others. They launched No. 1 lifeboat from the starboard side while the U-boat shelled the port. They rowed furiously away from the blazing collier, seeking the cover of darkness. Cartwright said, "The submarine passed our lifeboat about two hundred yards off, and after it passed us, it fired five or six more shells, then went around to the port side of the ship and fired two or three more times."

Now Cartwright discovered three dead bodies lying in the bottom of the lifeboat. The messboy was seriously injured, his side torn apart by steel shards. He soon died of his wounds.

The radio operator had stuck to his post for seven minutes, long enough to alert the nearby *CGC-218*, before he was killed at his key. Coast Guard cutter *Legare* observed the gunfire. As rescue craft sped for the action, the U-boat beat a hasty retreat seaward.

The three survivors and four bodies in lifeboat No. 1 were picked up by the *CGC-218* to be taken to Chincoteague. The *Legare* continued to patrol the area. Her crew saw the collier go down about an hour and a half later, leaving two feet of one mast showing above the water.

As the day dawned on a placid sea, the grim task of

recovering bodies began. A Navy blimp and a civilian plane dropped markers that directed the *Legare* where to look. She picked up thirteen bodies wearing life jackets marked *David H. Atwater*. *Eagle 56* picked up another.

That afternoon Oestermann torpedoed the *Otho*, a passenger-freighter on a voyage from Takoradi, Gold Coast, West Africa, to Philadelphia and New York. In addition to thirty-seven crew, ten armed guard, and six passengers, she carried 4,400 tons of manganese ore, 1,296 tons of palm oil, and 750 tons of lead in pigs.

The explosion broached the hull between No. 3 hold and the fire and engine room, wiping out the stokers and engine room crew to a man. The foremast collapsed from the shock, taking with it the radio antenna. The *Otho* went down quickly, taking with her twenty-five crew, nine gunners, and three passengers. Captain John Makkinje was among those lost. One lifeboat containing sixteen survivors drifted two hundred miles in five days. It was discovered by the USS *Zircon*, which took the weakened men to Cape May, New Jersey.

Topp found the ship he was saving his torpedoes for on the night of the fourth at 2300. The *Byron D. Benson* was bound from Port Arthur, Texas, for Bayonne, New Jersey, with a cargo of crude. Traveling with her were the *Gulf of Mexico* and two armed escorts: the USS *Hamilton* and the HMS *Norwich City*.

The torpedo slammed into the starboard side aft of the *Byron D. Benson*'s midship house. It blasted through tanks 7 and 8, creating a hole from considerably below the waterline up though the main deck. Blazing oil exploded over ship and sea. The steering gear and engine controls were wrecked. The tanker continued on a starboard tack, out of control, spewing oil and flames in a large pool aft.

The *Gulf of Mexico* veered out of the way, and again escaped destruction.

No order to abandon ship was given. With a hundred thousand barrels of burning oil engulfing the vessel, panic ruled. Within ten minutes the *Byron D. Benson* was a funeral pyre practically devoid of human life. Twenty-seven crew members got away in the aft port lifeboat.

Another lifeboat left the midship area with Captain John McMillian, three mates, the wireless operator, two A.B.s, and one ordinary seaman. It was last seen drifting into the flames.

One man was left aboard the tanker: Oiler John Austrauske. He waited thirty minutes, tossed a life raft overboard, and leaped in after he saw it was drifting away from the flames. He climbed aboard the raft. It provided a safe refuge until the burning came close and touched it off. Austrauske abandoned the raft. As he swam away he continually had to dive under patches of blazing oil. Eventually, he got far enough away so that he could "just lay to." The HMS *Norwich City* drove in close to the *Byron D. Benson*, looking for survivors. The armed trawler happened upon the lone oiler and effected the rescue.

The other lifeboat was not discovered until several hours later. All twenty-seven men were picked up by the U.S. destroyer *Hamilton*. Nine men remained missing and were presumed dead.

Fire raged out of control. The *Byron D. Benson* turned into a cauldron of flames and dense, black smoke that filled the sky with a spectacular display. Not until April 7, when the oil burned itself out, did the scarred, blackened cinder of a ship slip beneath the waves.

Lassen torpedoed the American tanker *Bidwell* early on the morning of the sixth. The explosion occurred amidships, blowing a huge hole in Nos. 7 and 8 tanks, knocking down the mainmast which carried the radio antennas, and destroying the steering control. Burning oil spewed out over the entire length of the ship. On the bridgewing, Second Mate Matthew Hehnen was showered with the hot, blazing oil. His clothes were instantly ignited, so he leaped overboard.

Burning oil and hissing steam lines prevented Captain Sedolf Heggelund from sending a messenger aft. Through the flames and white steam he could barely make out the stern lifeboat swung out. Assuming that the after crew was abandoning ship, he ordered No. 1 lifeboat launched. He and the bridge watch boarded it and pulled away.

Duty personnel aft knew nothing of their captain's

escape. Chief Engineer William Dalton called back the off duty personnel attempting to leave in the lifeboat. Under previous instructions to keep the engines going in the event of a torpedo attack, in order to outrun escaping oil, the engine room staff remained at their stations. The *Bidwell* cruised around in circles for thirty minutes while Dalton worked on the auxiliary steering gear. Once in operation, and without receiving any communication from the bridge, he steered a course for shore and shoal water.

Three hours later the captain's lifeboat caught up with the damaged, slow-moving tanker. He shouted for the ship to stop. He and those with him reboarded. He had just ordered slow ahead when the second mate was heard calling for help. The lifeboat was again lowered, and a rescue party sent out after him, but "the men in the lifeboat got within fifty yards of him and heard him say he couldn't last much longer, and when they reached the spot where he had been, he was gone."

The *Bidwell* headed for Hampton Roads, Virginia, at reduced speed. She was later repaired at the Sun Shipyards at Chester, Pennsylvania, and returned to service.

That night Topp had a two hitter. He first came across the tanker *British Splendour* and her escort, the HMS *St. Zeno*. Topp made a submerged attack to avoid detection. His torpedo ripped into the port side of the tanker aft of the engine room, blowing off the skylight. The entire aft superstructure was destroyed by the blast. Twelve men were instantly sent to their graves.

While the radio operator sent out a distress call, the rest of the crew rallied around the lifeboats and got three of them, and one raft, launched in the brief moments before the ship flooded and capsized. The *St. Zeno* rescued Captain John Hall, the remaining crewmen, and the gunners.

A few hours later, Topp found the Norwegian freighter *Lansing*. His torpedo blew in the steel hull adjacent to the engine room, destroyed two lifeboats and their davits, and killed Fireman Emil Hansen. Captain Johan Bjerkholt led the men in abandoning ship in the three remaining lifeboats. It took an hour for the *Lansing* to sink. Four hours later, the survivors were sighted by a patrol plane which broadcast their location. Twenty-eight men were picked up by the tanker *Pan-Rhode Island*, twenty-one by the HMS *Hertfordshire*.

Hardegen tried another double on the eighth but, although his aim was accurate, the gods of war were against him. His first target was the *Oklahoma*, an American tanker carrying 12,887 tons of petroleum and manned by a crew of thirty-eight. The torpedo hit her resoundingly, at about 0200, blowing a gaping hole in her stern. Water poured into the crew's quarters and engine room. Nineteen men were either killed by the blast or drowned.

The rest took to the lifeboats. As they were pulling away they heard shouts from the drifting tanker. Captain Theron Davenport turned his boat around and returned to the ship, where he found a wounded man trapped inside. The man was rescued, but later died of his injuries. As they were rowing away the second time, the U-boat surfaced and pumped a dozen shells into the hull and superstructure. All the survivors of the *Oklahoma* gathered in one lifeboat and steered for shore.

Hardegen then broke off the attack because he spotted the *Esso Baton Rouge* in the light of the rising moon. Within fifty minutes of attacking the *Oklahoma* he fired a torpedo at the second tanker.

Captain James Poche wrote in his report of the event: "From inside the chart room the shock felt as if the vessel had collided with some object. I returned to the bridge, where Second Mate Durdle informed me we had been torpedoed. The ship settled rapidly by the stern until the weather deck between the pumproom and the after house was awash and she apparently rested by the stern on the bottom in approximately seven fathoms of water. As the ship's radio was put out of order by the explosion, Radio Operator Michael J. Reilly was not able to send a distress message."

Three men who were on duty in the engine room were killed by the blast.

A joint report signed by all the officers takes up the story: "All hands rushed to their boat stations and released No. 1 and No. 3 lifeboats ready for lowering. The captain watched the launching of the two starboard lifeboats while Second Mate Durdle was standing on the boat deck supervising the fore fall of No. 1. When all were safely in the boats, the captain joined us in No. 1 lifeboat and we hauled away from the ship's side after seeing that No. 3 had cleared.

"We rowed until daybreak in a northwesterly direction and set sail. At sunrise No. 3 boat became visible in the far distance and we sent up a flare to signal our position. At 7 A.M., a patrol plane came out and circled over the ship. This plane was shortly followed by many others. At about 10 A.M., No. 3 caught up with us, together with a lifeboat from the torpedoed *Oklahoma*, Texas Company tanker, and the three boats sailed in company until we were sighted at noontime by a U.S. Navy patrol vessel.

"Second Mate Durdle went aboard with fifteen men from the boats. Captain Poche remained in No. 1, which was towed, with No. 3 and the *Oklahoma*'s lifeboat, to Brunswick, Georgia. We arrived there about 4 P.M." Among the survivors was Able Seaman Eugenio M. Gallego, who had been aboard the *E.M. Clark* when that vessel was torpedoed three weeks earlier.

While the story of the men is over, that of the ship is not. Captain Poche continued: "I reported to the U.S. Navy authorities. At about 6 P.M., a U.S. Coast Guard patrol boat took me back to the vessel, with First Mate Bill, Second Mate Durdle, and Chief Engineer Larsson, to inspect the general condition of the *Esso Baton Rouge*.

"At about 9 A.M., April 9, I called the company's office on the telephone, reporting the casualty and the possibility of saving the vessel. They said they would send Merrit-Chapman & Scott salvors to undertake operations as soon as possible."

In the meantime a Navy tug arrived, attached a one-inch cable to the bow, and tried to tow the grounded tanker. She was unable to move the ship. The *Esso Baton Rouge* had acquired an eighteen-degree list. The salvage tug *Resolute* did not get there until the fourteenth. *The Ship's Bulletin* for July-August 1943 tells the saga of salvage: "With enemy submarines a constant threat, salvage work was confined to daylight hours and there was fear that at almost any moment the Axis sub would return to finish the job. At night the tug and her people returned to port and at each dawn there was a sigh of relief when it was discovered that the submerged tanker was still there.''

The U.S. Navy kept a blimp over the area constantly to warn of an impending U-boat attack. A Canadian corvette conducted an antisubmarine patrol.

*The Ships' Bulletin*: "Air supplied by heavy compressors swung aboard from the pitching tug was used to blow cargo out of some tanks into others to correct the list. Oil was blown from aft forward to lighten the ship's stern and weight her bow. After seven days of strenuous effort under extraordinary circumstances, the ship was floated and brought into port, where divers made a more complete survey of the damage. It was found that the torpedo had ripped a twenty-five-foot hole in the ship's side, almost abreast of the engineroom; the main pumproom was open to the sea and the engineroom flooded.''

Most of the cargo was salvaged. Temporary repairs were made before the *Esso Baton Rouge* was towed to Baltimore. Six months of repairs at the Maryland Drydock Company made her whole again. Unfortunately, she made only two more successful voyages. On February 23, 1943, the ship was lost in the South Atlantic, along with three more men, when she was torpedoed by the *U-202* under Oberleutnant zur See Gunter Poser. Captain Poche survived that calamity as well.

On December 2, 1944, a brand new Liberty ship slid down the ways of the Delta Shipbuilding Company, New Orleans, Louisiana. Her name was the *James Eagen Layne*, after the *Esso Baton Rouge*'s second assistant killed on April 8, 1942. The story of the *Oklahoma* doesn't end here, either. That vessel was beached, and also salvaged and repaired. She met her ultimate end on March 28, 1945, when she was torpedoed by the *U-532*, Korvettenkapitan Ottoheinrich Junker, off the coast of South America.

The twenty-four-hour period covering the ninth and tenth was a busy one in the ESF: five ships were sunk by four different U-boats.

Hardegen started the streak by sinking the *Esparta* off the Florida coast. The freighter was bound from Puerto Cortez, Honduras, for New York, with bananas, coffee, and miscellaneous cargo. The first torpedo hit in the middle of No. 4 hatch, starting a fire and releasing 1,200 pounds of ammonia gas from the refrigeration system. The ship acquired a 15° starboard list and began settling. The escaping fumes forced some men to jump overboard. Lifeboats Nos. 1 and 3 got away, as well as a raft; one man drowned during the evacuation. The master and the radio operator were the last to leave; they leaped into the water, were picked up by a raft, and transferred to a lifeboat.

The *U-123* surfaced a quarter mile off, fifteen minutes after the attack, then left the scene. The *Esparta* did not sink until several hours later. When she finally went down with a 35° list, although the stern rested on the bottom, the bow and top of the bridge showed out of the water. The Navy Crash Boat *Tyrer* answered the SOS and, seven hours later, picked up the survivors.

Lassen took credit for the *Malchace*, a freighter carrying 3,628 tons of soda ash from Baton Rouge, Louisiana, to Hopewell, New Jersey. Captain Arnt Magunusbal was on the bridge when a tremendous explosion occurred amidships. As steam and soda ash erupted into the clear nighttime sky, the vessel listed to port. No. 2 lifeboat was destroyed. The radio equipment and antennas were demolished. A small fire started on the after boat deck, but this soon died down on its own.

Summoned by the shock, the crew poured out of the below deck spaces. One man panicked and leaped overboard. With the captain directing, the rest of the men calmly set about launching No. 1 lifeboat. This was accomplished in five minutes. The boat was crowded with twenty-five men, so Captain Magunusbal stayed aboard the *Malchace* with his two mates. They ran to the forward end of the freighter to launch a life raft. This was when the U-boat surfaced some three hundred feet dead astern. Half submerged, it slowly circled the motionless freighter. Said Second Mate Frank Sawyer: "It wasn't more than fifty feet from the ship. Why, I could have dropped baseballs on it."

The captain and chief mate escaped on the raft. Sawyer returned to where the lifeboat was waiting, climbed down the falls into the boat, and directed it to go around and take the raft in tow.

The men took to the oars and rowed away from the derelict. About twenty minutes after the first explosion, another torpedo ripped into the port hull alongside the engine room and boiler room. The *Malchace* rolled over on her side and slipped beneath the calm sea. The submarine was not seen again.

Captain Magunusbal and the chief mate transferred to the lifeboat. They set sail and steered for shore. About 0445 they heard a loud explosion. Looking west, about ten miles distant, they observed the flames of the furiously burning *Atlas*. They kept rowing, eager to get out of such U-boat infested waters. At 0830 they were picked up by the Mexican tanker *Fajo de Oro*. The only casualty was the lone fireman who had jumped into the sea from the *Malchace*'s deck.

Despite the proximity, it was Topp, not Lassen, who took out the *Atlas*. The American tanker was bound from Houston, Texas, for Seawater, New Jersey, with 83,000 barrels of gasoline. The first torpedo struck amidships. Captain Hamilton Gray ordered the engines stopped and abandon ship. Just as the crew was pulling away, a second torpedo ripped into the hull near where the first had struck, igniting the cargo. Instantly, the ship was a mass of flames. Fire raked the decks and superstructure: sure death for the merchant crew had they not acted promptly.

Even so, flaming oil spread by the current overtook one lifeboat, forcing the men to leap overboard and swim for their lives. Nine of them were picked up by the other boats, but two went to a fiery death. Coast Guard patrol boats converged on the scene and rescued the survivors soon after dawn. Several of the men, including the captain, suffered severe burns. The *Atlas* drifted for several hours before sinking.

At 2200, the *U-203*, Kapitanleutnant Rolf Mutzelberg, drove a torpedo into the British tanker *San Delfino*. The explosion blew in the main pump room on the starboard side, and instantly ignited some of the 11,000 tons of aviation gasoline that was bound from Houston, Texas, via New York, to the airfields in England.

Two lifeboats got away within five minutes. The high octane fuel spread so quickly that it caught up to one of the boats, burning every man to death. The other lifeboat was lucky enough to escape cremation. These men were picked up two hours later by the fishing trawler *Two Sisters*, and taken to Ocracoke. Twenty-one out of forty-nine survived. The ship burned quite a while before sinking.

Twenty-nine minutes after midnight, Topp sent a torpedo into the midships of the *Tamaulipas*. The explosion was so violent that it split the tanker in two. The midship buckled like a hinge, while the bow and stern rose high in the air. Two lifeboats pushed off the ship which was now ablaze. Lost were two lives and 10,200 tons of oil bound from Tampico, Mexico, for New York. An hour and a half later the survivors, including Captain A. Falkenberg, were picked up by the HMS *Norwich City*.

Hardegen struck again on the night of the tenth. The *Gulfamerica* was en route from Port Arthur, Texas, to New York, with 90,000 barrels of fuel oil. Although she was blacked out, Captain Oscar Anderson surmised that she was silhouetted against bright shore lights. Two torpedoes hit her starboard hull almost simultaneously: one in No. 7 tank, one in the engine room. The captain ordered abandon ship.

The U-boat surfaced and began shelling the ship, which was still sending out an SOS. What had been an orderly evacuation was turned into a rout as high explosive shells exploded everywhere, and machine gun fire raked the decks. Five men were killed outright. Another fourteen were lost either by drowning or by boiling oil in the water. The U-boat broke off the action when, after fifteen minutes, the tanker settled stern first to the bottom.

The twenty-nine survivors on rafts and one lifeboat were soon picked up by patrol boats. The *Gulfamerica* hung in there, refusing to sink all the way. It was not until six days later that she capsized and sank. Her cargo of crude from Port Arthur, Texas, never made it to New York.

Mutzelberg took care of the *Harry F. Sinclair, Jr.* with a single torpedo that exploded under the pump room and touched off part of the 68,000 barrels of gasoline and fuel oil. The ship erupted into flames, and twin streaks of burning oil fanned out aft as the headway gradually slowed. Although Captain William Collagen gave the order to abandon ship, he did not himself manage to get away; he was not seen again.

Two lifeboats were launched. Three men bounded over the taffrail: one was swept by a large swell into a patch of blazing oil and consumed; the other two swam around and ducked under the deadly flames until they happened on a raft. It was upon this refuge that they were found several hours later by the U.S. destroyer *Herbert*. The survivors in the lifeboats were picked up by the HMS *Hertfordshire*.

The *Harry F. Sinclair, Jr.* floated randomly for two weeks, burning all the time. It was not until April 23 that a towing hawser was attached to the tanker's bow. After four days of towing, she was beached east of Morehead City. Twenty-five days after the attack, fires still raged out of control inside the steel hull. There was no telling if, or when, she would blow up suddenly. On May 6, her after section was holed by shell fire in an effort to flood the stern and put out the blaze.

During the next two weeks the tanker was partially salvaged by fisherman Harry Willis, operating on his own. He turned over two hundred forty-nine cases of oil and 1,125 one-gallon cans of grease, requesting compensation. On May 20, the salvage tug *Relief* pulled the *Harry F. Sinclair, Jr.* off the beach, spent a couple days shifting the remaining cargo to trim the ship, and hauled the burned out hulk to Portsmouth, Virginia. After the tanker was pumped dry, she was towed to Baltimore, Maryland, where she underwent repairs.

It fell to Lassen to bag the largest ship lost in the history of the ESF, resulting in the biggest and most successful rescue operation of the entire East Coast war. In a daring daylight attack, Lassen fired two torpedoes into the starboard side of the 14,647 ton British liner *Ulysses*. The first one crippled the ship: the second failed to explode.

Traveling from Sydney, Australia, to Halifax and then Liverpool were one hundred ninety-five crew and ninety-five passengers, including thirty-seven women and twenty-four children ranging in age from eighty-six years to seven months. The 11,117 tons of general cargo consisted of pig iron, wool, butter, cheese, meat, rubber, and wine.

Captain J. A. Russell ordered abandon ship. High seas somewhat hampered the launching of lifeboats, but there were enough crew members to handle the task and keep the passengers orderly. Hastily but without panic, everyone got away in ten boats. The only casualty was passenger Bertram Barton, who was badly bruised when he jumped into a lifeboat.

Thirty minutes later, another torpedo delivered the coup de grace by exploding against the port side of the massive liner. The *Ulysses* went down in deep water, far off the Carolina coast. Two hundred ninety people, one cat, and three kittens, were left bobbing like clay ducks in the large Atlantic swells.

They had not long to wait. Patrol planes flew out in answer to the distress call, spotted the congregation of boats, and alerted a nearby destroyer. An hour and a half after putting to the boats, each and every person and animal was picked up and crammed aboard the USS *Manley*. They were soon landed at Charleston, South Carolina. What could have been the greatest tragedy since the sinking of the *Lady Hawkins* turned out, by the grace of fair weather and a fortuitously close patrol ship, to be little more than a happenstance in the lives of the stiff-upper-lip British.

On the twelfth, the Panamanian tanker *Stanvac*

*Melbourne* was torpedoed by the *U-203*. Captain Andrew Lagan testified at the "C" Marine Investigation Board held in Charleston, South Carolina:

"I felt a shock which seemed to come from an underwater explosion at 11:35 P.M. General alarm was given and the crew was mustered at the boats. The vessel was stopped seven minutes while an examination of the vessel's compartments was made. There was no evidence of any damage and I proceeded at full speed on the original course. At 12:13 A.M. Eastern Standard Time on April 12 a second explosion occurred on the port side about thirty feet aft of 'midships, apparently from a torpedo. This explosion blew in the side of the ship at No. 7 tank port, also bulkhead between wing and center, No. 7 tank. The damage extended on through starboard bulkhead and shattered shell plating. The vessel listed heavily to port."

Four lifeboats and all six life rafts were launched. The captain, one gunner, and an oiler remained on board. The ship slowly acquired a 30° list, but remained afloat. Captain Lagan "let go of the port anchor hoping that the boats might be able to get back but on account of the rough sea they were unable to do so."

At 0715, Patrol Boat *PC-472* hove to off the *Stanvac Melbourne*. Captain Lagan directed the boat to proceed in the direction of flares down current. After patrolling the area for signs of U-boat activity, *PC-472* took off. She returned at 1530 with twenty-eight survivors from the boats and rafts. Two men, who had died of exposure after being dumped in the water when their lifeboat capsized, were buried at sea. Later, the steamship *William Penn* picked up fourteen others. The steward remained missing and was presumed lost.

*PC-472* took off the captain and the other two, and took everyone to Wilmington, South Carolina. Two tugs were dispatched to aid the stricken tanker. They succeeded in towing the *Stanvac Melbourne* in to port. Temporary repairs enabled the American Bureau of Shipping to issue a seaworthy certificate. After a permanent refit, the tanker was returned to service.

She lasted only another five months. On September 12,

# April 1942

1942, the *Stanvac Melbourne* was torpedoed and sunk off Trinidad by the *U-515*, Oberleutnant zur See Werner Henke.

Mutzelberg was persistent. On the fourteenth he crossed paths with the *Empire Thrush* off North Carolina. The British freighter was carrying 5,000 tons of rock phosphate, 2,500 tons of citrus pulp, 60 tons of citrus concentrate, and 745 tons of trinitrotoluene (TNT).

The concussion was muffled by the rock in No. 5 hold, but the blast "blew off the hatch cover, tore a jagged hole in the plates, and buckled a portion of the deck." The radio equipment was damaged beyond repair. With all that explosive material in the holds, Captain George Fisk wasted no time in ordering abandon ship. There were no casualties; the entire crew got away in four lifeboats.

Four Coast Guard cutters witnessed the attack and rushed in to assist. Instead of picking up the survivors, who signaled that they were all okay, the cutters proceeded to search for the offending U-boat. The American tanker *Evelyn* picked up the survivors and took them to Norfolk, Virginia.

That same night, Kapitanleutnant Helmut Mohlmann in the *U-571* torpedoed and sank the *Margaret*. Although Mohlmann was prowling in the Bermuda Area, when he found the *Margaret* she had sailed over the boundary into the ESF. The freighter went down with all hands.

If this two-week plethora of sinkings seems too casually handled, it must be remembered that at this stage of the war there was so much stress and activity that it strained the resources of the intelligence task force. Ships were foundering under the weight of paperwork necessary to keep them at sea. The Navy as well as the public was calloused by the multiplicity of torpedoings, shellings, sinkings, suffering, and hair-raising survivals. Grand episodes that in the first months of the war would have made banner headlines and front page news were now shrugged off as passé and relegated to the back pages as fillers. This was not because life had become any less dear, but because too much else was happening. This was a world war in every sense of the word. The plight of the merchant marine was overshadowed by events on the European front and the Japanese conquest of the Pacific.

Besides that, there were no American victories in the battle on the Eastern Sea Frontier. The military campaign was strictly defensive. The only winners were those people who, set adrift in the broad reaches of the Atlantic, waged a fight against death—and triumphed against the odds. With winter yielding to spring, the horrible exposure to cold was diminished, thus easing the strife of seaborne sailors—at least it might have seemed so to those whose experience was only vicarious.

The only eventuality that could placate the depression into which the country had sunk, and help turn the tide of combat, was a confirmed and unequivocal offensive stroke against the German invaders. After three months of wearying resistance, the opportunity for retaliation presented itself on April 14. The Navy grasped it with a vengeance.

The USS *Roper* (DD-147) was conducting a routine antisubmarine patrol off Nags Head, North Carolina. The night was clear, the sea smooth, the wind Force 1 out of the southeast. The flush deck, four stack destroyer was a sister ship of the *Jacob Jones*, lost six weeks previously. She was headed due south at eighteen knots under a beautiful, starlit sky.

At six minutes past midnight, with Bodie Island Light and Bell Buoy No. 8 visible to starboard, radar contact was made with an object practically dead ahead and at a distance of 2,700 yards (a mile and a half). Soon afterwards, from his echo ranging station, the sound operator heard propellers at a range and bearing which coincided with the radar fixes.

As the range closed to 2,100 yards, lookouts on the *Roper* observed the wake of a small vessel running away at high speed. *Roper* increased revolutions until she was moving through the water at twenty knots. At first, the silhouette appeared to be like that of a small Coast Guard cutter. Lieutenant Commander Hamilton Howe was not taking any chances. He put out the call for general quarters. The crew manned their battle stations at the

The half-sunken *Persephone* is surrounded by a huge oil slick. Notice the survivors in the raft just below the blimp.

Oil-covered survivors of the *Persephone* wait for rescue. Fortunately, they are less than three miles from shore.

The captain of the *Persephone* stands alone on the bridge, preparing to climb down the falls into the waiting lifeboat.

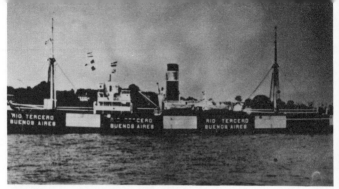

As this photograph shows, the *Rio Tercero* was boldly marked with flags denoting her neutrality.

The bow of the *Australia*.

Survivors from the *Empire Drum* in a lifeboat rigged with sails.

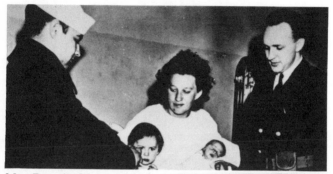

Mrs. Desanka Mohorovicic in the hospital with her two children after her ordeal of giving birth in one of the *City of New York*'s lifeboats.

Four of the seven naked survivors of the *U-701* after a raft had been dropped to them. For nearly three days they floated in the ocean before being spotted.

Flaming oil from the *Dixie Arrow* engulfs the ship as well as much of the sea.

The broken-off bow of the *Gulftrade*, floating away from the stern.

The stern of the *Esso Baton Rouge* rests on the bottom.

A tugboat struggles to tow the grounded *Tiger* to safety.

Men crowd the bridge and wintergarten of the *U-550* just before the enemy submarine takes its final plunge.

The British cemetery on Ocracoke Island, where four bodies from the HMS *Bedfordshire* are buried. (Photo courtesy of Gary Gentile)

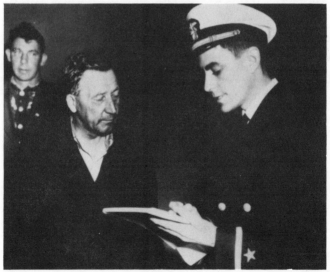

The captain of the *Lansing* (left) gives his report to an ONI officer.

Two *Libertad* survivors cling to bits of wreckage from their ship.

Lucky *Moldanger* survivors are about to climb aboard the rescue vessel.

The two *Chenango* survivors, after twelve days adrift, wave weakly at the rescue plane.

Lifeboats from the *China Arrow* are under tow.

three-inch deck gun, machine gun positions, depth charge batteries, and torpedo tubes.

The unknown craft started alternating its course from port to starboard to port. Howe feared a torpedo strike, so he conned the *Roper* to the starboard quarter of the vessel's wake. At seven hundred yards the track of a torpedo passed close by the port side and crossed the *Roper*'s wake close astern. It was almost a repetition of the *Jacob Jones* affair, except that this time the destroyer was on the alert and in hot pursuit.

Lieutenant William Vanous, executive officer, raced to the top of the bridge from which he could control the operation of the twenty-four-inch searchlight. At three hundred yards the target vessel veered sharply to starboard. A powerful beam of light stabbed through the darkness and illuminated in stark detail the light gray conning tower of a large submarine.

The U-boat continued cutting to starboard, inside the turning radius of the *Roper*. The searchlight beam tied the two vessels together like the string of a bola. Members of the enemy crew charged for their deck gun. Chief Boatswain's Mate Jack Wright opened up immediately with the *Roper*'s Number One fifty-caliber machine gun. He raked the hull and conning tower of the U-boat with such accuracy that men were seen to either jump into the water to escape the bullets, or were physically lifted off the deck by steel-jacketed shells. Tracers wove a web of destruction that kept the rest of the U-boat crew cowering behind the conning tower.

The three-inch deck gun came on line. The first two shells blew great geysers of water across the cornered U-boat. The third exploded at the base of the conning tower, right at the waterline. Men poured out of the hatches like rats quitting a sinking ship. Machine gun fire continued to strafe the U-boat from the stern quarter. Ensign Kenneth Tebo, officer-of-the-deck, continued to keep the *Roper* clear of the U-boat's wake in case it fired another torpedo or dropped mines in the destroyer's path.

Howe gave the order to fire a torpedo. Before the command could be carried out, the U-boat sank by the stern. Thirty-five or forty men bobbed in the gentle swells. The *Roper* passed so close that duty personnel could hear their shouts, although they could not distinguish the words.

Underwater, the U-boat appeared to be moving slightly forward. Howe took a bearing based on the still excellent sound contact and an estimate by sight. The *Roper* ran over the approximate location of the U-boat and laid down a barrage of eleven three-hundred-pound charges from her deck racks, Y-guns, and K-guns. During the course of twenty seconds, 3,300 pounds of explosives were detonated at a depth of fifty feet.

It was too dark to see oil slicks or floating wreckage. The *Roper* twice passed near the U-boat's survivors, but Howe was too well informed of wolf pack tactics to take a chance on stopping to pick them up, no matter how much intelligence might be gleaned from the interrogation of prisoners. He had no intention of losing his ship to the torpedo of another U-boat lying in wait. All night long the *Roper* crisscrossed the same stretch of ocean, seeking signs of the downed U-boat or a prowling cohort.

As dawn broke at sea, a Navy PBY patrol plane joined the search. Lieutenant C. V. Horrigan investigated slicks of oil and bits of debris. He dropped a depth charge on one suspicious target. The *Roper* dropped two. At 0700, Horrigan spotted bodies floating in the water. He released smoke floats to attract the attention of the *Roper* and to lead her to the spot.

Howe was still exercising caution. Knowing that vermin begets more vermin, he asked for protection. As many as seven planes at a time provided air cover, while the British armed trawler HMS *Bedfordshire* stood by. A blimp circled overhead and scanned the waves for the wake of a raised periscope.

The *Roper* lowered two lifeboats and commenced recovery operations. Within thirty minutes, one boat returned with positive proof of the nationality of their enemy: five bodies wearing German naval uniforms. A half hour later the second boat brought in fifteen more bodies. The *Roper* swung out a davit and one by one hoisted the dead aboard. They were laid out in neat rows on the deck.

Ever watchful, the sound operator detected an echo at a range of 2,700 yards. The *Roper* took off under full steam and seven minutes later dropped a four charge pattern over the suspected target. Fresh oil and large air bubbles rose to the surface. The blimp hovered over the spot and dropped marker flares. Bubbles kept rising from deep under the water.

The *Roper* returned to her boats. By 0930 she had recovered twenty-nine bodies. Two had been allowed to sink after the clothing was searched for objects of possible intelligence value. The rest of the bodies and personal effects were left unmolested for examination by Naval Intelligence personnel. Included among the recovered items were six escape lungs; two bodies still had the mouthpiece tubing clenched in their teeth, indicating that some German sailors had escaped from the U-boat after it had sunk.

At 1000, the *Roper* dropped two more depth charges over the site of the largest air bubble. Air continued to escape and rise to the surface. She then deployed a large orange buoy to mark the spot. An accurate sextant sighting was made and the position entered in the log. With job well done, the *Roper* headed for home.

At Lynnhaven Roads, Virginia, the bodies were transferred to shore. They were taken to a small hangar at the Naval Air Station where they were tagged, photographed, fingerprinted, and identified by identity discs, name tags in the clothing, or personal effects.

The next day the bodies were placed in individual caskets. A special truck convoy transported them to the National Cemetery in Hampton, Virginia. Twenty Military Police acted as pallbearers. Individual graves were prepared by fifty-two prisoners from Fort Monroe, Virginia. The burial service commenced after dark, at 2000, and was read by both Catholic and Protestant chaplains. With full military honors, a gun squad fired a twenty-one gun salute. Taps was sounded on the trumpet. The German sailors received a more dignified burial than they offered their victims.

Recommendations for citation were in the offing for officers and crew of the *Roper*. By coincidence, on the day before the action, the Navy circulated a secret memorandum in "recognition of successful anti-submarine warfare" to include prominent stack or fuselage devices, and sleeve devices for crew members.

*Roper* personnel were duly put in for the Distinguished Service Medal. The awards were approved, except where they were increased to the Navy Cross for Commander Stanley Norton, the commander of Destroyer Division Fifty-four, who was on the bridge of the *Roper* at the time of the action and who offered sound advice on pursuit of the adversary; Lieutenant Commander Hamilton Howe; Lieutenant William Vanous; Ensign Kenneth Tebo; Chief Boatswain's Mate Jack Wright; and Coxswain Harry Heymen, gun captain for the three-inch gun that hit the U-boat. In addition, each man of the gun crew was advanced a rating.

Learned from the effects of the German sailors was the designation of the U-boat. It was the *U-85*, Oberleutnant zur See Eberhard Greger. Greger's body was not found, nor his identity verified. Although his war log was lost, he is credited with sinking the Norwegian ship *Chr. Knudsen*, New York to Cape Town, on the way to his operational area in the ESF.

With the U-boat sunk only ninety-two feet deep, the Experimental Diving Unit was called in to conduct an underwater survey. The USS *Kewaydin* dragged for the wreck, snagged it, and sent down a diver who attached a descending line. A cursory examination revealed the U-boat listed to starboard practically on its side, angled at eighty degrees. A twenty-mm antiaircraft gun was mounted aft of the conning tower. The forward deck gun still had its tampion in place. The upper conning tower hatch was latched open. Lubricating oil was leaking out through the lower hatch, which was closed but not dogged. All compartments were flooded.

The salvage vessel USS *Falcon* arrived on April 29. Wearing bulky hardhat diving gear, Frank Miller squirmed into the conning tower. He was unable to get into the control room. Further attempts to enter the U-boat were considered unsafe. A complete exterior inspection was made. Salvage air lines were attached to the ballast tank manifolds. Air pumped into the U-boat failed to blow out the water due to depth charge damage and collapsed connection lines. The twenty-mm gun was removed.

Salvage connections were made to both the bow and aft torpedo rooms. When air was forced in, the divers noticed numerous small leaks from the conning tower to the bow, with a major leak at the torpedo loading hatch. Aft of the conning tower, air leaked out "like a sprinkling system." A large portion of the external piping was crushed from the effect of depth charges.

Divers recovered the sights from the eighty-eight-mm deck gun, as well as instruments from the bridge: the night firing device, the gyro pelorus repeater, and the gyro steering repeater. They inspected the ready ammunition locker, but found no ammunition. They tried to remove a spare torpedo stowed externally under the deck, but found it lodged in place and too dangerous to remove.

They also found painted on the forward high part of the conning tower a picture of a "wild boar with rose in mouth."

The most significant discovery was the open outer doors of the forward torpedo tubes, exposing torpedoes that were ready for firing. It explained Greger's final tactic. Caught in water too shallow to afford escape by diving, he attempted to circle around to get the *Roper* in front of his bow so he could sink her, or at least slow her down, with a torpedo barrage while he made good his escape.

Even though the hull and superstructure were essentially undamaged, after more than seventy-five dives Lieutenant G. K. MacKenzie, commanding officer of the *Falcon*, concluded that "combining the information contained in the USS *Roper* report of action with that gained by divers, it is my opinion that this vessel was thoroughly and efficiently scuttled by her crew, and that successful salvage can only be accomplished by extensive pontooning operations."

The Navy had more important things to do. The case of the *U-85* was closed.

Oddly, after all the false claims of U-boat sinkings reported in the newspapers, no mention of this genuine achievement was made. It should have made the headlines but, like the boy who cried wolf, the Navy had cried gray wolf so often that its impact on public morale would very likely have been negligible. The war went on without widespread acknowledgment of the first offensive success against the U-boat campaign in the ESF.

It was not until more than a year after the event, on July 22, 1943, that the Navy released the story (undated) of the sinking, along with photographs of the burial. The description in the communique led the reader to believe that the *U-85* had just recently been sunk. The purpose of such a tactic is unfathomable, and falls into the realm of "military intelligence."

Merchant ship sinkings continued unabated.

*U-572*, Kapitanleutnant Heinz Hirsacker, entered the growing list of U-boats operating along the U.S. East Coast. On the sixteenth he sank the *Desert Light* off North Carolina. The Panamanian freighter was carrying 3,800 tons of supplies, including 104 tons of ammunition and dynamite, from New York to the Naval Operating Base in Bermuda.

Two torpedoes in quick succession struck the starboard side amidships just forward of the boiler room, destroying one lifeboat, flooding the fire room, and severely damaging the superstructure. Captain Charles Dunn ordered abandon ship. Twenty-five men left in the port lifeboat, five got away on a raft. The survivors watched helplessly as their ship slowly settled by the bow. An hour and twenty minutes passed before the *Desert Light* disappeared completely, taking with her the body of Fireman Frank Clement.

The five men on the raft were taken aboard the lifeboat. A patrol plane noticed their plight, and dropped chocolate, a first aid kit, and flashlights to the survivors. The men expected a quick rescue. During the day two more planes flew overhead, reaffirming their expectations. But no rescue craft came after them. They spent an uncomfortable night huddled in the overcrowded boat.

The next day brought the Navy blimp *K-5*. The lighter-than-air craft swooped low, hovered, and lowered a line to which was attached a package containing apples, tomatoes, cigarettes, matches, and a compass. Again, the men expected salvation at any moment. They were disappointed once again. That night, a fierce storm blew them miles off their westering course, and dropped a torrent of rain on the bedraggled crewmen.

Then came five days of loneliness, with no planes or ships of any kind. It was not until noon of the twenty-third that the USS *Roper* hove into view and took them aboard.

Hardegen struck again, this time with shell fire. On the sixteenth, he caught the *Alcoa Guide* alone and unarmed, and pummeled her with his deck gun. Captain Samuel Cobb was hit by flying shrapnel. The sorely wounded master was placed in the port lifeboat by Second Assistant Engineer Charles McIver. Radio Operator M. E. Chandler tapped out a continuous sequence of distress calls until McIver warned him that the last lifeboat was leaving.

The shell fire stopped while two lifeboats and a raft were launched. As soon as they were clear, the U-boat's deck gun resumed firing. Some forty shells were poured into the starboard hull at the waterline until, pouring out smoke and flames, the *Alcoa Guide* slowly listed with the weight of the flooding seas.

Then it was noticed that a seaman was standing by the freighter's after rail. After the ship sank, he was not seen again. All this took some two hours, and by that time the three emergency craft had become widely separated. The men in the lifeboats were unaware that four men had escaped on a raft, so they raised sails and headed for land, over two hundred miles away. The next day, Captain Cobb and an injured fireman died of their wounds; they were given a seaman's burial. That afternoon, the U.S. destroyer *Broome* came across the two lifeboats and effected the rescue.

For the men on the raft, what followed was a month of horror. They endured the long days and cold nights in utter solitude. Only the sun and the stars kept them company. Once they saw a ship in the distance. Several planes flew overhead; one even dipped its wings in recognition. But no help came. On April 23, Chief Engineer Benjamin Fisher died of exposure. The next day a fireman passed away. The two survivors ran out of water and thirst became an insatiable, racking pain. The men took to drinking salt water. On May 17, writhing in agony, one more man perished. On the eighteenth, the British freighter *Hororata* happened by the raft. For the lone survivor, Able Seaman Jules Souza, the thirty-two day ordeal was over.

Kapitanleutnant Heinrich Zimmerman, *U-136*, torpedoed the *Axtell J. Byles* on the eighteenth. The tanker was the lead ship of a convoy of eight, escorted north along the coast by four patrol boats, the Coast Guard cutter *Dione*, and one plane for air cover. From the air, Lieutenant (jg) E. B. Ing noticed the torpedo "on the surface and splashing along like a high-speed motor boat."

Lieutenant Ing banked his plane and wiggled his wings. "Having the protection of the convoy uppermost in my mind, I instinctively headed for the convoy at top speed, diving from my original altitude of about 1500 feet to about 100 feet, heading down the track of the torpedo toward the leading vessel."

On the bridge of the *Axtell J. Byles*, Captain John Baldwin ordered hard aport, rang the general alarm, and blew the ship's whistle to warn the other ships to give way. There was not enough time for the ship to respond. The torpedo struck just forward of the bridge, blowing a huge hole in No. 2 tank. Considering her cargo of 87,000 barrels of crude oil and 27,000 barrels of fuel oil, it was miraculous that no fire ensued.

Six tankers and a freighter executed a right turn, away from the direction from which the torpedo had come, while patrol boats converged on the spot where the track began. The *Dione* dropped two spreads of four depth charges. As many as eight planes made bombing runs over a suspected sonar target, but Zimmerman made good his escape.

Aboard the *Axtell J. Byles*, the men swung out the lifeboats and stood ready to abandon ship. The tanker settled by the bow, then stabilized. Captain Baldwin found his ship still had power. He broke off from the convoy under escort and headed for shoal water. Then he worked his way up the coast until he made Hampton Roads, Virginia. The ship required extensive repairs. After a long layup, she was returned to service.

Next came the *U-84*, Oberleutnant zur See Horst Uphoff. He was some seventy miles off Cape Henry, Virginia, when he sighted a Panamanian freighter. The *Chenango* was carrying a cargo of manganese ore from Rio de Janeiro to Baltimore, via St. Thomas. Around 1900 on the evening of the twentieth a single torpedo blasted into her port side between No. 4 and No. 5 hatches. The hull plates were blown out so violently that the ship plunged down stern first in two minutes.

Most of the men did not make it topside. Crew members on deck were catapulted overboard by the force of the explosion, and either drowned or died of their wounds. James Terrence Bradley and Joseph Dieltiens, suffering internal injuries, swam to a raft which floated free from the sinking vessel. They clung to the refuge in a choppy sea and winds of Force 6.

They were afloat on the raft for twelve days with no food and only one cask of water.

On May 2, an Army bomber spotted them. The plane could not land in the water, but it radioed its position back to base. Commander Richard Burke jumped into his Coast Guard PH-2 seaplane and soared out to the location some ninety-five miles southeast of Oregon Inlet, North Carolina. Confusing cross seas did not prevent him from setting his plane down in the water and taxiing to the semiconscious and delirious survivors.

Dieltiens was so far gone from sunburn and dehydration that, even though he was able to stand up and wave at his rescuers, he died three days later in the Marine Hospital at Norfolk.

Oberleutnant zur See Karl-Ernst Schroeter, *U-752*, also put in his appearance on the twentieth. Shroeter had no difficulty spotting the *West Imboden*, Durban, South Africa, to Boston, Massachusetts. A fire in the freighter's smokestack belched out glowing cinders that landed on the canvas tarpaulin covering the hatches. Within minutes the ship was ablaze with the light of a serious but not uncontrollable fire. Able Seaman William Gibbons said the flames "illuminated the ship like Forty-second Street." It was nearly midnight.

From the bridge, Captain Antone Anderson saw the wake of a torpedo approaching his ship. There was no time to avoid it. The torpedo hit forward and, because the whole crew had been roused to help fight the flames, no one was below decks where the explosion occurred. Two minutes later the U-boat surfaced and began shelling the already burning vessel. A distress call went out and was received. Captain Anderson ordered abandon ship. The *West Imboden* was a mass of flames as the men pulled away. The fire was not doused until the freighter slipped beneath the waves.

Schroeter maneuvered his U-boat alongside the lifeboats, and inquired about the status of the ship and her personnel. He particularly wanted to know if anyone had been killed. Then he left them to their own devices.

Said Chief Officer Frank Jasper: "Some of the men in my boat were scantily clad. Some were without shoes and some even without pants. After the lifeboat's sail was hoisted, its canvas cover was cut up and shoes and other clothing improvised to help keep the men warm."

The next afternoon, they were all rescued by the U.S. destroyer *Bristol*.

On the twenty-second, the passenger-freighter *San Jacinto* ran afoul of the *U-201*, Oberleutnant zur See Adalbert Schnee. Schnee's torpedo struck aft of midships in No. 5 hold, demolishing staterooms and the recreation hall, tearing up the deck, and destroying the radio room so that no SOS could be sent.

With the loss of power the vessel began to lose headway. Captain Robert Hart ordered abandon ship. One hundred four passengers on their way from New York to San Juan, Puerto Rico, plus seventy-nine crew, were aboard. As they launched lifeboats, *two* U-boats surfaced on opposite sides of the *San Jacinto*, circled counter-clockwise, and fired incendiary shells into the ship full of helpless people. Unbelievably, most survived under cover of darkness. The captain had a battery operated radio in his lifeboat, but was afraid to use it for fear of being shelled. The *San Jacinto* went down four hours later, ablaze and on an even keel.

In the morning, Captain Hart put out a call for help. At 1304, the U.S. destroyer *Rowan* found the six drifting lifeboats and attendant rafts, and crowded her decks with survivors. When the final toll was taken, nine passengers and five crew were missing.

Schroeter engaged the armed merchantman *Reinholt* on the twenty-third. The Norwegian freighter was on her way from Santos, Brazil, to New York, with a general cargo, when the U-boat opened upon her from two or three miles astern. The U-boat's eighty-eight-mm deck gun fired furiously, hitting the *Reinholt* twenty to twenty-five times.

The *Reinholt*'s gun crew was not sitting idle. They returned fourteen shots. Just as they ran out of ammunition, a Navy plane arrived in response to the freighter's SOS and drove off the attacking U-boat. Further help came in the form of a U.S. destroyer, which delivered a concerted depth charge attack that produced no positive results.

The *Reinholt* was in a bad way, drifting and afire, but she refused to go down. One man had been killed by enemy shell fire, and two others wounded. The crew got the fires under control. The Navy tug *Sagamore* passed a towing hawser to the freighter's bow which the crew made fast to the forward bit. After a long haul, the *Reinholt* was eventually towed in to port and her damage repaired.

The *Tropic Star* led a charmed life. Kapitanleutnant Hans-Dieter Heinicke, *U-576*, hit her dead to rights with the first torpedo he fired in the ESF. It was a dud, and did not explode. The Norwegian steamship continued on her way only slightly dented.

That same night, the twenty-fourth, the *Empire Drum* did not fare as well. She was one day out of New York, carrying a general cargo that included 1,270 tons of explosives. Two lookouts were on watch as she zigzagged according to Royal Navy Pattern No. 37. But the lookouts did not see nor the zigzagging ship avoid the torpedo that ripped open No. 1 hold on the port side.

It was a sure bet that a ten-knot freighter could not outrun a German submarine. Even though the British ship was not seriously damaged, Captain John Miles ordered the engines stopped, a distress call sent, and preparations made for abandoning ship. He did not allow the gun crew to man any of the two twin Marlins, the two-inch U.P. Gymbol, the two Lewis guns, or the four-inch deck gun. Within ten minutes the *Empire Drum* was a derelict. Her forty-one man crew was spread out in four lifeboats.

Two minutes later a second torpedo struck the port side at No. 2 hold. The blast detonated some of the explosive cargo. The secondary explosion was so violent that it capsized one of the lifeboats. No one was lost, however; they were all picked up quickly and distributed among the remaining three boats.

With her bottom torn open, the *Empire Drum* went down by the bow in thirty seconds. Out of the water rose the *U-136*. Zimmerman maneuvered his U-boat close to the lifeboat which was in the charge of the *Empire Drum*'s second officer. He asked the name of the vessel he had sunk, and whether they had gotten out a call for help. All the time, four astute lookouts scanned the ocean and sky from the protection of the conning tower. After a brief interrogation, the U-boat eased away at slow speed.

Several hours later, Zimmerman returned to the scene. He was attracted by a light shown by one of the lifeboats. Possibly, he hoped to bag a rescue vessel. Ascertaining that nothing had changed, he left under cover of darkness.

The lifeboats stayed together all night long. At dawn, Captain Miles decided they should strike out for land. The boats set sail. Because of different sailing characteristics, they soon became separated. The boats were well-provisioned so there was little discomfort, and none of the men were injured. The day passed.

On the twenty-sixth, the lifeboat with the captain and thirteen crew was sighted by the Swedish steamship

*Venezia*, which picked them up. The second lifeboat was not found by the USS *Roper* until the twenty-ninth.

The thirteen men in the third lifeboat spent a week at sea, squinting and burning in the bright, hot sun, crammed together uncomfortably and wondering if they were ever going to be rescued. When their food ran low and salvation did not come, they rationed what little was left.

Forces ashore knew of the missing lifeboat, and every day conducted aerial patrols. It was not until May 1 that Lieutenant Commander W. B. Scheibel, flying Coast Guard Airplane No. 183, spotted the lonely lifeboat in the broad, blue Atlantic. Scheibel radioed his position to base. He flew close overhead and dropped an emergency container with rations, medical supplies, and blankets. The parachute opened and checked its fall, but the canister sank on impact with the water.

Chief Officer Lee, in charge of the lifeboat, signaled with an Aldis lamp that one of his men was in serious condition. Despite a large swell thirty degrees out of the wind, Scheibel landed on the choppy sea and taxied to the beleaguered seamen.

Scheibel exchanged his medical kit and all the rations and water he had for two men: John Pratt, who was delirious, and First Radio Operator Frank O'Reilly, in case military authorities wanted to question him immediately about their plight.

Later that afternoon, eleven anxious crewmen were located by surfboat *#5429* from the Caffeys Inlet Lifeboat Station. *CGC-407* soon caught up with them and took off the men, while the surfboat towed in the lifeboat. The crew of the *Empire Drum* was, at last, safe and sound.

This incident furthered the erroneous belief that Italian submarines were operating in the western Atlantic. The German commander's broken English was mistaken for an Italian accent, and witnesses thought they saw an "I-44" painted on the U-boat's conning tower.

After a three-day lull in activity, the New Jersey shore again became the focus of attention. Zimmerman was back for another score. U-boats were notoriously peripatetic, and the *U-136* was no exception. After having sunk the *Empire Drum* some three hundred miles off the mouth of the Chesapeake Bay, he made a long, fruitless haul westward and northward, until he caught the Dutch freighter *Arundo* practically inside New York Harbor.

With Rommel sweeping unchecked across North Africa, the Allies were in desperate need of war material. The *Arundo* left New York with essential supplies such as 4,995 boxes of beer, 6,844 cases of canned herring in tomato sauce, 4,545 drums of lubrication oil, 54,711 bags of nitrate, 2,000 cases of evaporated milk, 123 one-and-a-half ton Ford trucks, and 2 steam locomotives and their tenders. Her destination was Alexandria, Egypt. Because the Suez Canal was closed to shipping, the *Arundo* would have to take the long route around Capetown, South Africa.

She left port not in convoy, but within a five mile radius were two tankers, two freighters, and a U.S. destroyer, all visible under excellent conditions that bright spring morning. The *Arundo* was only fifteen miles past Ambrose Light, the guardian of the harbor, when the torpedo track was seen. It was a white turbulence of water three feet high, and extending out as far as half a mile.

The official memorandum states "the torpedo struck below the water line on the starboard side under the bridge, approximately amidships. The explosion was not loud but resulted in a violent concussion shaking the ship from stem to stern and causing a high column of water to be thrown up on the starboard side. The hull at No. 2 hold was extensively damaged, the hatch covers in No. 2 hold were blown off; No. 1 lifeboat destroyed, and the radio equipment damaged. The only hold known to have flooded was No. 2. No fires were started. The ship developed a sharp starboard list, practically ninety degrees, sinking by the bow within five minutes."

The *Arundo* was heavily armed, but had no chance to defend herself. The U-boat was never seen. Fortunately, the destroyer (USS *Lea*) turned back to rescue the men struggling in the water, but not before sounding out the area thoroughly with her hydrophones. It was two hours before the survivors were picked up.

Captain A. C. Trdelman's statement concerning the six fatalities was summed up by a Naval Intelligence officer: "Two individuals, a trimmer and a fireman, were not seen subsequent to the attack, and the other four men may have lost their lives either in the lifeboats that were faultily launched or because one of the locomotives, which were a part of the deck load, tipped into the water among the swimming survivors."

The *U-402* made its debut off the coast of North Carolina on the twenty-ninth, when Kapitanleutnant Siegfried von Forstner spotted the Russian freighter *Ashkhabad* through the lenses of his periscope. The freighter, converted into tanker, was traveling in ballast from New York to Matanzas, Cuba. Her escort was the HMS *Lady Elsa*.

The U-boat was seen by sharp-eyed lookouts on the antisubmarine trawler: a gray shape outlined in the glistening light of the moon. The *Lady Elsa* fired a four-inch shell, forcing the U-boat to submerge.

One minute later, despite a zigzag pattern that carried her as much as 22° from her base course, the *Ashkhabad* was struck by a torpedo at No. 4 hold. The upward force of the explosion peeled out the hull plates, and strewed the deck with wreckage. Water flooded in through the shaft alley.

The freighter's gun crew opened up on the resurfaced U-boat. They recorded no hits. Soon, the *Ashkhabad*'s engine room was filled with water. Captain Alexy Pavlovitch gave the order to abandon ship. The stern sank until it rested on the bottom, leaving the bow afloat. The decks were awash up to the forward part of the bridge. The crew, including three women, got away in two lifeboats and a raft. They were soon picked up by the *Lady Elsa*.

The situation on the *Ashkhabad* had not changed by the next morning, so the captain and some of his men returned to the vessel. They were shocked to find that sailors from the HMS *Hertfordshire*, thinking the ship had been abandoned, had rifled the bridge and taken off valuable navigational instruments. Captain Pavlovitch protested, since it seemed that his ship could be salvaged.

Not knowing that a salvage tug was on the way, the U.S. destroyer *Semmes* came upon the half-submerged freighter on May 3, and, following standing orders to destroy any wrecks considered a hazard to navigation, pumped the *Ashkhabad* full of four-inch shells. The bridge caught fire and burned furiously until the next day. The Russian freighter still did not sink, but as there was little left to salvage, she was later put out of her misery.

Two hours after midnight, making it the thirtieth, Heinicke found the Norwegian freighter *Taborfjell* off the Massachusetts coast, bringing 16,000 bags of sugar from Matanzas, Cuba, to Montreal, Canada, via New York and the Cape Cod Canal. The freighter was a hundred miles east of Cape Cod when a torpedo slammed into her hull, gouging out a hole fifty feet long and ten feet deep below the waterline.

It took only two minutes for the massive weight of inrushing water to take her to the bottom. The bow rose up to a 60° angle before the barnacle covered hull disappeared forever, taking down seventeen of her crew. The only survivors were three men who jumped overboard and located a raft that had floated free. They were later picked up by the British submarine *P-552*.

The last sinking of the month, indeed, for nearly two weeks, was the Norwegian freighter *Bidevind*. She was bringing to New York a cargo of spices from Bombay, India, and wool and goat skins from Karachi. After rounding the horn and crossing the entire South and North Atlantic Oceans, she was within sixty miles of her destination when she slipped into the sights of the *U-752*. Having failed to bag the *Reinholt*, Schroeter made sure of getting the *Bidevind*.

At 2250, Schroeter surfaced his U-boat off the starboard bow of the *Bidevind*, aimed, and fired. Observers on the freighter saw the enemy, but had no time for evasive maneuvers. The torpedo struck amidships. Five minutes later, another exploded aft.

During the fifteen minutes it took the ship to sink, the entire crew managed to get away in two lifeboats. The U-boat was not seen again. One lifeboat was motorized; she took the other in tow and began the long haul westward. Fourteen hours later, when they were only eight miles from the beach, they were spotted by a patrolling Coast Guard surfboat. The stranded seamen were immediately taken ashore. Four who were injured were transported directly to the hospital.

As April ends we notice some differences in the direction of the East Coast U-boat war, both offensive and defensive. More U-boats than ever encroached upon the domain of the ESF, but the amount of time spent there by each one was shorter. For the most part, the East Coast was but a way station, a sniping point. Men who had been cooped up during the long Atlantic crossing were given the opportunity to shake out the doldrums of inactivity by attacking merchant shipping while the U-boats moved on toward their final operational areas southward: the Caribbean and the Gulf, where fat tankers abounded. It was an ever-moving treadmill. While simply "passing through," the U-boats created havoc by popping up all over the ocean, like gophers out of their holes, only to disappear quickly after the damage was done. This potshot technique was telling on merchant marine morale.

On the other hand, public awareness was on the wane. The Navy was clamping down on merchant ship casualty information released to the press. Even if a story was surrendered to the media, it was played down. A typical newspaper clipping might state that "a medium sized merchant vessel was sunk off the Atlantic coast last week, and the survivors taken to an undisclosed east coast port." The time lag for media consumption could be as long as a month.

For this reason, most civilians were made to believe that the U-boat campaign against merchant shipping along the East Coast was dying down. Coupled with the numerous "sinkings" and "probable sinkings" of U-boats by the Army Bomber Squadrons, Navy and Coast Guard planes, and the antisubmarine craft of the home fleet, an effective propaganda program left the American people blissfully unaware of the true success of the U-boat crusade.

Members of the merchant marine harbored no such

delusions. They were well aware of the chances they were taking every time they left port. Many men had had more than one ship shot out from under them; some kept notches on their belts.

It was a not uncommon practice to travel with lifeboats already swung out on their davits. This undoubtedly saved many lives, especially on heavily laden vessels that plummeted like rocks.

Merchant ships were also becoming better equipped: with life saving gear, with radio transmitters, with increased lookouts, with deck guns and armed guards. The most important defensive tactic, however, was the convoy system. Ships were now grouping at their ports of call, and leaving in the company of armed escorts. While U-boats might be attracted to the concentration of sluggish targets (the speed of the entire convoy was determined by the slowest member), the presence of fast patrol craft fitted with guns, depth charges, hedgehogs, and the most sophisticated surveillance equipment then available, was usually enough intimidation to keep German periscopes well under the waves. This protective screen surrounding a covey of cruising ships was unattractive to any U-boat that wanted to survive the action.

Added to this was the increasing experience the U.S. Navy was gaining in offensive warfare. As the Navy's technique improved, U-boat commanders were forced to become more wary of approaching vessels, especially in shallow water where their path of retreat was limited.

A single ship, on the other hand, beckoned to the U-boat as a sick, lonely caribou enticed the hungry wolf. The relative safety of the convoys increased the hazards of those ships running independently.

Despite the high number of ships attacked and sunk—roughly equivalent to the number sunk in March—the proportion of survivors to fatalities shifted in favor of survival. While the statistics might appear to be slewed by the amazing rescue en masse of the entire complement of the British liner *Ulysses*—contrary to the immense loss of life accompanying the sinking of the *Lady Hawkins* in January—the *reason* for the success of rescue operations is more important: the sheer quantity of seagoing craft and airplanes maintaining stations.

There was now a much better chance of being picked up by a passing patrol boat, or being spotted by an aerial lookout from a blimp or plane, than there was in January. Added to this were the summery temperatures as the season progressed. Sunburn was a discomfort not to be scoffed at, but it was not as deadly as soaking in freezing water. A man might live only a few minutes in frigid winter seas before going numb and unconscious. Even though the water temperature in April was lower than the average person could withstand for very long, a man momentarily immersed could at least dry off in the sun once aboard a lifeboat or raft. It certainly was not a pleasant experience, but at least it was one that a hardy seaman could live through.

After he had, he was usually more than willing to return to his trade along the dangerous routes of the sea.

# MAY

"Captain Edward Vincent Peters, master of the tank steamer *Esso Nashville*, for outstanding heroism in line of his profession when his vessel was torpedoed and broken in two by an enemy submarine off the U.S. Atlantic coast on March 21, 1942. After giving the order to abandon ship and ascertaining that all men were in lifeboats, Captain Peters, in attempting to embark in the last boat, slipped on the oil-covered deck and fell into the sea, sustaining chest injuries and a fractured leg. Observing that the boat was about to be crushed against the side of the ship, he ordered it to get away and pick him up later, if possible. Realizing that his painful injuries rendered him incapable of swimming to the boat, he floated himself over the awash midship section of the tanker, made his way aft to the engineers' quarters and bandaged his broken leg. After a short rest he hoisted a distress signal and later was rescued by a Navy vessel. Without regard to his personal safety, Captain Peters, in ordering away the boat, undoubtedly prevented the loss of the lives of many of his shipmates. His act of courage and bravery above and beyond the call of duty will be an inspiration to the men of the U.S. Merchant Marine."

Citation for the American Legion Medal
Awarded May 3, 1942,
at the Maritime Exchange

Washington was quick to recognize the invaluable service rendered by the men of the merchant marine. As far back as the 1700s, Thomas Jefferson told Congress that the country needed "workmen of every kind who may be found at once for peaceful speculations of commerce and for the terrible wants of war." That attitude has not changed. In the 1900s, President Theodore Roosevelt reiterated Jefferson's admonition to have "seamen of our own to convey our goods to neutral markets, and in case of need, to reinforce our battle line."

When the shipbuilding industry began on the North American continent in 1607, the Colonies were under British rule and shipping was dominated by the parent country. The virgin forests of New England provided an abundant supply of good, strong lumber necessary for building wooden hulls capable of withstanding the vagaries of rough, Atlantic Ocean weather. By 1681, the American fleet consisted of nearly a thousand sailing vessels: fishing, plying the coastwise trade, and engaging in foreign commerce.

After the Declaration of Independence, a 1790 Act of Congress inaugurated the first of many legislative measures to sustain and regulate the merchant marine of the newly founded country and to protect American seamen. The United States backed up its resolve by waging war against the Barbary States of North Africa, who were pirating American shipping in the Mediterranean.

Through the years, various Acts were passed in order to encourage the manufacture of vessels, strengthen foreign trade, and ensure safety at sea. As shipping technology progressed from wooden hulls to steel, and means of propulsion changed from sail to steam, the plight of the seaman, as in all cultural advances, was sadly lacking. The days of the Captain Blighs, and punishment by lashing before the mast, lingered on until wedged out by the rise of maritime unions. In the United States, the LaFollette Seaman's Act of 1915 set the standards for higher wages and better working conditions.

# TRACK OF THE GRAY WOLF

Today, with the advent of sophisticated electronic equipment and complicated mechanical devices, officers and seamen attend the Merchant Marine Academy in order to learn their specialized trades. With continuing shipboard education, and evaluation, testing, and advancement based on time in grade, what was once merely a job for the ignorant has become an honored career.

On April 6, 1942, Congress enacted a resolution that authorized the Maritime Commission to award medals to members of the American merchant marine who, during the course of the war, had distinguished themselves by "outstanding conduct or service in the line of duty."

Civilian seamen were dying on the vast ocean battlefront just as soldiers were dying in the fields. In many cases their travails were more severe than those suffered by trained combatants. The Congressional bill was open acknowledgment of the country's indebtedness to the mariners responsible for transporting through hostile seas the troops and materiel necessary for the pursuit of the war. Dodging torpedoes and gunshells was no easier than dodging bullets and artillery.

The *Fredden* was an unarmed Swedish ship whose men got a close-up view of the war at sea. At 2130 on May 4, the deadly track of a torpedo passed a ship's length in front of them. The U-boat that had launched the attack was nowhere to be seen. Thirty minutes later, another torpedo came their way. This one passed right under the ship, but at such a depth that it did not detonate. The U-boat still was not spotted, but it doggedly kept after them. An hour later, a third torpedo streaked toward the tramp steamer. It ran shallower than the second, but not shallow enough: it passed underneath the barnacled hull just forward of the bridge. Thirty minutes later yet another torpedo closed on the freighter. It was so close to the surface that it broached the waves. It missed the bow of the *Fredden* by only a few feet.

Four torpedoes expended on a nearly worthless quarry was obviously more than the U-boat commander could bear. He surfaced half a mile off the port beam. The master of the *Fredden* placed the stern of his vessel toward the enemy submarine, to present the smallest possible target. The fires were dampened, the engines stopped, and the crew abandoned ship before the inevitable bombardment occurred.

The U-boat submerged in the darkness. Nineteen men in two lifeboats followed along meekly behind their ship. The U-boat did not reappear. Finally, at 0830, after drifting ten or fifteen miles, they reboarded, started the fires, and continued on their way. They made New York on the eighth with an unbelievable tale: that of a sitting duck that had been left sitting.

On the ninth, Cape Hatteras was enjoying a rare day of quiet seas lifted gently by long, smooth swells. Despite an overcast sky, visibility was a good nine miles. The men of the Coast Guard cutter *Icarus* were anticipating an easy, if lonely, cruise from New York to Key West.

The only man experiencing any agitation was the sonar operator: the southward journey was full of sound contacts. So many ships had been sunk during the past four months that the ocean bottom was littered with wrecks whose high, steel hulls reflected pips with a constancy that was ever growing as the *Icarus* rounded the Diamond Shoals. The target he picked up at 1620 was not strong or worthy of notice. Still, he continued observing it as it passed the cutter's beam. The signal was growing stronger. Lieutenant Maurice Jester, commanding officer of the *Icarus*, was off duty at the time. He was called and, at 1625, he took over the conn.

At 1629, a tremendous explosion rent the calm sea only two hundred yards off the port quarter. Water spouted high in the air, the *Icarus* reeled with the concussion. She was saved from calamity by the torpedo's untimely detonation. Jester rang general quarters. The crew manned their battle stations as he spun the cutter in a sharp arc that would take her toward the sound contact. The sonar operator then heard for the first time on his listening gear distinct propellor noises.

The *Icarus* steamed over the spot and dropped five depth charges in a diamond pattern, wreaking havoc below. The initial salvo was accurate, and trapped the

*U-352* in shallow water. "The first explosions destroyed the periscope and killed an officer in the conning tower. Gauges and glasses were smashed in the control room. The deck was littered with broken gear. Lockers burst open. Crockery and other loose objects were flung about the boat. . . . All lights except the emergency system failed."

The *Icarus* ran a reverse course and dropped three depth charges in a "V" pattern. Large air bubbles burst to the surface. Jester homed in on the telltale swirls and dropped another depth charge. As the cutter swung away for another pass, the bow of the U-boat broached. Its stern was down, and it appeared to be unmanageable. Men poured out of the conning tower hatch.

From a distance of a thousand yards, the *Icarus* opened up with the thirty-caliber machine gun on the flying bridge, and with the starboard fifty-caliber machine gun. The three-inch deck gun was brought to bear as the distance closed. The first high explosive projectile fell short, but ricocheted through the fairweather. With frenzied rapidity, the gunnery officer called out the ranges as the gun crew continued firing. Six direct hits on the hull and conning tower were recorded.

The crew of the *U-352* had no opportunity to man their gun. Under a hail of fire they abandoned ship and quickly swam away from the boat. At 1714 it was all over. During its three minutes on the surface, the U-boat had disgorged thirty-three German sailors. In a gush of air it sank into the warm, blue water.

Jester ran his ship over the spot and delivered a parting shot, a single depth charge dropped directly on the wreck. Another large air bubble and a slick of diesel oil came to the surface. This time the U-boat stayed on the bottom, a tomb for thirteen German sailors.

In the meantime, Lieutenant Jester called for instructions. With the possibility of another U-boat lurking nearby, he needed authority to stop and take on survivors. The *Icarus* broadcast a plain language message, "Have sunk submarine. Thirty to forty men in water. Shall *Icarus* pick up any of men." What followed was a half hour of no responses, Jester's repeated transmissions, and one acknowledgment of receipt with no message. Finally the commandant, Sixth Naval District, radioed, "Pick up survivors. Bring them to Charleston."

The situation of the men in the water was not desperate, except for Maschinistenmaat Gerd Reussel. While abandoning ship, his leg had been severed by a shell from the *Icarus*. Kapitanleutnant Hellmut Rathke, captain of the *U-352*, removed the belt from his own pants and used it as a tourniquet for the wounded man's bleeding stump. All the German submariners wore lungs and life jackets. As the Coast Guard cutter approached slowly, Rathke warned his men against divulging military secrets.

The *Icarus* stopped dead in the water. The starboard gangway was lowered. The four wounded men were the first brought aboard. Reussel and another were found too seriously injured to suffer much movement. They were placed on litters and kept topside. Reussel died four hours later. The other man, who had lost an arm, slipped into delirium but survived. The rest of the prisoners were carefully searched as they boarded, and all personal items were deposited in a barrel. Then the men were escorted to the crew's quarters where they were quarantined under guard until the ship reached port the next day.

Neither Hellmut Rathke nor the *U-352* had ever sunk a ship. Between her only two war patrols, the *U-352* had been docked at St. Nazaire during the time of the famous British commando raid; it was not damaged. Reussel was buried with full military honors at the National Cemetery in Beaufort, South Carolina. Rathke and the remainder of the crew spent the rest of the war as POWs.

Very little of intelligence value was gleaned from the reticent German sailors. The Navy hoped to learn more by salvaging the sunken U-boat. On May 19, the Navy salvage tug *Umpqua* headed out for the site of the *U-352*. It took four days to locate the wreck. A cursory examination was made by divers during the next two days. The U-boat was found listing to starboard at an angle of 60°, in one hundred ten feet of water. Divers were unable to fit through the hatches in their hardhat gear. The lack of escort vessels precluded the *Umpqua* from continuing diving operations. In the immediate vicissitudes of war, no further attempts to visit the site were made until August. At that time, divers found five live depth charges lying around the wreck—it had apparently been attacked during the interim. Two-and-a-half-knot bottom currents halted further exploration. The *U-352* was abandoned.

On May eleventh, the convoy system was introduced for coastal running. The ports were already choked with ships aggregating for the long Atlantic crossing, and this additional change increased the bunching up of merchant vessels awaiting escort. Naval authorities considered the system important as a deterrent against lurking U-boats waiting to pick off the slow, solitary tramps. With the arrival in March of the British armed trawlers, and the increased number of converted yachts and submarine chasers now available, coastal patrol and escort service was undertaken in earnest.

The HMS *Bedfordshire* was one of twenty-four commercial fishing vessels loaned by the British to help fill the gap left by the fifty destroyers they had taken on lend-lease. Four officers and thirty-three ratings manned the one hundred seventy-foot-long trawler. Her fishing gear was replaced with depth charge racks and throwers; overlooking the stern equipment was a thirty-caliber machine gun inside a tub. Mounted forward on a raised platform was a four-inch deck gun.

Her Majesty's trawlers operated under strange jurisdiction. They maintained Admiralty status, were run by a British crew, but took orders from the U.S. Navy. They represented a situation of staunch Allied cooperation.

On the night of the twelfth, Kapitanleutnant Gunther Krech, *U-558*, exacted retribution for the loss of his fellow U-boat commander, Helmut Rathke. He fired a torpedo at the patrolling trawler and hit her square amidships. The *Bedfordshire* blew up violently.

The first the Navy knew of the calamity was on the morning of the fourteenth. The body of the *Bedfordshire*'s second in command, Sub-Lieutenant Thomas Cunningham, washed up on a deserted Ocracoke beach. Coast Guardsman Arnold Tolson was on patrol when he spotted a fully clothed body in the surf. He waded out and recovered it. He loaded it into the back of his truck and dashed off to make his report. On the way, he was stopped by a fisherman who had spotted another body in the inlet. Tolson charged into the water again and brought back the second body. Because the *Bedfordshire*'s crew had spent the previous month in the area, and fraternized with the locals, the chief of the Ocracoke Coast Guard station recognized Cunningham.

A week later, two badly decomposed bodies were recovered from the ocean by Coast Guard cutter *63-067*. They were unidentifiable, but wearing the same sweaters the other British seaman wore, and were assumed to be from the *Bedfordshire*. These four men were buried in a special cemetery on Ocracoke Island. Weeks later, the trawler's nameboard washed ashore, tangible proof that the ship was gone.

On the fourteenth, the Greek ship *Stavros* was torpedoed by the *U-593*, Kapitanleutnant Gerd Kelbling. She was in ballast from Lisbon to New York, via Bermuda, when a torpedo ripped into her port bow at the waterline. Moments later, with incredible accuracy, Kelbling placed another torpedo into the hole made by the first. This one went through the ship and blew out the starboard side.

Fire broke out in the forecastle storerooms. The forepeak tank filled with water, but the collision bulkhead prevented further flooding aft. An SOS went out, and the captain ordered abandon ship. All thirty-two crew men got away in two lifeboats. They sat at their oars for twenty minutes, watching the flames and expecting at any moment that the U-boat would surface and complete the destruction of their vessel. When nothing happened, they reboarded, broke out the fire hoses, and put out the flames. The Second Engineer lost two fingers. The *Stavros* limped into New York under her own power.

Three days later the *Skottland* was torpedoed by the *U-588*. Vogel was back for his second American tour, one which would prove more fruitful than his first. The Norwegian freighter was carrying over a million and a half board feet of lumber from the United Kingdom to Philadelphia, via Halifax. The second mate saw "a flash of white water" two hundred yards away. The torpedo hit between Nos. 3 and 4 holds under the after mast. One fireman on engine room duty was killed instantly by the blast. The ship heeled to port, split in two, and sank in five minutes.

The twenty-four surviving crewmen managed to shove off the starboard lifeboat and some of the rafts. Fortunately, because the attack occurred during the day, they were spotted thirty minutes later by a Canadian patrol plane. An hour passed before the men were rescued by a Canadian lobster boat, the *O.K. Service IV*. They were taken to Boston, where the six injured received medical treatment.

That night, at 0200, Vogel torpedoed the *Fort Binger*, Liverpool to New York in ballast. The tracks were spotted from the bridge of the British ship, which went into evasive maneuvers with the helm hard aport. The first torpedo hit on the port side, but did not explode. The second passed twenty yards astern. The U-boat surfaced nearby. The *Fort Binger* turned to ram as the U-boat opened fire with machine guns and its deck gun.

Despite shells exploding against the hull and superstructure, killing one and wounding four of the sixty-one free Frenchmen aboard, the *Fort Binger* continued to circle and tried again to ram. Vogel drew away from the aggressive merchantman. As soon as the *Fort Binger*'s four-inch deck gun could be brought to bear, she retaliated in kind, forcing the U-boat to break off the action and submerge. That was one wolf that was beaten off with its tail between its legs.

Vogel left the northern waters and on the twenty-first, well out to sea and hopefully out of range of coastal support, found the *Plow City*. Again he pursued a daylight attack, but this time with a ruse.

The freighter was en route from Port of Spain, Trinidad, to New York, with 4,971 tons of bauxite, running independently. Captain George Hazeleaf related the incident: "At 9 A.M. we sighted what appeared to be a lifeboat about five miles away. Naturally, we did not want to pass up anybody in distress, so we headed for it. Suddenly we saw smoke come out and the sail it seemed to have been carrying disappeared. We figured it was no lifeboat, and put our stern to it and ran.

"But he kept gaining on us. Then, after a while, we lost sight of him. Pretty soon, however, at 9:45 A.M., we sighted a periscope and we tried to leave that far astern. I knew we were going to be chased and we couldn't seem to outrun him."

All this time the *Plow City*'s radio was emitting an SSS. It was not until 1430 that the track of a torpedo was sighted. Captain Hazeleaf grabbed the helm and threw his ship into a wildly zigzagging course. The first torpedo narrowly missed the bow, reportedly by only five feet. But the second one in the spread caught the *Plow City* at the waterline aft of No. 2 hold. Fred Martin, the second mate, was blown off the bridge. Communications with the engine room were severed. The captain ordered abandon ship. As the wounded vessel slowed to a halt, a third torpedo slammed into her.

The thirty survivors got away in the lifeboats, and not a minute too soon. The *Plow City* plunged beneath the waves as the men made good their escape. Captain Hazeleaf: "The sub had surfaced in the meantime. It went to the port lifeboat, which had capsized during launching attempts. Then the sub crew helped right it and took aboard one man clinging to it. They asked him a few questions and then came alongside the rest of us and put him aboard.

"The commander asked the name of our ship, cargo and ports bound, to and from. He spoke good but German-accented English. 'Do you want any cigarettes? Do you want any rum?' " The offers were not refused. As the exchange took place, the U-boat crew snapped pictures, "apparently so they could make propaganda out of it at home."

He then left the merchant seamen to their fate. Although the *Plow City*'s distress call had been received, it was five days before the lifeboats were located. The armed yacht USS *Sapphire* picked up the men who, because of good weather, were still in good condition.

Vogel must have loved daytime encounters. On the twenty-second, at 1530, he fired a torpedo at the British freighter *Margot*. Her cargo was 6,000 tons of valuable war materiel: planes, tanks, and explosives, bound from New York for the Middle East. The explosion blew in the starboard stoke hold, flooding the engine room, knocking out the radio, and collapsing the funnel.

The *U-588* then surfaced and engaged the freighter with her machine gun. This forced the crew to abandon ship. Vogel waited patiently until the evacuation was complete, watching idly as one lifeboat left from the port side, two from the starboard. As soon as the men were clear, he fired twenty rounds from his deck gun into the vessel. The *Margot* started to settle by the stern.

Vogel approached the lifeboats. He stopped by the one containing the second officer, and asked for particulars of his prey. In gracious compassion, he handed over a supply of rum. Then he moved to the boat with the *Margot*'s captain. With typical British aplomb, the captain asked to be towed to shore. Vogel did not comply, but did give him a ration of rum.

Two and a half hours later, the *Margot*'s bow was still protruding from the water. The *U-588* slowly circled the mortally wounded freighter while its gun crew pumped a couple dozen shells into the forepeak to let out trapped air. She finally sank by the stern.

The three lifeboats were not picked up until five days later by the Swedish steamship *Goland*.

There was no such thing as perfect protection against a sufficiently courageous U-boat commander, as proved by the demise of the Panamanian tanker *Persephone*. She was traveling in convoy and only two and a half miles off the New Jersey coast, nearing the end of a journey from Aruba to New York with a cargo of fuel oil, when Kelbling attacked her in broad daylight.

Said Captain Helge Quistgaard, master: "At 2:58 P.M. a torpedo hit the *Persephone* on the starboard side in way of the engineroom. A thick, black smoke covered the entire ship. About forty-five seconds after the first explosion, another torpedo struck the *Persephone* at No. 8 tank, starboard side, causing large quantities of oil to spout onto the ship. The stern of the tanker settled immediately and rested on the bottom, leaving the bow and midship house out of the water.

"I went to the bridge and gave orders to abandon ship. No. 1 lifeboat had been partly lowered by officers and crew members who were amidships at the time of the torpedoing. It got safely away with seven men. I noticed that a large raft was already floating about 300 feet from the *Persephone*, with seventeen men on it. This raft was carried away by the backwash caused by the rapid settling of the ship's stern. A number of the crew, caught by the explosion as they were having coffee in the messroom, jumped onto this raft and were thus saved before it washed away.

"As I realized that the tanker's stern was resting on the bottom, I decided to collect all the navigation instruments I could carry and put them in lifeboat No. 2, which I lowered myself after making sure that all hands had left the ship. I was unable to row away alone, but was picked up by one of the escorting Coast Guard vessels. Other Coast Guard craft, which put out from shore in response to our distress signal, rescued the survivors in lifeboat No. 1, together with others who were in the water and those on the after port side life raft."

Seeing that his ship refused to go down any further, Captain Quistgaard changed his mind. "At my request, I was returned to the *Persephone* to salvage twenty-three bags of U.S. Mail. The Coast Guard crew assisted in this work."

Out of a convoy of some twenty vessels, stretching from horizon to horizon, the *Persephone* was the only ship torpedoed. Escorting craft prowled the ocean, and airplanes from shore filled the sky, but the marauding U-boat was not seen. Nine of the *Persephone*'s engine room gang went to their graves.

A Navy memorandum made note of Quistgaard's dissatisfaction: "The Captain feels that his ship was in a crude convoy. There was no uniform speed, and although patrolled by a blimp and other aircraft, as well as surface vessels, the ships in the convoy were so extended as to make adequate patrol impossible."

# TRACK OF THE GRAY WOLF

Part of the *Persephone* lived on. A salvage crew managed to sever most of the hull from the sunken after section, and tow it to Gravesend Bay, New York. Twenty-one thousand barrels of the eighty thousand barrel cargo were recovered. A year later, the tanker *Livingston Roe* caught fire at dock in Recife, Brazil, burning out her midship house before firemen got the flames under control. The hulk was towed to Baltimore, Maryland, for repairs. The *Persephone*'s midship house was removed intact and also towed to Baltimore. The two parts were mated—like Frankenstein's monster—and the new vessel was sent out to once again ply the seven seas.

In addition to salvaging and refitting sunken vessels, U.S. ship production was reaching an all-time, world-wide high. The Liberty ship construction program was in full swing. Not counting tugs, minesweepers, sub chasers, and patrol boats, in the month of May U.S. shipyards put into service fifty-eight full-sized ships aggregating 632,000 tons: nearly two ships a day. One 10,500 ton ship, from keel laying to commissioning, was built in only forty-six days. Tonnage construction had not yet equaled losses, but American know-how and ingenuity were finding more shortcuts in building, and were eliciting in addition to increased manpower—womanpower. Not content to do only clerical and secretarial work for the war effort, women were now becoming welders and shipwrights. This represented more than a mere technological revolution—it was a cultural revolution as well: one that was a long time coming, but, once arrived, was here to stay.

Judging by the action reports in the ESF for the month of May, it appears that the U-boat campaign was dying down. Nothing could be further from the truth. True, only five ships were sunk, and more than half of the *Persephone* would eventually be salvaged; only four other ships were attacked. Weighing these meager losses against those of previous months, and against the sinking of the *U-352*, the tide seemed to have turned against the enemy.

But the Caribbean and Gulf Frontiers were taking a beating. The war against merchant shipping was not easing up, it was merely changing venue. Florida was the new shooting gallery.

June would prove that the northern states still had plenty to worry about, and that Doenitz had the imagination, and his U-boat commanders the courage, to find new ways of wreaking terror against American shores.

# JUNE

"We are some twenty-five of the thousands of 'clay pigeons' who man the tankers carrying oil and gas up and down the coast. We make perfect targets for Adolph's subs to improve their aim on. So far, and we are still a few hours out of port, our ship is still unshelled and untorpedoed. Our course has taken us past a veritable graveyard of vessels less fortunate. Five big ships have been sunk within rifle shot of our coast and hailing distance of our largest naval bases.

"In money, the ships we are on represent millions of dollars. In cargo, they represent many hundreds of thousands of dollars in value to the national defense and no one knows what the aggregate of ship and cargo is worth to our United States.

"The lives of the crew must have some value. It is a lead pipe cinch that we and the other tankers and freighters would at least mean an iron cross on the chest of one of Hitler's submarine commanders if we should happen upon the wrong end of one of his torpedoes.

"The Atlantic coast sea lanes are full of merchant-marine ships just like this one. We are told and are happy to feel that we are doing our bit by keeping them sailing."

The Crew, Steamship Rubilene

After a week without activity, a new pack of wolves started arriving on the East Coast. The first of these was the *U-404*: von Bulow was back for his second tour. He struck at 0615 on the first.

The *West Notus* was bound from Buenos Aires, Argentina, via Trinidad for New York. At the helm was Chief Officer Lambert Kat. A Naval gunner climbed up to the bridge with a cup of coffee, handed it to Kat, and glanced idly out at the sea and the rising sun. "What is that bearing down on us?"

Kat did not know, but traveling alone through U-boat infested waters he wasted no time in putting down his coffee, spinning the helm hard to port, and ringing the alarm bell. As the ship slowly swung its stern toward the unknown craft, he ran and got the captain. By the time they were back on the bridge the U-boat was in full view, running on the surface. Its deck gun burped once. The first shell exploded in the radio shack.

As the U-boat raced ahead it caught up with the freighter. It pumped incendiary shells into the bridge, killing Captain Hans Gerner, damaging the controls, and setting the room afire. The Naval gun crew returned fire with machine guns and the after deck gun until the ship was ablaze from the U-boat's accurate fire. With shrapnel peppering the deck and superstructure, the men got ready to abandon ship. The third mate was shot down. One lifeboat was blasted full of holes. With too much way on the vessel, another boat capsized when it hit the water.

Dodging flames and flying metal, two lifeboats got away on the protected side with most of the men. The rest were forced to leap for their lives into the water. Radio Operator Wilfred Clarkson drowned.

Kat and several others climbed aboard a half-submerged lifeboat whose stern was afire. They were unable to save it, and it sank, full of holes. Since the shelling had stopped, this small group of men swam back to the ship. Third Engineer Victor Wallcom was not seen again.

Kat testified, "We discovered that No. 3 lifeboat was alongside and just hanging on by one part of the falls. She was full of water and full of holes, so we started to gather blankets, clothes and food and water. We couldn't find the water beaker. I don't know where that went to.

We gathered the food and some snow off the pipes in the ice box, and we put off from the ship. We didn't know when she would blow up. She was smoking so badly. We started bailing the boat out, and started plugging the holes up, and oh, I don't know how much later, half an hour later or so, the sub came back and came right up to us and the first thing he asked us is 'was there anybody killed?' Then he asked the name of the ship. Oh, yes, he knew it already. He says, 'Isn't this the *West Notus*?' I guess he saw it through the painting. The letters were painted grey and I asked him if he would give us some water and he said he would see if he could spare some, so then he said, 'I will give you a line. I will tow you to your other two lifeboats.' He gave us a heaving line and we gave him the painter and he towed us over to the other two lifeboats, in the meantime, asking us questions, asking if he was towing us too fast.''

The survivors were given water, as well as a piece of paper with distance and bearings for Cape Hatteras, written in English. The U-boat left. The men reshuffled themselves in the two good lifeboats, and let the third one go. Kat returned once again to the still burning ship, grabbed a watch off the second mate's desk, then beat a hasty retreat. The time was now 1130.

"About 3:00 in the afternoon, we heard four loud explosions spaced more or less at regular intervals, maybe a couple of seconds in between. The next explosion we saw a long column of flames. It must have went up two hundred or three hundred feet high. We couldn't see the mast of the ship then and we saw a puff of white smoke and a big flame, and I guess about 4:00 in the afternoon, we saw the sub come back and the other lifeboat was a little bit astern of me and oh, maybe half a mile or so, and we saw the sub pull alongside of him, and we saw a sail go down, so we thought he must have picked up somebody out of the water and he had.''

Von Bulow was wisely saving his torpedoes for targets that required stealth. He sent a demolition party onto the *West Notus*, and sank the ship with explosives.

The lifeboats got separated, each sailing toward the East Coast some three hundred miles away. Kats' testimony is purely factual: "I set watches on there and gave out food and water and the next day, we sighted some wreckage and a Norwegian ship, and outside of that, we didn't see a thing, that day. That was Tuesday, the second. On the third, about a quarter to 7:00, I guess, in the morning, we sighted a steamer and then he went in the other direction, and then he came back. He was a Greek. We had made up in the lifeboat that we didn't want to go with any ship going to South Africa or South America. We figured we could make the coast, and then the Greek threw us a heaving line and I went up and spoke to the captain and asked him where he was going and he said he was going to Bermuda. I asked him for cigarettes and he said you better go along to Bermuda. I told the boys we better go with the Greek to Bermuda, so the boys came aboard."

Kat also told the investigation board, "I couldn't tell the sub from our lifeboat. His conning tower looked similar to our sail, except we knew our sail was red, and if you saw the two together, you would swear that there were two lifeboats together. . . . The Greek thought we were a sub at first."

Eighteen men were safely ensconced aboard the *Constantinos H*. The other lifeboat, containing eighteen survivors, was picked up on the fourth by the Swiss steamship *Saentis*.

On the second of June the *Berganger* came to grief. For three and a half hours that morning she was stalked by the *U-213*. The inexperienced Kapitanleutnant von Varendorff fired as many as five torpedoes at the Norwegian vessel. All missed. It seemed as if the 48,000 bags of coffee, one thousand bales of linters, and hides and sunflower seed oil laded at Santos, Brazil, were bound to make it to New York.

Veteran submarine commander Rehwinkel, *U-578*, was not as poor a shot. The *Berganger* crossed his path that afternoon. His first torpedo went true, exploding between the engine room and No. 3 hold on the port side, and killing four duty personnel. As the freighter gradually slowed and swung to port, out of control but losing way,

Rehwinkel surfaced and engaged the freighter with his deck gun from a mile and a half away.

The *Berganger*'s crew was still on edge from the morning attacks, when they had been unable to return fire on their unseen adversary. Now the gun crew rushed into action, placing six rounds so close to the U-boat that it was forced to submerge. Rehwinkel sneaked around the ship and fired two more torpedoes into her hull.

With their ship out of control, some of the men were abandoning ship when the second attack occurred. Their lifeboat was capsized by the blast. No one was hurt. They were all able to swim to a raft. After the *Berganger* went down, the U-boat approached one of the boats and asked for particulars about the ship. The men reported seeing an insignia on the conning tower that reminded them of Ferdinand the Bull.

Despite the SOS, rescue was not effected until the fourth, separately for each vessel. The thirteen men on the raft were picked up by the USS *Madison*, seventeen in one lifeboat by the *Bavaderos*, thirteen in the other lifeboat by the fishing vessel *Mary J. Landry*.

Yet a third U-boat veteran returned to the ESF on the third. This was Schultze in the *U-432*. His object here must have been harassment rather than serious tonnage accumulation, for he attacked two small fishing boats off the coast of Maine. Both draggers were headed for the fishing grounds off Seal Island, Nova Scotia, from their home port of Gloucester, Massachusetts.

The *Ben and Josephine* was attacked first. Captain Guiseppe Ciaramitaro first saw the U-boat at 1500. "He came right alongside at 4 o'clock. We heard the machine gun fire. They fired not for our boat. They fired on the water between our boat and the submarine. And I told the boys, 'Let's get the dories overboard. We might have a chance to save ourselves.' "

One shell hit the forecastle. Four men got into each of the two dories. After the men pulled away, the machine gun fire concentrated on the wooden hull. The force of the shells turned the boat around, so that both sides were raked. The engine room was penetrated, and a huge tongue of flame shot out as sparks ignited oil from the fuel tanks. Bow first, the *Ben and Josephine* slipped beneath the waves.

While he was making good his escape, the boat's cook grabbed the two-quart coffee pot off the stove. This was the only water they had with them between the two dories. For food the cook brought four packages of coffee rolls wrapped in cellophane. The two dories stayed side by side during their eighty-mile haul.

Captain Ciaramitaro wrapped it up succinctly: "We started to row to make land. After thirty-six hours we made Mt. Desert Rock, Maine."

John Johnson, captain of the *Aeolus*, was only a few miles away during the attack on the *Ben and Josephine*. He heard gunfire, then saw the flames. When he realized what was happening, he altered course and beat a hasty retreat. The crew donned kapok vests. Ten minutes later "the first shell burst overhead so I ordered the engineer to stop the engine—after a second shot across the bow another struck right across the stern—he came closer and closer. By the time we had the first dory out he started to fire again—the fourth shot hit the bow on the starboard side."

Johnson counted some seventeen shots, of which eight or nine struck. The *Aeolus* caught fire forward. "By that time we were away from the vessel. We rowed away from the vessel—when we were about a quarter of a mile or half a mile away she sank. After that we rowed to Mt. Desert Rock, Maine."

Although the dog was killed by shellfire, the six men suffered no injuries. Both thirteen-foot dories stuck together, actually lashed by a painter during the night. They made it to shore along with the crew from the *Ben and Josephine*.

The psychological effect this had on Maine and Nova Scotia fishermen can well be imagined. Previously, they had all thought their boats were too small for U-boats to bother with. Now, they were understandably stirred by concern for their lives as well as their livelihoods. The impact on the fishing industry was yet another aspect of the U-boat campaign that went far beyond the mere sinking of ships and cargoes.

# TRACK OF THE GRAY WOLF

Schultze raised his sights on the ninth, this time going after a Norwegian steamer *Kronprinsen*, Baltimore to Manchester, England. He fired a torpedo that gouged a large hole between Nos. 1 and 2 holds, blew the poop deck to pieces, and knocked the crew's quarters askew so the wreckage hung overboard. Both holds flooded quickly. The ship could not maneuver, and went dead in the water.

Schultze did not follow up the attack. After a muster was taken on the *Kronprinsen*, it was found that one man had been killed by the blast. Since the ship was not in immediate danger of sinking, the crew remained aboard. Eventually, the ship was towed to Shelbourne, Nova Scotia, and repaired.

U.S. ports and coastal inlets had long been protected by mine fields. Maps were drawn in meticulous detail so that Allied vessels could avoid destruction. Swept channels usually described a circuitous route through the stationary explosive devices. On the night of the tenth, many reported enemy sightings along the coast. A Coast Guard patrol boat closed on the northbound tanker *F.W. Abrams* as she approached the Diamond Shoals, and semaphored instructions to follow her to a safe anchorage for the night.

The next morning, while being escorted out of the inlet in a heavy rainfall that reduced visibility to a quarter mile, the *F.W. Abrams* strayed from the path. Her voyage from Aruba to New York was curtailed by an explosion that tore a gaping wound in her bow. Witnesses swore they saw the track of a torpedo, then later thought they saw the submarine that had fired it. In truth, the tanker had blundered into the Hatteras minefield. Once she was in it, she could not find her way out. Before long, the tanker detonated two more mines. She went down by the head without loss of life.

A similar incident occurred on the fifteenth, at the approaches to the Chesapeake Bay. A northbound convoy was proceeding past the mouth of the bay when the fifth ship in a thirteen-ship column, the *Robert C. Tuttle*, suffered an explosion about a hundred feet aft of the stern. With water pouring into the hole, the vessel swung out of control to port. Captain Martin Johansen ordered the engines stopped; he dropped all confidential documents over the side in a weighted steel box. As the tanker went down by the head, the forty-seven man crew abandoned ship. Ruben Redwine, second assistant engineer, drowned. In ten minutes the ship's bow rested on the bottom in fifty-four feet of water, with the decks awash to midships and the part abaft of midships out of the water. *PC-474* rounded up the three lifeboats and took the survivors into Norfolk, Virginia.

Immediately behind the *Robert C. Tuttle* was the *Esso Augusta*. In addition to a merchant crew of forty-four and a thirteen man gun crew (she carried both a three-inch and a five-inch deck gun), a party of five including the Vice-Commodore of the convoy were aboard. Captain Eric Blomquist ordered hard right and full speed ahead in order to avoid collision with the tanker, and to outwit any torpedoes. With thoughts of enemy submarines on his mind, Lieutenant Commander W. S. Carrington, vice-commodore, recommended that each vessel break her cruising pattern by zigzagging, and that the convoy take a long, sweeping clockwise curve that would bring it into the mouth of the Chesapeake while the undersea culprit was put out of action. The *Esso Augusta* was swinging in a broad arc as instructed when an explosion rent her stern. The tanker's engines made two more revolutions, then ground to a halt. The only injury was to one of the gun crew, who had been thrown on his back by the force of the blast.

Captain Blomquist's vessel drifted seaward. "I requested Chief Engineer Hall to go below and investigate the damage. He informed me that our rudder and stern post had been blown off; there were holes in the hull under the tail shaft; all auxiliary machinery foundations were cracked or shattered; electrical communications were disrupted, and fuel and steam lines broken. The main engine was disabled and the steering engine inoperative." Seeing that his ship was maintaining buoyancy, Captain Blomquist requested tugs to tow him into port.

Still suspecting U-boats in the area, the destroyer USS

*Bainbridge* dropped a pattern of depth charges on a suspected site. Surprisingly, her eight depth charges resulted in nine detonations. The extra blast was so close that it sheared rivets in her hull, and sprung leaks in lubrication lines, exhaust lines, suction lines, fresh water tanks, and fuel oil tanks. Her rudder was damaged, and the propeller shaft bearing pedestal was cracked. The *Bainbridge* was forced to break off action. She limped into port for repairs. Other escorts prowled the area.

Into this mass of confusion came the HMS *Kingston Ceylonite*, escorting the tug *Warbler* and her tow *Delisle*. The British armed trawler hit a mine that blew up her magazine. The double blast tore the ship apart. The bow forward of the bridge listed to starboard and sank immediately. The stern settled on an even keel. Within two minutes the entire ship was gone. Fifteen British sailors either floated about or clung to an overturned boat. The blimp *K-5* dropped a raft, onto which three men climbed. They were picked up quickly and rushed to the hospital. Three bodies later washed up on shore, but fourteen men remained missing and were presumed dead.

Back at the *Esso Augusta*, the tug *Keshena* arrived to take the wounded tanker in tow. The ship was too much to handle, so they had to wait until another tug, the *Coyote*, could lend the power of her diesel. The *Esso Augusta* moved slowly. An hour after midnight, a third tug wound a hauser cable around her towing bit and latched onto the tanker. They weighed in at Hampton Roads, Virginia, at 0645. The 119,000 barrels of diesel oil bound from Texas City, Texas, for the United Kingdom were discharged. Temporary repairs enabled the tanker to make it to Baltimore where she was laid up for six months.

The *Robert C. Tuttle* was also subsequently salvaged, and half of her 142,700 barrels of crude oil saved, although not without travail. The *Robert C. Tuttle* was a sister ship of the *E.H. Blum*, and suffered almost as much indignity before becoming again a seaworthy ship. As she sat at dock after her salvage, her upperworks burst into flames. Fire fighters shrouded the decks with foamite and dry ice and succeeded in containing the blaze.

She was moved to another anchorage. The strain of mining, sinking, salving, and burning finally took its toll. The ship broke in two aft of the bridge. Both halves sank, but in such shallow water that neither part was submerged. The sections were raised, towed to the Navy Yard drydock for temporary repairs, then towed to Baltimore for permanent reattachment. She was eventually returned to service.

What really happened to convoy KN-109? No U-boats were detected. All ships were well clear of the protective minefield. The only conclusion was that it had run into a nest of enemy-laid mines. To test this theory, minesweepers were sent out to clear the area. They detonated four more mines in the vicinity of the previous day's casualties.

The intrepid U-boat commander was Kapitanleutnant Horst Degen, *U-701*, who on the night of June 12 had boldly sneaked into the shallow bay approaches to lay down explosives. The Germans had now added another device to use against the merchant marine. Even though two of the vessels did not count as tonnage losses for Degen, the overall effect was devastating. It meant that the U.S. Navy, whose resources were already strained, was forced to take on yet another task. Mine sweeping operations would now have to be conducted on a regular basis.

While this new tack on the war was being evaluated, the torpedoing of ships on the high seas went on unabated. That night, at 2320, both the passenger-freighter *Cherokee* and the British freighter *Port Nicholson* fell to the machinations of Kapitanleutnant Joachim Berger, *U-87*.

Convoy XB-25 was en route from Halifax to Boston. With unerring precision, Berger chose two victims and got them both. The *Port Nicholson* was hit in the engine room, killing two men. With his ship mortally wounded, Captain H. E. Jeffry ordered abandon ship. Since the vessel maintained an even keel, lifeboats were launched without undue difficulty.

Captain Twiggs Brown, master of the *Cherokee*, was in the chart room behind the wheelhouse when "I heard an explosion out on the port bow, and I knew it was either a torpedo or a depth charge some escort had dropped, which depth charges in convoys are very frequent things (you hear them any time day or night.)'' He threw the alarm switches to scramble the gun crew to their stations, and to rouse the passengers and crew. He hardly had time to observe the *Port Nicholson*'s troubles when his own ship was hit.

The first torpedo struck under the port bridge wing, blowing most of it clean away. The wheelhouse floor buckled up from the force of the explosion. ''The steering wheel was laying over almost 45°, and the foremast was back over the top of the wheelhouse, and the lights all went out. I tried the loud speaker; that was gone. I tried the whistle; it wouldn't work. In the convoy we had a whistle signal in case you were torpedoed; we tried that, and that wouldn't work.''

Seconds later another torpedo hit. The radio room aft of the chart house fell apart, doors were twisted in their frames. The ship started to list and never stopped. Control of his ship was taken away from him, Captain Brown lamented pitifully.

''I tried to get out of the starboard side of the bridge, and that whole thing was wrecked too. The whole wheel house was a wreck. I got as far as the door and slipped and landed out on the port wing of the bridge, and I couldn't get word. I couldn't talk to anybody; there was nobody there you could talk to. There were men around, of course. When I seen the ship was going, there wasn't a thing in the world I could do, or anybody else could do. She had listed then until the top of her house, that is where the bridge was, was under water. That is where I was standing. The port wing of the bridge submerged, and she had almost gone 90° then. Her stack was just about laying in the water, and then I jumped.''

It took only three minutes from the time of the first explosion until the *Cherokee* reached 90°; in another three minutes she was gone. None of the ship's ten lifeboats got away. Captain Brown floated in the darkness amid floating wreckage for a half hour before he was picked up by a raft containing thirteen bedraggled men.

After daylight, at 0700, they were picked up by the Canadian corvette *Halifax*. Others were rescued by the U.S. Coast Guard *Escanaba* and the SS *Norlago*. Of one hundred sixty-nine passengers, crew, and armed guard, eighty-six were lost.

The survivors from the *Port Nicholson* were also picked up. Third Officer Paul Stansbury said that since the *Port Nicholson* was still afloat, Captain Jeffry decided to see if she could be saved. "He got into a lifeboat with six men and an officer from the rescue ship and rowed to his slowly sinking vessel. Shortly after that the ship settled quickly at the stern. I guess they weren't able to pull away in the lifeboat, for the men and the lifeboat were dragged under as the ship sank."

On the seventeenth, the *Santore* discovered that all the mines sown by the *U-701* had not been swept up. Leaving Norfolk, Virginia, with 11,095 tons of coal for Cristobal, Canal Zone, the ore carrier took tenth place in the single column of Convoy KS-511. As Captain Eric Nyborg maneuvered his ship along the swept channel a tremendous explosion occurred amidships on the port side, flinging coal some fifty feet into the air.

The gun crew manned their gun, and got as far as loading it, before the *Santore* rolled completely on her side and sank. There was no time to launch lifeboats; one raft got clear. The ship was gone in four minutes, leaving forty-three men swimming and three men missing. Escort vessels soon plucked the doused crewmen out of the water, and took them back to port.

Since the *Santore* had a fifty-seven-foot beam, and sank in fifty-four feet of water, three feet of her starboard side protruded above the waves. She also rested directly in the middle of the channel: a severe hazard to navigation. She was found unsalvageable, marked by buoys, and eventually demolished by the Army Corps of Engineers.

The Office of Naval Intelligence (ONI) started an investigation, the main impetus of which was to discover how mine-laying U-boats knew where to deposit their explosives with such accuracy. It was no accident that the mines were sown exactly in the shipping lanes. Yet, routing instructions were issued on the spot by convoy leaders to their escorts and charges, or in the form of sealed orders only for the eyes of merchant ship captains running alone. It was one more ploy used by the enemy to cause confusion and uncertainty among Allied shipping, and it proved once again that the Axis powers had resources far more extensive and insidious than previously suspected.

Although her mines were wreaking havoc along the Chesapeake Bay approaches, the *U-701* was by no means taking it easy. Degen conducted a diligent patrol along the coast as far south as the Carolinas. In the wee hours of the nineteenth, he engaged the converted fishing trawler USS *YP-389* in a bloody, running gun battle.

The *YP-389* was slow (nine knots) and lightly armed: she carried one three-inch gun on the bow, two thirty-caliber Lewis machine guns, and six depth charges. She performed escort duty on occasion, but was found woefully inadequate because she had trouble keeping up with the convoys. Therefore, she was consigned to patrol duty, her primary task being to warn merchant shipping of the Hatteras minefield.

When the *YP-389* left Morehead City on the seventeenth, her three-inch gun was not in working condition. It had refused to fire on the previous patrol because of faulty ammunition and a defective firing pin. A new part was requisitioned, but the patrol boat was ordered out to sea before it arrived.

On a dark night with no moon, nothing was visible from the bridge of the *YP-389* until tracer bullets appeared suddenly like speeding fireflies and stitched a jagged path across the superstructure. Lieutenant Roderick Philips, commanding, rang the general alarm. As the men tumbled out from below, incendiary shells exploded against the wooden hull and deck. Seaman C. F. Hensley and Fireman J. C. Doucette raced for their battle stations at the three-inch gun, to see if the new ammunition would fire. They were cut down as soon as they stepped out of the hatch.

Fires blazed everywhere. While the two Lewis guns returned fire, aiming wherever the gunners saw the incoming tracers originate, the rest of the crew fought the flames and tried to duck the shelling which had switched to common and shrapnel shot. Suspecting that his deck gun was useless, Lieutenant Philips decided upon a course which kept the patrol boat's stern toward the enemy, thus presenting as small a target as possible. Fireman W. B. Cole rolled depth charges out of the rack as a way of forcing the U-boat to keep its distance. Riddled with bullets and shrapnel, he was killed at his post.

The Coast Guard responded to the distress call with the message that help was on the way. In the meantime, the U-boat's superior speed allowed it to fire first from one quarter then from the other. It was black, and impossible to see, while the *YP-389* was kept alight by flames. What is a few minutes in the telling was an hour in the fighting.

With his ship sinking from under him, Lieutenant Philips ordered cease fire. He personally conned the helm in the exposed wheel house, keeping the U-boat off his starboard quarter while the men gathered on the port bow. Going full speed to disguise the fact of her abandonment, the *YP-389* maintained her course while the men jumped overboard in groups of two and three, the uninjured helping the wounded. When Lieutenant Philips left his ship, she was a fiery cauldron. She went on for half a mile, with the U-boat shelling her most of the time, until she sank.

Lieutenant Philips kept the men together. They floated in their life jackets on the gentle Atlantic swells. Doucette died from his wounds during the four-hour wait. After dawn, they were found by two Coast Guard boats and taken to the station at Ocracoke. The wounded were moved to the Naval Hospital at Portsmouth, Virginia.

It is interesting to note that a Court of Inquiry studying the incident recommended Lieutenant Philips be brought to trial by General Court Martial on the charges of "(1) failure to seek encounter with the enemy; and (2) culpable inefficiency in the performance of his duty." The three judge panel was of the opinion that he should have rammed the U-boat or forced it to submerge, "by reason of which failure the said USS *YP-389* was sunk and the enemy submarine escaped.''

The June 22 sinking of an Argentine freighter was followed by a wave of international repercussions. The *Rio Tercero* was carrying a cargo of newsprint, asbestos fiber, and insulation board from New York to Buenos Aires when she was torpedoed by the *U-202*, Kapitanleutnant Hans-Heinz Linder.

The attack occurred in full daylight, at 0645, off the New Jersey coast. The explosion blew in the hull adjacent to the boiler room, killing four duty personnel and demolishing the starboard side lifeboats. Captain Luis Pedro Scalese ordered SOS and abandon ship. The crew rushed into action and got two lifeboats launched in seven minutes; the *Rio Tercero* went down four minutes later. One seaman was dragged down with the ship.

A confidential report to the Commandant, 4th Naval District, gives particulars on subsequent events. "At 0715, the Captain of the *Rio Tercero* was taken aboard the submarine, which he described as being about 1500 gross tons and of the *U-27* class. The submarine commander took the ship's log from him, and stated that the *Rio Tercero* had been torpedoed because her name did not appear on a list of Argentine ships. The Captain was offered three glasses of cognac and a pair of shoes, which he took. He saw the submarine commander's chart, upon which the route of the torpedoed vessel outward from New York was marked with a zig-zag line. The Captain was then put back in his lifeboat, and four sailors from the submarine appeared on the deck with two machine guns. The Captain believes that he and his crew were going to be machine gunned, but this was prevented by the appearance of a U.S. Army plane at 0730. The submarine immediately crash dived.''

The plane dropped seven depth charges. The *U-202* got away. Rescue craft were dispatched immediately. By 1045 the *PC-503*, the HMS *Northern Chief*, the HMS *Lady Rosemary*, and the yacht *Niagara* converged on the site. Said Captain Scalese of his rescue: "To the Air Force and the Navy of the United States we all want to give our heartfelt thanks for the help extended us.''

Argentina was not a belligerent in the war. As a neutral nation, the government took "a serious view" of the sinking, and sent an "energetic" protest to Berlin. This was the third Argentine ship sunk by German U-boats, and came at a time when President Roberto Ortiz was resigning, when Acting President Ramon Castillo was under violent Congressional fire for his "conciliatory policy toward the totalitarian States," when the government was trying hard to avoid breaking diplomatic relations with the Axis powers, and when shipping circles were deeply concerned that the German blockade of the Atlantic coast would restrict Argentine free trade.

Only five days previously, Germany had sent a letter of apology for "accidentally" torpedoing the Argentine ship *Victoria*, and had agreed to pay indemnity for damages. This solution was accepted as satisfactory only as long as the high seas remained free to Argentine vessels. In the case of the *Victoria*, Berlin claimed that "it was a lamentable error of a submarine commander." That could not possibly be accepted in the case of the *Rio Tercero*, which displayed "thirteen plainly visible Argentine flags painted on various parts of the vessel."

Imitating the events following the series of sinkings of Chilean ships three months earlier, anti-Axis sentiment ran high. Riots in Buenos Aires necessitated reinforcement of the German embassy police guard. Argentina was full of political unrest.

The U-boat attacks continued. On the twenty-fourth, von Bulow in the *U-404* found himself off Cape Lookout, North Carolina, with a Yugoslavian freighter in his sights. His first torpedo was a dud, bouncing off the steel hull with a rattle that roused Captain Henry Cantin to action. He broke off his zigzag course, swung to port, and went to half speed—all in an attempt to throw off the calculations of his pursuer. It did no good. Eight minutes later, at 0330, a second torpedo struck the *Ljubica Matkovic*. The resultant explosion blew a spout of water into the air as high as the mast top. Captain Cantin sounded the general alarm and ordered abandon ship. The entire crew got away in two lifeboats.

They rowed frantically but were still only two hundred

yards away from the ship when a third torpedo slammed into the listing hull. The ship broke in half and quickly went down. Five hours later, in the light of day, the lifeboats were spotted by a Navy blimp. Two hours later the *CGC-470* picked them up, none the worse for wear.

That afternoon, the tug *John R. Williams* was entering the Delaware Bay at 1620 when, according to Second Assistant Engineer Harold Jorgensen, "there was an immense explosion, which seemed to occur on the port side approximately amidship I would say from what I observed. The boat lifted up and then headed down. That was the last I seen of her as I was blown over the side. All I could see was pieces flying. Then I was gradually being drawn down by the suction. I finally got away. I swam away and got a hold of a mattress and pulled myself up on the mattress. After a while the bottom of the mattress fell out, and I got a hold of the ventilator that had blown off from the upper deck, the end of it where it was attached to the house. I grabbed a hold of that, and I worked myself over to the life raft."

Chief Engineer William Lacoy got sucked underwater, and "was so long coming up I thought I'd never get to the top again."

Seaman William Balfour said the tug "just disappeared in a flash and there was nothing left of her."

These three men who made it to the raft, plus Seaman Homer Pendleton floating nearby, were the only survivors of the crew of eighteen. They were lucky enough to be sipping coffee on the stern deck of the tug when she contacted a mine laid by the *U-373*, Oberleutnant zur See Paul-Karl Loeser. The *YP-334* picked them up.

The Coast Guard immediately issued a warning to pleasure craft, and cordoned off the area until the following day when minesweepers carefully checked the mouth of the bay. They found four more mines. The shock value of this second incursion into home waters was out of proportion to the tonnage loss—exactly what Doenitz planned.

The day's war actions were not yet over. Von Bulow dallied off Cape Lookout during the day. When he rose to the surface that night he found himself in the middle of a northbound convoy. Eleven merchantmen and seven escort vessels inched along at eight knots. Von Bulow took careful aim and fired a spread of deadly missiles into the three overlapping columns of ships.

First struck was the Panamanian freighter *Nordal*, running in the starboard column. No. 3 hold was broached, and dark smoke from the cargo of hides was blown out along with the spray of water. The signal to disperse was given. Ships frantically changed course in a random fashion, to avoid any follow-up torpedoes, while the escorts charged through the procession after the enemy.

Four minutes later, in the center column, the *Manuela* was struck between the engine room and boiler room, killing two men outright. Thick oil was thrown upward, dousing the upper decks and the men outside enjoying the cool night air. The starboard lifeboat, swung out for rapid deployment, was destroyed by the blast.

The *Nordal* was sinking rapidly, settling by the stern with a strong starboard list. Captain Hans Hansen, master, ordered abandon ship. Thirty-one crewmen got away in three lifeboats. Able Bodied Seaman Olaf Svendsen fell overboard and missed the boats. He was rescued fifteen minutes later by the *CGC-483*. The others were picked up by the HMS *Norwich City*.

On the *Manuela*, Captain Conrad Nilsen also ordered abandon ship. The port lifeboat left with twenty-two of the crew. Nine others, plus the six men of the armed guard, jumped off the stern and swam to hastily launched rafts. The *CGC-483* plucked the men out of the water, while the *Norwich City*, completing her rescue of the men from the *Nordal*, crowded her decks with those from the lifeboat. In addition to the two men killed in the engine room blast, two others were missing.

The *Nordal* was gone, but the *Manuela* remained afloat. She listed so far over that the ocean lapped at her hatch coamings. A Coast Guard cutter hovered around the struggling ship. The next day, a lonely figure was found waving from the steeply canted deck. Antonio Figuerosa, a fireman, had been knocked unconscious by the blast. When he came to he found the ship abandoned.

Suffering from shock and from compound fractures of the left arm and right leg, he took hours to crawl along the companionways and up the ladders to reach the deck. *CGC-252* took him off and rushed him to the hospital.

The Navy rescue tug *P.F. Martin* was dispatched to the site and started to tow the freighter to shore. Together they plodded along slowly until, twenty-four hours after being torpedoed, the *Manuela* rolled over and dipped beneath the waves.

On the night of the twenty-fifth, Captain Even Bruun-Evensen, master of the Norwegian passenger-freighter *Tamesis*, misread the buoys marking the Hatteras minefield and became hopelessly lost. A large explosion blew a hole in the bottom of the ship. No lives were lost. The ship was abandoned, then reboarded and run into shallow water where she was lightered and patched. The *P.F. Martin* was again called into service, and towed the *Tamesis* to Norfolk for permanent repairs.

Investigators determined by mapping the vessel's route and triangulating her distress call that she must have hit a defensive mine. On the other hand, German records give credit to the *U-701* for torpedoing the *Tamesis*. Degen was still in the area, and it is entirely possible that he did fire a torpedo at the *Tamesis*. However, in a subsequent interrogation with the U-boat commander, during which he outlined the times and places of his attacks, he failed to mention any activity at that time and in that place.

While the case of the *Tamesis* is open to conjecture, it is certain that Degen torpedoed the *British Freedom* on the twenty-seventh. The British tanker was one of a thirty-one ship convoy, KS-514, standing out of Lynnhaven Roads, Virginia, and headed for Key West, Florida. As the nine columns moved southward with ponderous precision, armed escorts shuttled to and fro, their sounding gear in constant use. Leading the pack was the converted yacht, USS *St. Augustine*.

Despite the intimidating array of armed merchantmen and fast, prowling escorts with stern decks bulging with depth charges, and a bright, sunlit day, Degen boldly brought the *U-701* into attack position. He fired a two torpedo spread at the *British Freedom*. One torpedo missed; the other caught the tanker just forward of the bridge in the No. 3 tank. The blast ripped out hull plates below the water line, bulged up the main deck, demolished the bulkheads to the adjacent tanks, and destroyed the main pipeline. The tanker was in water ballast, so there was no secondary ignition of oil or gasoline.

There were no injuries or casualties. Since the escorts were aware of the *British Freedom*'s situation, Captain Francis Main kept radio silence. The engines were stopped. As soon as the ship's way ceased, all fifty-five crewmen left in two lifeboats. After a quarter of an hour, with the ship floating high in the water, the captain and chief officer reboarded and conducted an examination. They found the flooding contained; a small fire in the galley was caused by a pan of grease left on the stove. Since the ship was in no imminent danger of sinking, the rest of the crew were recalled. The engines were restarted, and the *British Freedom* returned to Norfolk for extensive repairs.

This was by no means the end of the action. The *St. Augustine* picked up a solid sound contact and delivered a five-depth-charge attack before losing the submerged U-boat. With techniques perfected over the months and studied and passed on through Naval ranks, the *St. Augustine* continued her echo ranging. A couple hours later she heard propeller noises retreating. She chased the elusive signal until she was directly over the U-boat. Four more depth charges rolled off the stern deck. Air bubbles and small discs of white wadding about four inches in diameter came to the surface.

Deep underwater, the *U-701* was squirming like a worm on hot pavement. Glass in the conning tower gauges was shattered, and the electric motor was temporarily put out of action.

The *St. Augustine* continued prowling. When sound contact was made again she dropped four depth charges at a range of depths: one hundred feet, one hundred fifty feet, two hundred feet, and three hundred feet. The *U-701* escaped with minor damage which its crew was able to repair. But the important factor was the continued aggressive action on the part of the escort craft, and improved sounding and depth charging techniques.

In the past, when merchant ships ran unescorted, the U-boat had every opportunity to surface, aim, and fire at will. With the convoy system this was no longer possible. In the first place, the mere presence of escorts severely limited the amount of time a U-boat could keep its periscope showing. The commander could not take a chance on being spotted by ever alert Naval gun crews. Then, once he fired his first spread, he was hounded so vigorously that he was unable to follow up his attack. Forced to remain submerged, precious electricity was wasted as the U-boat threaded an escape course on battery power. Even if the U-boat survived the counteroffensive, it could do no more damage. It limped away like a whipped dog, with its tail between its legs.

In the deadly game of U-boat warfare, the hunter was evolving into the hunted.

About the time the *St. Augustine* was depth charging the *U-701*, a brother sea wolf was operating far off the New Jersey coast. This was von Bulow, on his way home after a fruitful patrol. Crossing his path was the Norwegian freighter *Moldanger*, carrying vegetable oil, tallow, wool, and hides, from Buenos Aires to New York.

The foremast lookout saw the track of a torpedo and called out. A few seconds later, an explosion rent the bulkhead adjacent to the engine room, disabling the engines and knocking out the power. The radio went dead. Captain Frode Hansen gave the order to abandon ship and dropped the confidential papers overboard in a weighted bag. As the crew readied the lifeboats, and waited for the vessel's forward motion to give way, another torpedo slammed into the hull under the poop deck. Thirteen men were launching the port lifeboat, just above the point of impact. They were wiped out by a blast that nearly blew off the stern. The starboard boat swamped. A small dory and two rafts got away, but most of the men were in the water. The *Moldanger* sank by the stern in eight minutes.

The U-boat cruised slowly into the group of thirty-one survivors, stopping long enough to ask the name of the vessel, her cargo, and their destination. After the U-boat left, the men of the *Moldanger* managed to right the overturned lifeboat. Personnel were distributed among the four craft.

For three days and nights they stayed together, drifting aimlessly. During that time not a single plane or ship was sighted. The pleasant weather and the warm Gulf Stream water eased the discomfort of cramped spaces. Finally, they decided that if rescue was to be effected, they had more of a chance of being spotted if they separated and each went in a different direction. They did this on July 1, the fourth day.

The warm sun was a mixed blessing. Instead of suffering from cold and hypothermia, the men endured heat, dehydration, and sunburn. At least, by this time in the war, rafts and lifeboats were adequately provided with food, water, medicine, and clothing.

On July 7, the HMCS *Buctouche* happened across the lifeboat. One of its men had died and had been buried at sea. The fifteen survivors were in poor condition and were treated for exposure. The word was out, and the broad ocean was searched for the remainder of the crew.

It was not until July 15 that an Army bomber on routine patrol spotted the dory. It radioed immediately for help. They were so far offshore that no shore-based rescue craft were in the vicinity, or could reach them in any reasonable amount of time. The PC-495 was deployed from a southbound convoy. The next day the patrol craft picked up six men "so dehydrated and weak from exposure that a week's rest would be necessary before they could be moved."

The two rafts were given up for lost. But the men were still very much alive. They were wearing rubber exposure suits that kept them dry.

Each catamaran raft measured six feet by nine; the buoyancy tanks were six empty drums, three per side. Each was equipped with four oars, a sail, and a sea anchor. Twelve-inch-high poles, with canvas stretched around the perimeter, offered a reasonable protection from the wind and sea. Provisions included biscuits, chocolate tablets, malted milk tablets, peppermint tablets, and water.

During the day, the men sat exposed to the awful sun. At night, when the temperature dropped, they donned their life saving suits. Both rafts stayed together, expecting rescue any moment. But as the days dragged on and no ships were sighted, the men grew weaker and weaker.

On the twenty-second day their tablets ran out. The biscuits lasted only a few days longer. They stretched out the canvas sail to catch rain water. They survived three full-fledged gales, one lasting forty-eight hours. The two rafts were tossed in pounding seas like corks in a child's swimming pool.

The men fashioned hooks from safety pins, and made lines from the threads of the canvas. They subsisted mainly on raw fish. They even managed to catch sea turtles: they not only ate the meat, but the liver, the fat, and the blood. July came and went.

It was not until August 14, after forty-eight days at sea, that all nine men, miraculously still alive, were found by the steamship *Washington Express*. In the annals of survival at sea this story of the struggle to live, of the unwillingness to yield to the comfort of death, is a true tribute to the men of the merchant marine. What these nine Norwegian sailors endured serves as an example of the suffering others must have borne—others who were not so fortuitously found, and who died when their bodies failed them. This is the plight of all those men whose ships disappeared without a trace.

Degen was back in business on June 28. This time he stumbled upon a lone merchantman accompanied by one escort. The large tanker *Wm. Rockefeller* was bound from Aruba to New York with 136,697 barrels of fuel oil. Because of the attack on the *British Freedom* the day before, as the *Wm. Rockefeller* approached Diamond Shoals she was instructed by a Coast Guard patrol boat to heave to for the night. Captain William Stewart duly anchored his vessel off Ocracoke Lighthouse. The next morning he was given new routing instructions.

"At about 12:26 P.M. I was in the chart room laying

off a position, when I heard an explosion which I concluded was the result of a torpedo.'' He raced outside to check the damage. Through a black pall of smoke he was barely able to discern that the ship had been hit ''on the port side amidships in way of the pumproom.''

Engine room personnel were forced to abandon their stations so that, when Captain Stewart rang for full speed astern in order to lose way for the launching of lifeboats, he got no response. Instead, he had the helm swung hard aport. With steam escaping from ruptured lines, the din was so loud that conversation was nearly impossible. The vessel was aflame for half her length, from the bridge aft. Two lifeboats capsized due to excitement of the crew and undue haste in launching. The entire fifty man crew got away safely in rafts and two other lifeboats. Coast Guard cutter *470* raced off to deliver a depth charge attack, without effect, then returned and picked up the *Wm. Rockefeller*'s men.

Captain Stewart: ''It was my idea to ask the Captain to stand by the ship for some time; it appeared to me that the fire was subsiding; but due to the fact that several members of the crew had been smeared with fuel oil in their eyes, and completely smeared with it, I could see that they required attention, and the Captain steered for the shore, and I didn't interfere with him.''

The *Wm. Rockefeller* continued to burn throughout the day, but by night the flames were subsiding. A salvage tug chugged out of Norfolk and headed for the Diamond Shoals. However, Degen was not yet done with the tanker. Although he had been forced to flee, he returned eleven hours later under cover of darkness. An hour before midnight, he fired another torpedo into the drifting hulk. The *Wm. Rockefeller* joined the shipyard cemetery at the bottom of the sea.

The last action of the month was the sinking of the *City of Birmingham* by the *U-202*. Just four hours before midnight on the thirtieth, Linder fired two torpedoes into the side of the heavily laden passenger-freighter: one in the bow in No. 1 hold, and one under the bridge. The ship sank in four minutes.

Yet in that short time, six lifeboats and five rafts were

launched. Some passengers, slow in reaching the deck from their staterooms, literally walked off the ship as she slipped beneath the waves. Nearly a hundred people floated in the water or clung to flotsam. Fortunately, Captain Louis Borum had instructed his passengers to wear life jackets, so loss of life was kept to a minimum: two passengers and seven crew members.

The U.S. destroyer *Stansbury*, escorting the *City of Birmingham*, steamed into the floundering mass of humanity and effected a quick and efficient rescue, despite the possibility of a secondary attack. Bright moonlight aided the Navy sailors in locating solitary survivors. After the lifeboats and rafts were picked up, Captain Borum found that three hundred seventy-two passengers, crew, and armed guard had lived through the sudden sinking: a remarkable achievement due in part to daily lifeboat drills.

June ended with the enemy still having the upper hand. In addition to the continued sinking of merchant ships, U-boats were sowing mines along the inlets and convoy routes. They also threw a scare into the local fishermen, who now had to keep in mind that trawlers and draggers that were too small for the expenditure of a torpedo were at least worthy of a good shelling.

It was difficult to assess at this time the efficacy of the massive air and water patrol. But, as wave after wave of undersea marauders beat against American shores, beach erosion had reached its zenith.

The tide was about to change.

# JULY

"Even before Pearl Harbor, American seamen were under hostile fire from air and sea. Ever since then, the merchant marine as a whole has been constantly in action, meeting the enemy, day in and day out, from the Arctic to the south Pacific. There is no more heroic saga in the annals of man than the story of the courage and stamina of our merchant seamen, without whom we could not hope to be victorious."

Rear Admiral Howard L. Vickery, USN,
Vice Chairman, U.S. Maritime Commission,
and Deputy Administrator,
War Shipping Administration
National Maritime Day dinner, May 21, 1943

The Liberty ship *Alexander Macomb* stood out on her maiden voyage, bound from New York to Archangel, Russia, with 9,000 tons of sorely needed military supplies: tanks, planes, ammunition, and explosives. She was traveling under escort with a convoy of forty-one ships. Due to a dense, nighttime fog and the fear of collision, she gradually fell behind.

At 0630, a torpedo struck aft between Nos. 4 and 5 holds, where the cargo of explosives was stored. A titanic blast ripped the ship apart and spread fire along the decks and superstructure. Chased by flames, men were driven overboard in order to escape the fiery cauldron. Three boats and a raft were launched, and these went around and picked up men clinging to floating wreckage.

Three escorts turned and headed for the conflagration.

With the fog lifting, the *Alexander Macomb* was clearly visible under the smoke and flames. As the HMS *Le Tigre* approached, she made a sound contact with a submerged object moving slowly across her bow. The echo remained strong.

Lieutenant C. Hoodless stated in his action report that "at three hundred yards Submarine turned towards and approached at very high speed. A pattern of depth charges was fired at appropriate moment. He did undoubtedly pass down our Starboard side but it seems probably he was damaged, as in the next attack, movement was nothing like so fast.

"Having run to 1100 yards only just maintaining contact we turned towards and ran in to attack, once again he appeared to pass to starboard and for this reason only the starboard thrower was fired. There seems no doubt that this was a direct hit or within two or three feet as submarine immediately became stationary and all H.E. ceased."

Three crewmen from the *Alexander Macomb* watched the counterattack from their raft, half a mile away. While columns of water and the smoke of the underwater explosions hid the departing armed trawler from view, they saw the U-boat broach, roll over, and disappear.

"Both these attacks were made very close to the survivors of the torpedoed ship, and they were all the time getting closer, so much that when we ran in to deliver the coup de grace we were unable to fire as a life raft had drifted almost directly over the submarine."

The *Le Tigre* then picked up survivors, as did the HMCS *Regina*. Ten of the crew and armed guard were lost. With the men out of the water, the HMS *Veteran* picked up a faint, stationary ping on her echo ranger. She dropped more depth charges.

The British antisubmarine trawlers did their job well. They sank the *U-215*, Kapitanleutnant Fritz Hoeckner, with all hands.

Unaware of the loss of a fellow wolf, Degen kept up his patrol off the Diamond Shoals. Four days later found the *U-701* running on the surface in the afternoon, on a flat sea under clear skies. The boat loped along easily on her diesel engines. Fresh air was sucked into the compartments, to replace the stale blend the men had been breathing for the last ten hours since submerging at dawn. Along with Degen on the bridge were three other lookouts, each in charge of a 90° quadrant.

Oberleutnant zur See Konrad Junker, the executive officer, dropped his binoculars and shouted, "Airplane, there!"

Leutnant zur See Bazies and Obersteuermann Gunter Kunert reacted immediately by jumping down the ladder. Junker and Degen were right behind them. Degen spun closed the hatch as he ordered a crash dive. Crammed together in the conning tower, Degen said, "You saw it too late." Junker replied, "Yes."

In the clouds, Second Lieutenant Harry Kane was the pilot of an Army A-29 bomber armed with three three-hundred-twenty-five-pound depth charges and two machine guns: a fifty-caliber and a thirty-caliber. He and his crew of four had left Cherry Point Field, North Carolina, four hours earlier for a routine patrol mission off Cape Hatteras.

"I was flying in lower broken clouds with visibility about ten miles, when off to my left at a distance of about seven miles, I first sighted this boat through an opening in the clouds."

He turned his plane to investigate, and soon became convinced that "it was a submarine running with decks awash." The crew prepared for an attack.

"At a distance of approximately two miles, the submarine commenced to dive, taking about fifteen seconds to get under the water. When we got over it, we were at an altitude of fifty feet and our speed was two hundred twenty mph. The submarine was then about ten to fifteen feet under water and his swirl from diving was quite pronounced. The navigator and bombardier could easily discern all its outlines and superstructure. We dropped three depth charges, in train; the first fell twenty-five feet short, the second one hundred feet further on, and the third fifty feet beyond the second. Both second and the third depth charges either fell on the submarine or slid off the left side. The second was aft of the conning tower and the third between the bow and the conning tower.''

Inside the U-boat the instruments were smashed by a tremendous explosion aft of the conning tower. The men were inundated as water poured in through a large hole torn in the pressure hull. The main lighting failed, and dim emergency lights flickered on.

Degen ordered all tanks blown. ''Within one to two minutes control room and conning tower filled with water. Ship had list to starboard of approximately twenty degrees. C/T hatch opened easily. Ship is at a depth of about fifteen to twenty meters and no longer able to surface. Depth of water about eighty to one hundred meters.'' The *U-701* was hovering in an untenable condition below the surface, unable to rise and still losing buoyancy.

During this time a torpedo machinist's mate, who was asleep in the bow compartment during the attack, made his way to the control room, where he discovered they were about to abandon ship, then ran back to his bunk. By the time he returned, water in the control room was waist deep. The U-boat was on an irreversible downward course.

Air burped through the conning tower hatch as, one at a time, eighteen men crawled out and kicked hard toward the open air. Kane noticed that ''a light blue substance appeared about twenty-five feet to the left of the slick caused by the third depth charge. This started a slight bubbling on the surface. As it increased in intensity, a man popped up in the middle of it.''

The survivors had among them only three escape lungs and one life preserver. They huddled close together, treading water. Kane circled his craft and dropped a rubber life boat and four life vests. The Germans managed to retrieve two of the life preservers, with as many as five men at a time holding onto each one.

Meanwhile, Kane noticed another group of survivors numbering about fifteen. These men had escaped through the bow torpedo loading hatch only minutes after the others. They came up about a hundred yards away from the first group, but because of high seas the two groups were unable to see each other. Kane dropped a smoke bomb to mark the site, then winged off toward a Coast Guard cutter some five miles away.

Using Aldis lamp and radio, he alerted the *CGC-472* of the predicament and asked that the vessel follow him back to the location of the sinking to pick up survivors. Kane flew back, but could not relocate the floundering U-boat crew. Since he was low on fuel, he was forced to abandon his search and return to base.

Degen saw the bomber again, but determined that the large rolling waves prevented the Americans from seeing him and his men. Alone in the vast ocean, his only course of action was to keep his companions as close together as possible, to increase their odds of being spotted. But two men, Fahnrich (Ing.) Lange and Oberbootsmannsmaat Kurt Hansel decided to strike out on their own. They were last seen swimming toward shore some thirty miles away.

*CGC-472* hunted diligently for the German sailors. Some twenty-five miles distant, the *PC-480* was ordered to break away from her convoy duties to aid in the search. Together, the two ships scanned the sea until long after dark, but saw no signs of debris, oil, or survivors.

The Germans were in good spirits, as they expected to be rescued momentarily. But when Bootsmann Etzweiler, who did not know how to swim, weakened and was unable to keep his head above water, he drowned. As night settled in, the eighteen in Degen's group had withered to fifteen.

At dawn, after treading water for an unbelievable fifteen hours, the German submariners saw a Coast Guard vessel come into view. The men shouted and waved their arms, but the boat did not come any closer than a mile, and the men were not spotted. At that point some gave up hope, others lapsed into delirium.

As their strength gave out, the death toll rose: Maschinenmaat Damrow, Maschinenmaat Schmidtmeyer, Obermaschinist Grundler, Oberleutnant Karl-Heinrich Bahr, Matrosenobergefreiter Weiland, Maschinenmaat Schuller, Maschinenmaat Bosse, Maschinenmaat Fischer. The survivors kept seeing planes in the vicinity, flying search patterns, so they knew they were being sought. But no aircraft came close enough to discern them in the water.

Some time during the afternoon of the eighth another survivor joined their group. He was Matrose Laskowski, who had escaped with the group from the bow. He was wearing two escape lungs, and was still very fresh. This was the first Degen knew that other men had escaped from the sunken U-boat. Laskowski reported to his captain that among others, both the first and second watch officers had gotten out of the sunken U-boat.

The midsummer heat beat down relentlessly, baking the men and burning their skin. Salt water continually washed over them, stinging chapped lips. They suffered horribly from thirst. Yet somehow, they managed to stay afloat, still huddling together and clinging to the two slender life preservers. For the second time, the sun set upon them.

At last the sea moderated. During the night they caught a lemon and a coconut that were floating by. Maschinistenmaat Ludwig Vaupel smashed open the coconut husk with an oxygen flask from an escape lung, and passed it around so that each man received a swallow of milk and a piece of meat. They took turns sucking the delicious juice of the lemon. Even so, three men became delirious and yelled horribly from their suffering. Three apprentice seamen, Leu, Michalek, and Laskowski, joined the ranks of the dead.

Obersteuermann Kunert supported his captain in the water. Degen's strength was running out. "I seem to recollect that I talked nonsense and that Kunert kept on quieting me. As the sea was still like a pond, I kept up the practice of discarding my life preserver, saying that I would swim to shore. I assumed that with a few strokes I would feel bottom under my feet and would be able to stand up, but every time I tried this I went under. That would bring me to again and I would swim back to my life preserver. This occurrence must have happened many times. Then I lost consciousness."

Their main problem was the Gulf Stream. While the water was warm, and undoubtedly helped preserve them from hypothermia, it was slowly but assuredly carrying the men northward—away from where their U-boat had gone down and where the search for survivors was being concentrated.

A full two days after the sinking, the Navy was still conducting search operations. That morning a blimp, the *K-8*, left the Naval Air Station at Elizabeth City, North Carolina, under the command of Ensign G. S. Middleton, and began its search pattern at the Wimble Shoals Light Buoy. At a steady two knots the nonrigid airship cruised along the Gulf Stream in a northerly course that was determined by a faint oil slick and pieces of debris.

At noon the first survivor was sighted, ninety miles from where the sinking occurred. Jubilantly, a flare was dropped and a radio call went out to the Coast Guard at Elizabeth City. Middleton reported that the sea was calm enough for a float plane to land on the ocean. Soon, two more men were spotted nearby, and a quarter mile away, a fourth. *K-8* cruised at fifty feet and carefully lowered a life raft to the strongest looking survivor, and directed him toward his companions. The airship also dropped food, water, a first aid kit, blankets, and a knife.

Degen regained consciousness when he heard his name called. "About thirty meters away sat Kunert, Vaupel and Grootheer making for me in a white rubber boat. I was taken into the boat as Kunert was about to open a can of pineapple with a knife. Out of a can already opened Grootheer gave me tomatoes to eat, and all the while a Zeppelin airship circled about us."

Once the men appeared to be stabilized, the *K-8* rose and headed further along the slick. At first the aircrew found only three dead bodies. But on the way back to the raft they came across three lone individuals still tenaciously clinging to life, separated from each other by half a mile. The blimp dropped flares beside each one.

By this time the seaplane had arrived. It was piloted by Lieutenant Commander Richard Burke, intrepid rescuer of the *Chenango* survivors. He scouted the area around the blimp. The seven survivors were scattered over an area of eight miles. Delicately, he landed his plane on the water near the farthest German, Mechanikerobergefreiter Werner Seldte, picked him up, then taxied to each of the other two: Mechanikerobergefreiter Gerhardt Schwendel and Mechanikerobergefreiter Bruno Faust. These were the only survivors from the group that had escaped from the bow.

Burke then taxied his plane for five miles until he reached the four men on the raft. In short order the sunburned, oil-soaked men were brought aboard. Among the seven survivors, the only personal effects were four pairs of swimming trunks, two escape lungs, and one rubber life jacket. Three of the men, including the captain, were completely naked.

Out of the forty-three man crew of the *U-701*, only these seven survived.

In the flying boat, a pharmacist's mate tended them with water, coffee, and sandwiches. Degen, delirious and close to death, was given a mild stimulant. He rallied after the hypodermic injection, happy to be alive after the forty-nine hour ordeal.

A bare three hours later, the men underwent interrogation by Naval Intelligence at the Naval Air Station, Norfolk, Virginia. Their resolve was weakened by their condition, and much general information was obtained about their U-boat, the twenty-two day Atlantic crossing, and their operations in U.S. territorial waters. The Navy was satisfied that the men were not lying because their stories of attacks coincided with what was already known from previous reports.

Degen verified that he had shelled a cutter off Cape Hatteras (the *YP-389*), had torpedoed the *British Freedom*, had been depth charged by one of the convoy's escorts (the *St. Augustine*), and had torpedoed the *Wm. Rockefeller*. The Navy was satisfied with his sincerity. But at no time did Degen ever admit to laying mines in the approaches to the Chesapeake Bay. This information was not obtained until postwar records were debriefed. Under interrogation, "Degen held the opinion that shallow waters presented opportunities to mine-laying U-boats, both in the paths of convoys and at harbor entrances. He admitted the possibility of large U-boats carrying mines, but said such matters are held secret."

So, by stating what he suspected was already known by U.S. Intelligence, and telling his interrogators what they wanted to hear, Degen managed to keep secret his mine-laying operations.

Degen also stated wryly that, although twelve husbands or fathers went down with the boat, the seven survivors were bachelors.

After interrogation, the men were transferred to the Naval Hospital where they slowly regained their strength. Their skin peeled off in great patches, as they were all suffering severe sunburn. Medical authorities believed that if they had not been coated by their own diesel oil, their sunburn would have been much worse.

On July 11, Lieutenant Harry Kane and his bomber crew visited with Degen, to pay their respects to the captain and to those men who had died so terribly. For publicity purposes, the five Americans posed with the U-boat commander for photographs. Despite his pajamas and peeling face, Degen maintained his heraldic bearing.

The next day the Germans boarded a train for Fort Devens, Massachusetts, "where we shall now pass the days of our detention as prisoners of war. We are being correctly handled and receive good treatment. There is plenty of good food to eat."

The seven German survivors did not remain at Fort Devens. They were split up and transferred to various POW camps across the country. But they did receive good treatment for the next four years. They were finally released in June 1946 and returned to their native land.

It is interesting to note that forty years after their first meeting, Kane flew to Germany to meet his old adversary, Degen. Both men were retired, both were grandfathers, both recalled the war as a dim and distant memory of their youth. Neither harbored any animosity. In 1942, when their countries were at war, they were enemies. In 1982, they were allies and friends.

After months of false claims and a plethora of commendations and promotions, a U-boat had finally been sunk by an airplane. Nor was this merely a matter of luck. Partly it was due to the continued evaluations that followed each unconfirmed sinking. Partly it was due to experience gained by flying crews making hundreds of offshore missions. Partly it was due to increased training. But mostly it was due to the sheer numbers of aircraft available for coastal patrol. Army, Navy, and Coast Guard planes flew overlapping sorties that filled the sky with the noise of unmuffled engines.

Since almost all shipping was running in convoy along the shore, U-boats were lured to shallow water like moths to a flame. Here they had to run the gauntlet of destroyers, patrol boats, and antisubmarine trawlers. When they came up for air, they had to watch the skies with the intensity of gophers watching for hawks. They could not relax their vigil for a moment. Whereas five and a half months earlier they were enemies to be feared, now they were in fear themselves.

Attacks against U-boats became more aggressive. On the twelfth of July, Coast Guard plane #5772, pilot Lieutenant E. B. Ing, drove down another U-boat off Cape Hatteras. He saw a disturbance in the water he identified as the swirl of a diving U-boat. Ing figured he had been spotted. Instead of pressing home an abortive attack, he lingered high over the area and waited patiently for the U-boat to reappear. He was rewarded by the wake of a periscope. Because the water off the Carolinas is so clear, once overhead he could discern the entire outline of the U-boat. He dived down at high speed, leveled off at two hundred feet, and dropped two three-hundred-twenty-five-pound depth charges that straddled the cigar-shaped hull. He observed that the bow of the U-boat was kicked sharply to the side by the force of the blast, and later noticed a light film of oil on the surface of the sea. He had severely damaged the undersea marauder.

The next day, Army plane B-17-E patrolled the same sector. Captain A. H. Tuttle "established an instrument contact and almost at once sighted a submarine." It appeared to languish on the surface almost motionless. It was either the same U-boat damaged the day before by Ing, or another caught completely offguard. Tuttle called to his bombardier to get ready. The plane swooped down from eight hundred feet, leveled off at two hundred, and, still traveling at one hundred sixty miles per hour, released six depth charges in rapid succession. The U-boat was straddled with explosives. The tail gunner saw the U-boat roll first to one side, then to the other as plumes of water shot into the air.

After the U-boat submerged, Tuttle saw unidentifiable debris and a large oil slick staining the clear blue water. He circled the spot for five hours, keeping a visual as well as a radar check on the area. Despite the severity of the attacks, and the proximity of the depth charge explosions, the U-boat survived. But its patrol was prematurely ended. As it headed for home, it left behind an ocean that was lorded over by antisubmarine warfare units. Its report to Doenitz could have nothing but a paralyzing effect on the future of the U-boat war in the ESF.

Into this angry wasp's nest charged the *U-576*, Kapitanleutnant Hans-Dieter Heinicke. On the night of the fifteenth, he surfaced in the middle of Convoy KS-520. The nineteen vessel convoy had assembled in the Chesapeake Bay for the journey south. The escort consisted of two destroyers, two patrol boats, a Canadian corvette, and two Coast Guard cutters. In addition, a Navy blimp tagged along in the air, while patrol bombers offered fast offensive protection.

Heinicke had much to contend with. The heavily escorted convoy system offered very little opportunity for a sneak attack, much less a sustained assault. Every Allied warrior knew his part and played it well. Even though the sun was still adorning the afternoon sky, Heinicke could not afford to pass up such a golden opportunity. He let loose a barrage of torpedoes that scythed through the parallel columns with deadly accuracy.

First struck was the *Chilore*, lead ship in the second column. At thirty-second intervals the *J.A. Mowinckel*, second ship in the fourth column, and the *Bluefields*, third ship in the fifth column, were hit. This was the textbook convoy attack, shot from the leading forward quarter, so that any torpedo that missed the closest target had a prime opportunity of hitting an overlapping target

in the farther columns. Heinicke had delivered it fault-
lessly.

The *Bluefields* went down in four minutes; her crew
was rescued by the USS *Spry*.

The *Chilore* suffered no casualties. Her forepeak was
blown in and flooding, but not dangerously. The *J.A.
Mowinckel* shuddered with the shock that tore a twenty-
by-twenty foot hole in her stern and disabled the steering
gear; one seaman was killed by the blast, twenty others
injured. Both ships lost way as the rest of the convoy
dispersed.

Immediately following the detonations, the bow of the
*U-576* broke the surface in the middle of the convoy.
Possibly it was forced upward by the nearby concus-
sions, or perhaps Heinicke had not compensated
adequately for the sudden weight loss of so many torpedoes. He might even have thought that the merchantmen
would shield him from view of the escorts that
surrounded the convoy.

In any case, the U-boat was spotted from the air by
two alert Navy planes, and by the gun crew of the
steamship *Unicoi*. As the planes dived on their target, the
deck gun of the *Unicoi* burst into action: one well placed
shot hit the U-boat aft. The *Unicoi* ceased firing as the
planes dived in for the kill.

From the action report: "Ens. Lewis attacked immediately from ahead, dropping two Mark 17 depth charges
in salvo with a fifty-foot depth setting which detonated
in a perfect straddle of the conning tower. One charge
actually slid off the starboard side of the submarine. At
the instant of detonation the submarine's deck was just
under the surface. The submarine's speed was about three
knots at this time. After this attack the submarine was
observed to veer to the right and to list to starboard.
Black oil and bubbles came to the surface. Ens. Webb
attacked shortly after the previous spray had subsided
diving from the starboard quarter and dropping two Mark
17 depth charges in a salvo with a fifty-foot depth setting.
Both charges detonated very close to the submarine on
the starboard side just forward of the conning tower. At
this time the submarine was sinking fast and was

completely under at the time of the second set of explosions but with little headway. Shortly thereafter the scene of action was completely covered with oil and debris making it difficult to determine whether this was from the submarine or the sinking ship.''

Sometime during the confusion, several merchantmen opened up with their deck guns against the exposed conning tower. Afterwards, the U.S. destroyer *Ellis* made a well defined sound contact, and drove in with two full patterns of depth charges.

The *U-576* went straight to the bottom; there were no survivors.

The last reports Doenitz received from Heinicke were "13/7/42 damaged from A/C bombs. Am attempting repairs, moving off to eastward," and, the next day, "Repairs not possible." It seems as if, this time, Lieutenant Ing got his man, and succeeded in weakening him for his final conflict.

Three U-boats were sunk in twelve days. This was not just a turning point in the U-boat campaign, it was virtually the end. From this point on, U-boat action in the ESF was anticlimactic: a mopping up operation. Planes, armed merchant ships, and well equipped escorts, all working in unison, were too much for the lone gray wolves.

Despite a well planned attack, Heinicke had not been able to follow up the onslaught as U-boats had in the past. The *Chilore* was listing to port, the *J.A. Mowinckel* down by the stern. From the bridge of the *J.A. Mowinckel*, the Commodore of the convoy, Captain Nichols took charge. He ordered the U.S. destroyer *McCormick* to transfer her doctor to the *J.A. Mowinckel* to attend to the wounded. Now a curious incident occurred.

Joseph Sokolowski, a wiper on the *J.A. Mowinckel* reports that he "was wounded in the left shoulder by flying metal fragments and was blown overboard. I swam for about twenty minutes without a life jacket; then a crew member of a passing tanker spotted me and tossed down a life preserver. About an hour later I was sighted from the destroyer USS *McCormick*. Her crew threw me a line, pulled me aboard, and administered first aid. Afterward, the *McCormick* came alongside the *J.A. Mowinckel*. Most of my shipmates thought I was lost. They were amazed at my sudden appearance aboard another vessel.''

The convoy regrouped under the guidance of the Vice Commodore, and continued on course. The *Chilore* and the *J.A. Mowinckel* headed for shoal water.

Captain Harold Griffiths, master, described the condition on the *J.A. Mowinckel*: ''A survey of the damage ascertained that we had been hit about eight feet below the waterline and right aft, the explosion tearing a twenty-by-twenty-foot hole in the plates and blowing through the after peak and the steering engine room. The steering engine and capstans, the galley, the messrooms, and the after gun platform were wrecked.

''There was a six-inch hole in the after bulkhead in the engineroom. All of the rivets were leaking badly and the engineroom began filling up. Chief Engineer Cecil M. Guthrie ordered his men to stuff a mattress in the hole and brace it there with planks, but the water kept coming in with considerable force. The chief engineer had to put all his pumps on the bilge to try to keep the water down.

''He found, however, that both engines were operable and I therefore decided to make for shore in the hope of saving my ship. As the steering engine was useless it would be necessary to steer with the twin screws. I ordered Chief Mate Reckstin to drop a mooring line over the starboard quarter to assist with the steering. He also attempted to trim the ship by shifting water from No. 6 starboard to No. 3 port tank.''

The *Spry* acted as escort and led the way for the ore carrier and the tanker. After all the peregrinations following the dispersal of the convoy, the lagging of the damaged merchant ships, and the antisubmarine activity of the *Spry*, there was some doubt as to the actual position of the vessels when they turned and headed for the safe anchorage of Hatteras Inlet. Since a minefield protected the approaches, it was critically important that the swept channel be entered from a specified direction. The Commodore was nominally in charge of this three vessel detached convoy. His "dead reckoning" course was laid out with an erroneous starting position, with the result that the ships were not following the course he thought they were.

To complicate matters, for a variety of reasons the three boats that were supposed to be patrolling the minefield perimeter were not there at the time the merchantmen arrived. Although last in the jagged line, the *Chilore* was the first to discover the truth. A tremendous explosion occurred on the port side amidship, followed a moment later by another further aft. Then the *J.A. Mowinckel* was struck on the starboard side by No. 2 tank. The Commodore thought they were under another U-boat attack, and passed on to Captain Griffiths the order to abandon ship.

On the *J.A. Mowinckel* everything was orderly. Captain Griffiths: "All the injured men were placed in the boats and as comfortably cared for as possible. I put all the secret documents and codes in a special sealed container and threw them overboard. All four lifeboats were safely launched."

Some of the *Chilore*'s crew panicked. Even though Captain George Moodie had issued no such order, a few men took it upon themselves to abandon ship. In their hurry to get away, two men were drowned as one of the lifeboats capsized. The captain and most of the crew remained aboard until the next day.

By this time it was dark. Two of the *J.A. Mowinckel*'s lifeboats were found by a Coast Guard cutter and towed to Ocracoke Inlet. The others rowed until they reached Ocracoke on their own. Six days later, Seaman Raymond Wolfe, a member of the Naval gun crew, died in the hospital from wounds received in the torpedo blast.

The debacle was not yet over. Over the course of the next few days, as the two ships swung at anchor, a channel was swept through the minefield so the merchantmen could be safely moved. As the tug *Keshena* lashed herself to the stern of the *J.A. Mowinckel*, to act as rudder as the *J.P. Martin* carried out the tow, she contacted another of the defensive mines and was blown up and sunk. Two men were killed.

Finally, both ships were towed safely into Hatteras Inlet and beached. Several days later, while repairs were underway and after the *J.A. Mowinckel* was refloated, she dragged anchor and drifted back into the minefield. No. 7 starboard main tank was blown in and flooded. After temporary patches put the vessel in seaworthy condition, her repair odyssey began. She was towed around the Diamond Shoals and taken to Norfolk, repaired well enough to get her to Baltimore, repaired again so she could be moved to New York, and there refitted permanently. She was not put back into service until March 12, 1943.

The route of the *Chilore* was not quite so circuitous. While rounding Cape Henry, a watertight bulkhead gave way and she capsized in shallow water. Torpedoed once, mined twice, and foundered for good: ultimately, Heinicke got the credit.

With the loss of the *U-576*, the six-month reign of terror that began with the sinking of the *Norness* had gone full cycle. The American public knew nothing of these latest U-boat sinkings, and might only have shrugged them off anyway after reading all the "cry wolf" episodes of the previous half year. With the strict news curtailment, it was difficult for the public to understand what was going on off the East Coast. For the average American citizen, the U-boat war, if it had ever existed, was long since out of mind.

Since most ships were now armed and carried a full Naval gun crew, even an unescorted merchantman had a good chance of winning a surface engagement against a U-boat's deck gun. The U-boat was much more vulnerable to shelling, since one well-placed round could puncture its pressure hull and prevent it from making its escape underwater. The merchant ship had the advantage in sighting a fully surfaced U-boat, since a lookout in the crow's nest was a hundred feet above the water, as opposed to the U-boat lookout's ten or fifteen feet. Nor was it necessary for the merchantman to sink a U-boat in order to effect a successful retreat.

Running on its diesels, a Type VII-C could make seventeen knots. Forced underwater by gunfire, it could make only seven and a half. In order for a U-boat to press home a successful torpedo attack, it had to lie in wait in the path of an oncoming victim. If it found itself adjacent to or aft of an unsuspecting merchantman, it had to race ahead of its target on a parallel course until it reached a favorable firing position. Therefore, an alert, armed merchant ship could find a way to outwit an undersea predator in the oceanwide cat-and-mouse game.

Close to shore, land-based aircraft kept the U-boats ducking for cover, rarely giving them the opportunity to surface long enough to recharge batteries. Some U-boat commanders returned to Germany with long-winded reports of short surface intervals broken by terrifying crash dives as planes swooped down from the clouds: a gambit that went on for hours, or days, until both boat and crew were utterly exhausted.

Added to this was the intelligence factor. With the breaking of the German machine ciphers, and information gleaned through Ultra, communication between Doenitz and his wolf packs not only offered insight into how the Admiral was running the U-boat war, it often gave the exact location of a U-boat that was transmitting its position to U-boat command.

The U.S. took this data a step farther by assigning a submarine tracking officer to make course interpolations based on reported sightings as well as enemy transmissions. On July 22, a U-boat was spotted in the Georges Bank area. The STO laid out a plot like a child's connect-the-dot drawing, indicating a probable course. A Q-ship, the USS *Captor*, was dispatched to an intercept area where it was suspected the U-boat would arrive two days hence. Sure enough, as the disguised merchant ship patrolled the designated tract, a torpedo crossed her bow. The U-boat was not sunk, but the value of the Submarine Tracking Officer was accentuated.

On the twenty-seventh, the last U-boat casualty of the year within the boundaries of the ESF occurred off the coast of Maine. The fifty-four ton Canadian fishing boat *Lucille M.* was working her way from Lockport, Nova Scotia, to the Georges Bank. She lay adrift in the gentle Atlantic swells, awaiting daylight so the eleven man crew could resume fishing. The sound of running diesel engines carried across the water. Captain Percy Richardson thought it must be a patrol boat, but in actuality it was the *U-89*, Kapitanleutnant Dietrich Lohmann, charging its batteries.

At 0300, the *U-89* opened fire on the lowly schooner. The first shot was high, hitting the sails and the top hamper. This was enough to rouse the fishermen into action. Under an intense hail of gunfire, they jumped into two dories and pulled away from the boat. During the first two minutes of the attack, the *U-89* pumped twenty shells into the *Lucille M.* from less than a hundred yards away. This was accompanied by irregular bursts from twin machine guns.

Four men were wounded. The stern of the schooner was shot completely away, the wheelhouse was demolished, shells punctured the hull and hit the blocks of ice within. Captain Richardson could hear the gun crew working the breech and the cartridge cases clanging to the deck. The dories had water but no food. The fishermen rowed for thirty-six hours until they reached the safety of Cape Sable Island, off the southern tip of Nova Scotia.

In this pathetic action for the German war effort, the *U-89* victimized one wooden schooner and twenty-one swordfish. What had begun so triumphantly six and a half months earlier ended ignominiously.

# AUGUST–DECEMBER

"Each month about 75,000 seamen transport ten tons of supplies for each soldier our country has fighting overseas, and bear in mind we are fighting on fronts as far apart as New Guinea and north Africa, as Iceland and the Solomons. Day after day, week after week, the ships ply steadily through storms and mine fields and the concentrated attack of the submarine wolf pack. Our protective technique is better than it was, but the casualties are the evidence that it must be further improved. Over 4,500 seamen, about six percent of those engaged, are dead or missing from enemy action, a greater number proportionately than the combined losses of our armed forces. That figure alone, however, does not give the full measure of the merchant seamen's courage. To the valorous deeds under fire must be added the tenacity with which they make the long, slow voyages with the grim knowledge that torment or death may strike at any moment."

> Captain Edward Macauley, USN
> Deputy War Shipping Administration
> Propellor Club of the United States
> May 22, 1943

While the keel of the U-boat campaign against the ESF had been effectively broken, there was no relaxation of defensive measures. It was only the continued aggressive patrolling that kept the wolves at bay. Antisubmarine warfare was an ongoing process. The slightest hint that a prowling U-boat might be in the area brought on concerted depth charge attacks from planes and surface craft. After action, evaluations often revealed that the objects of attack were wrecks or fish (whales, porpoises, and large schools of small fish), but this did not meet censure. The Navy maxim was "attack first."

They did. The idea was to nitpick the U-boats to death, forcing the enemy underwater so it could not set up its target bearing transmitter, so it was forced to use up its oxygen and power reserves. The constant vigil was expensive in terms of manpower, equipment, and explosives, but it paid off.

Blimps had become a common sight to beachcombers and seaside vacationers. The slow but dependable gas bags offered an ideal platform for observation. With radio communication, they could bring in a flotilla of fast planes or sub chasers to bomb or depth charge any suspected enemy contact: no oil streak, wake, or swirl was safe. Instrument contacts (echo ranging, hydrophone, and radar) were not just investigated, they were trounced. The Atlantic Ocean was a dangerous place for anything larger than an ocean sunfish or basking sea turtle. Doenitz went so far as to admit publicly that the blimp was one of the greatest hazards his U-boatmen faced.

Because of the clarity of the Gulf Stream waters, especially off the Carolinas, Georgia, and Florida, pilots from their mobile aeries often spotted shipwrecks resting on the white, desertlike ocean floor, and mistook them for enemy submarines. Many a sunken hulk was pounded to pieces by depth charges. Sound contacts that echoed a ping similar to that of a U-boat's hull were repeatedly depth charged. Some of these intact wrecks were leftovers from the First World War.

Then someone came up with the brilliant idea that German submarines could *hide* alongside a previously torpedoed vessel. This thought undoubtedly originated in the minds of those officers debriefing action reports, and who made recommendations that up-to-date charts showing wreck sites should be kept on board patrol craft to eliminate the attacks on known shipwrecks. Their own paranoia resulted in the mistaken belief that an ingenious U-boat commander would take a chance on steering his boat blindly into the shadow of a sunken tanker or freighter. So they went on blowing up these hulks on the off chance that the Germans were using them as rest stops and hideaways.

Germany did not have sufficiently sophisticated detection gear that would allow them to try such a tactic with any hope of success. However, it must be conceded that Naval Intelligence had no idea of what technological advances had been made by German scientists, so they could not afford to take any chances.

Merchant seamen had become so used to having ships shot out from under them that the crew of one vessel actually refused rescue because the merchantman that picked them up was not "going our way." The crew of the *West Notus* may have been expressing post-survival bravado, but those of the *Mattawin* certainly were not. They accepted gasoline, cigarettes, and a navigational chart from an African bound freighter, and nursed their lifeboat's auxiliary engine with Vaseline and massage oil for sixty-three hours during their hundred mile journey. Their engine conked out twenty yards off a New England beach.

The one-hundred-ten-foot, twenty-one-knot, wooden hulled submarine chasers were coming off the production line at a prodigious rate. Beginning in the summer of 1942, delivery increased rapidly until by the end of the war some four hundred fifty were in service. As the U-boats were beaten off American shores, and slipped into the Caribbean and the Gulf, the SCs went after them. Only one substantiated U-boat sinking was attributed to SC actions, but their real value lay as a deterrent: their constant and ubiquitous presence kept the U-boats submerged and out of the rink.

On July 25, Secretary of the Navy Frank Knox issued the following proclamation: "Patriotic yachtsman and small-boat operators now have the opportunity which they have been so earnestly seeking: to serve their country and combat its enemies in the sea-going manner for which their experience fits them.

"The Coast Guard has for some months been taking numbers of yachtsmen and their boats into the Coast Guard Reserve and its civilian auxiliary. And now many more are needed. The process of enrollment is to be speeded to the utmost.

"The Navy and Coast Guard hope to add one thousand small boats to the Auxiliary Patrol. These boats are needed right now—not only for the captain of the Port and Harbor Patrol duties but for actual offensive operations against enemy submarines.

"Those Americans who feel themselves qualified to perform this type of duty are asked to get full details of enrollment from the nearest Coast Guard office."

Contrary to the usual stiff military enlistment practices, the Navy announced that "physical requirements are limited only to immediate ability of the men to serve." This was no mere placebo to mollify fishermen outraged at German encroachment on their fishing preserves. "Boats found to be qualified will be equipped with radio, armament and suitable anti-submarine devices as rapidly as possible." Like their revolutionary forefathers who had taken up the arms of war, American civilians were prepared to trade their plowshares and trawler gear for swords and depth charge racks.

The building of the "mosquito fleet" is what freed the larger military vessels for convoy duty, and it was the escorted convoy which forced the U-boats to move into unprotected southern waters. As the lag in East Coast defense measures grew shorter, antisubmarine craft jumped onto the same southbound conveyor belt the U-boats were on, and nipped at German rudders in the Caribbean and the Gulf.

At a Senate committee meeting discussing the U-boat menace and the Navy's counter-measures, Knox admitted that no U-boat had ever been sunk by aircraft. (This was prior to the sinking of the *U-701*.) When one Senator reminded him that he himself had decorated a pilot (Donald Mason) for just such an act, Knox had to retract his statement. It was obvious, then, that the Navy knew the facts from the hype, and that the long list of U-boats supposedly sunk in the ESF was just another fish tale.

In order to prove to the public the reality of Allied success against the U-boat campaign, and to increase civilian morale, the government released a belated bulletin backed up with heart-wrenching photographs. Previously, the only quasi-authentic tale of U-boat annihilation was a brief Navy communique issued three weeks after the triumph over the *U-85*. (The names of both the *Roper* and the *U-85* were withheld.) It differed little from other pumped-up Navy communiques except that it disclosed in tantalizingly meager detail the capture of part of the crew, when in fact they had all been depth charged to death.

(Coincidentally, this story was released only two days before the genuine capture of the survivors from the *U-352*—an amazing if unplanned prescience.)

Now, three *months* after the event, the Navy revealed the sad fate of the crew of the *U-85* (again, without mention of the U-boat's name): interred rather than interned. Written with glib pathos, the account left out any mention of when the U-boat was destroyed, nor did it distinguish this story from the previously released story that claimed the false capture of survivors. (They read as two separate events.) It was as if the Navy were saving the story for a rainy day.

If anything, it served as an advertisement for the aid of civilian pilots and volunteers with their own radio-equipped planes. As Americans have shown in the past, when the chips are down the people are even stronger in answering the call.

Rear Admiral Emory Land, Chairman of the Maritime Commission, was pessimistic. "You can't cure the submarine menace. You can ameliorate it. That's the history of the last war and that's going to be the history of this war."

Other people thought differently. In order to fill "the vital need for more officers for American ships," the State of New York wanted its State Maritime Academy and those of other states to receive government subsidies that could "offer the same inducements to prospective students as is done by the United States maritime academies."

The ship building industry was doing its best to supply ships for those newly trained officers to command. On National Maritime Day, May 22, 1942, in nineteen shipyards across the nation, *twenty-seven* ships slid down the ways. Every newly constructed ship was armed, and supplied with a trained Naval gun crew.

Ships were being sunk at a rate of just over one a day. To help private companies share the burden of loss of those vessels to Axis powers, the Appropriations Committee increased the marine and war risk insurance fund of the War Shipping Administration by $210,000,000.

To help protect the sailors of those vessels, stringent rules went into effect involving lifeboat drills, new and better life saving equipment, and provisioning of lifeboats and rafts. Portable radio units were to be included as part of the survival gear.

Blackouts among shore communities were strictly enforced. Dimouts as far inland as fifty-five miles were essential because of sky-glow. Said torpedoed Seaman Leon Haskell to War Council members, sailors "cursed every bit of light from shore that silhouettes ships and makes the ships targets for U-boats," and, civilians should "stop griping about the gasoline shortage and start protecting the ships, supplies and troops that have to reach overseas bases."

As proof of the effectiveness of the antisubmarine campaign, not a single ship of any kind was sunk or damaged in the ESF for the rest of the year. The concentration of vessels forming up for convoys brought the inevitable accident through collision, and groundings took place with fair regularity because of inshore routing, but this was acceptable in light of the alternative.

By August, Brazil was totally frustrated with its persistent attempts to find a peaceful but honorable way of avoiding the clash of German torpedoes. On the twenty-second, Brazil declared war on the Axis powers. Chile, despite the depredations it had suffered at the mercy of unrestricted U-boat warfare, remained neutral throughout the war. The fascist element dominated the Argentine government until Germany's defeat was imminent; in the spring of 1945, Argentina opted for the side of the winners.

Aside from continued sightings of periscopes and the detection of unknown submerged objects, the only genuine U-boat operation conducted within the bounds of the ESF was the September mining of the Chesapeake Bay approaches. Because of persistent German propaganda, some people today still believe that U-boats *entered* the Chesapeake Bay and drove as far north as the Potomac River where they observed the lights of Washington, DC. Like Hardegen's portrayal of his infiltration into New York Harbor, this is the sheerest fantasy. The seven mines detonated by *YMS 55* on September 12, 13, and 16, were well off Cape Henry.

However, the truth of the situation is even more fascinating than the myth. As the Plot Room of the District Intelligence Office followed the U-boats' tracks, it was noticed that a decided lack of U-boat activity occurred before and after the discovery of the mines. The explanation: the Germans knew that any other kind of action would result in fierce countermeasures with an almost guaranteed result.

But the real intrigue unfolded when neutral vessels were inspected at the port of Baltimore, and found to have different routing instructions than those issued by the United Nations. The Greek steamship *Helene Kulukundis* and the Swiss steamship *Calanda* had been instructed by the Swiss Legation in Portugal to avoid the specific area where the mines had been swept up—and these instructions were dated two months prior to the actual mining.

The Coastal Information Section's report stated, "It is most unusual that a neutral nation, supposedly with no first-hand information of the approaches to a belligerent harbor, would undertake to issue routing instructions for the entrance to the harbor in direct contravention to the instructions issued by nations charged with keeping a channel into such harbor open and free of mines."

Clearly, Germany was trying hard not to antagonize

the European neutrals by telling them which places to avoid. Just as clearly, Doenitz planned well in advance exactly where these mines were to be sown. Because of rigorous submarine defenses, it was the only way he could use his U-boats off the U.S. East Coast without losing them.

Chairman Vinson of the House Naval Committee admirably summed up the condition of antisubmarine warfare operations when he stated that the organization "has now passed through its period of growing pains, is well established and is functioning efficiently."

Once again, Doenitz was better informed than U.S. intelligence. He already knew this.

# 1943-1945

> "If Hitler and his partners in crime can be said to have made one outstanding error, it was in neglecting to reckon with the courage of the men who go to sea in American ships."
> Rear Admiral Howard Vickery
> Vice Chairman of the Maritime Commission
> May 22, 1942

Unrestricted U-boat warfare was still going strong worldwide, and merchant seamen were still dying horrible deaths overseas. With the Liberty ship program in full swing, more tonnage was coming off the ways than was being sunk. There were always more men to replace those lost in pursuit of their dangerous trade.

The ESF was a secure area. The skies and sea lanes overflowed with heavily armed patrol craft that struck at a moment's notice at anything that did not respond in kind to coded transmissions. U-boat sightings still occurred, but the raiders were beaten underwater so soundly that none encroached closer than a hundred miles to shore, and none was able to press home any attacks.

After the shelling of the *Lucille M.*, the next real scare did not occur until March 27, 1943, when the Coast Guard cutter *Catamount* (CG-85006) exploded and sank some thirty miles southeast of Ambrose Lightship. Five of the eleven man crew were blown clear, but only one survived the night by clinging to a piece of wooden wreckage. The *Charles B. Aycock* picked him up the next day, and alerted Naval Intelligence of the casualty.

While rescue craft searched for other survivors, the *Esso Manhattan* came to grief only a few miles away when "a great shock was felt throughout the vessel." The crew safely abandoned ship. The tanker folded up like a jackknife, with the bow touching the stern. The two parts separated and drifted away. Eventually, both halves were towed into New York and reunited.

Since these incidents took place in a milling area for

ships waiting to join convoys, the obvious cause was either enemy mines or torpedoes. The port of New York was closed for two days for investigation and mine sweeping operations. No mines were found. Ultimately, the blowing up of the *Catamount* was determined to have been caused by a faulty gas line that had been giving the cutter trouble. The *Esso Manhattan* broke up due to structural failure.

The Submarine Tracking Officer continued to correlate data. On May 1, he proclaimed that only one U-boat was then operating within the ESF: "one recently unlocated, probably patrolling Savannah to Hatteras." A massive search by air and sea craft turned up nothing. High winds and heavy seas that swept along the coast on May 3 slowed down the hunt.

The bad weather that day also hit hard Convoy NG-359, New York to Guantanamo Bay, Cuba. By 1700, the *Oneida* fell behind as she took on more water than her pumps could discharge. At 2239, a distress call went out with the monition that she was sinking fast by the stern. Since she was then some eighty miles off Norfolk, Virginia, Captain Carl Flygare turned his ship for the beach. The shaft alley flooded; slowly, the water in the engine room reached the floor plates. By 0230 of the fourth, all hope was lost. Captain Flygare ordered abandon ship. A lifeboat and three rafts were lowered into tumultuous seas.

While the men were going over the side, a white light focused on the *Oneida*'s port quarter. Some of the men reported hearing two dull thuds, after which the vessel went down quickly by the stern. However, it is unlikely that torpedoes were fired at the foundering freighter since no U-boat reported such action. The sixty-two men fought to keep their craft afloat in storm-ridden seas. When they were rescued seventeen hours later by the newly commissioned U.S. destroyer escort *Andres*, only half the ship's complement could be found.

On May 5, the *Panam* was blown up and sunk. But in this instance it *was* due to enemy action. The *U-129*, Kapitanleutnant Hans Witt, had overstepped the boundary of the Bermuda Area, where he was operating, and got as close as two hundred miles from the North Carolina coast. He chanced across the path of Convoy NK-538, Norfolk to Louisiana. The convoy was so heavily guarded that there was no opportunity to launch an attack without suffering sure destruction.

The *Panam* developed engine trouble, lost speed, and was soon left behind in the darkness. By morning, her capable engineers got the engine back on line. The Panamanian tanker struggled along in rough seas. At 0800, a torpedo blast blew in the port bulkhead of the engine room, completing the damage that had only hours before been repaired, and killing two duty personnel. The radio was wrecked by the explosion. Ten minutes later, another torpedo struck the vessel; it exploded amidships, wrecking the pump room and buckling deck plates. The men barely scrambled away in lifeboats before the ship sank beneath the waves.

An Army B-25 bomber reported sighting three lifeboats at 1847, and put out a call for help. *SC-664* intercepted the transmission, dropped back from the convoy, and picked up the survivors. This was Witt's only encroachment into the ESF. He quickly retreated to the broad, safer reaches between Bermuda and the Caribbean.

Kapitanleutnant Klaus Bargsten, *U-521*, cruised into the ESF at the end of the month. He started his patrol off the North Carolina coast, then prowled northward until he was as close as a hundred miles off Virginia. While Bargsten lay in his bunk reading a travel book, immersed in a chapter entitled "Middletown, U.S.A.", the sound operator reported propeller noises. Since it was daytime, and because of the previous sightings of planes and destroyers, the U-boat maintained a depth of a hundred feet.

Overhead, Convoy NG-355 was on its way from New York to Guantanamo Bay, Cuba, when one of her escorts, the *PC-565*, picked up a sound contact. She veered off for a routine check, set her depth charges according to her ranging gear to explode at one hundred feet, and dropped a standard five depth charge harassment pattern.

Inside the *U-521*, the accuracy of the depth charges

shattered instruments, knocked out breakers, blew out the lights, stopped the electric motors, and disabled the diving planes and rudder. Cold seawater spurted into the conning tower through ruptured pressure gauges. Amid the debris and darkness, Bargsten gave the order to dive for cover.

After a few seconds, Oberleutnant (Ing.) Henning reported that the boat was sinking. It was already down to five hundred feet and dropping rapidly. Even though it did not make sense to Bargsten that the U-boat could plummet so quickly on an even keel, he gave the order to blow all ballast. The main depth gauge must have been knocked askew by the depth charge blast for, before he knew it, the *U-521* broke the surface. Bargsten snapped open the conning tower hatch and rushed outside to assess the situation.

The *PC-565* was only a quarter mile away. She opened up with her 20-mm gun, and turned to ram. Shells burst on and around the U-boat's conning tower. The *PC-565*'s gun jammed. The USS *Brisk* let loose with her deck gun, but got only one shot off before the *PC-565* got in her line of fire.

Realizing that his boat was done for, Bargsten shouted down the conning tower to open the sea cocks and abandon ship. He saw Henning climbing up the ladder, but before the engineering officer reached the hatch, the U-boat suddenly sank out from under the captain's feet. The last thing Bargsten saw was a maelstrom of water pouring into the open conning tower hatch. Then the *U-521* was gone, and Bargsten was left floating in the ocean.

With professional conduct the *PC-565* turned as the U-boat slipped beneath the waves, ran a parallel course, led the swirl by a hundred feet, and dropped another depth charge. Huge bubbles of air rose to the surface, followed by iridescent slicks of oil. Chunks of freshly broken wood and pieces of vegetable fiber littered the sea.

Bargsten was the sole survivor. Several large pieces of human flesh were recovered, leading to the belief that other German sailors had been making a free ascent when the last depth charge went off among them.

A week later, Kapitanleutnant Friedrich Markworth entered the ESF in Zapp's old boat, the *U-66*. The duck shoot days of early 1942 were long gone, but Markworth managed to make a couple marks and get out alive. On June 10, he saw through his periscope the first of the T-2 tankers built for the Maritime Commission only a year before. The *Esso Gettysburg* sported two guns, bow and stern, and a typical twenty-seven man armed guard in addition to her forty-five man merchant crew. She was en route from Atreco, Texas, to Philadelphia, Pennsylvania, with 119,726 barrels of crude oil.

A joint report compiled by Chief Mate Herman Kastberg, Second Mate Thomas H. Chapman, and Third Mate Victor Crescenzo, stated that "the ship was suddenly struck by two torpedoes on the port side, about four seconds apart. The first torpedo struck in the vicinity of Nos. 6 and 7 tanks and the second torpedo at the forward part of the engineroom space. Immediately the vessel burst into flames and almost instantly settled by the stern.

"When the torpedoes struck, Second Mate Chapman left the bridge to put the sextant and chronometer in No. 2 lifeboat. He hurried back to the bridge, from where it was observed that the fire was sweeping rapidly forward.

"The second mate then launched Nos. 1 and 2 life rafts and proceeded toward No. 1 lifeboat, which was being lowered into the water with the assistance of Chief Mate Kastberg and Third Mate Crescenzo. The second mate joined them to lend a hand and the boat was about a foot above the water when the falls suddenly jammed and the heat and flames became so intense that the men in this group were forced to leave and run forward. They dived from the bow into the water. Two other men dived from the stern of the ship."

Kastberg was among a group of six who had to swim for it. "Suddenly a shark was among us. As I had previously got rid of my shoes, I felt him brush past my bare feet. Only three of us had life jackets, and we were supporting the other men. The shark circled off toward the ship, but came back again and charged. Chapman grabbed a knife, but we cautioned him against using it except as a last resort. We all kicked and splashed and the shark again swerved away, but a few minutes later he made a second charge. We repeated the kicking and thrashing in the water and he went off.

"When well clear of the flames we saw some other men swimming to the north of us; we hailed them and told them to join us so that we could all keep together. Soon afterward we saw Third Mate Crescenzo towing Ensign Arnold. Finally, several other men joined us. We decided to swim closer to the burned out area, figuring that the oil would keep the sharks away.

"This decision was fortunate, as it resulted in our finding two lifeboats that had drifted clear of the flames. Chapman and I swam toward the boat which seemed usable—lifeboat No. 3. On the way I picked up a Navy issue first-aid kit; it belonged in the flare box and had apparently been blown overboard. The metal lifeboat was so hot that we had to splash water on it to cool it off. In reality it was just a burned-out hull and it had shipped a considerable quantity of water. The water saved submerged material from the flames. We found the remains of three bodies in the boat." They gave the three unfortunate men a burial at sea.

Over the next few hours they paddled around searching for other survivors, and in all fifteen men finally got aboard the blackened lifeboat. They were nearly a hundred miles off the Georgia coast, drifting quickly in the Gulf Stream. Kastberg administered first aid. Ensign Arnold was "stoical and uncomplaining, waiting until daybreak for treatment of his burns. When there was light enough for me to see clearly, he asked me to cut some of the hanging flesh away from the burns. I did this carefully and applied a dressing from the first-aid kit. I also applied it to two other men."

The seven Navy gunners and eight crewmen were picked up after nineteen hours, by the SS *George Washington*. Among the survivors was Able Seaman Jessie McDonald, who had survived the sinking of the *Wm. Rockefeller*. Fifty-seven fine men, including Captain

Peder Johnson, perished in the torpedoing and subsequent burning of the *Esso Gettysburg*.

Markworth hung around the area, but it was not until three weeks later that he was able to strike again. This time his target was the *Bloody Marsh*, a tanker bound from Houston, Texas, for New York with 106,496 barrels of Navy fuel oil. The position was only thirty-seven miles from where he torpedoed the *Esso Gettysburg*.

In addition to her crew of fifty, and an armed guard unit of twenty-eight to man the bristling array of guns, the *Bloody Marsh* carried the latest in American ingenuity and vacuum tube technology: a torpedo indicator. At 0408 on July 2, a red warning light indicated the approach of a torpedo on the port side. Captain Albert Barnes issued a short blast on the foghorn, then swung his ship hard aport directly into the face of the oncoming torpedo in a maneuver that might have pivoted the tanker out of the way. The ship moved too slowly. The torpedo caught the port quarter of the engine room, blasted in the bulkhead, and killed three duty personnel. The force of the explosion blew off the stack, while fragments of steel wrecked No. 6 lifeboat and demolished the davits. No. 4 lifeboat was holed, but still seaworthy.

One minute later a distress call filled the airwaves like the bleat of a terrified sheep running from a hungry wolf: "SOS SSSS SOS BLOODY MARSH 31-33N/78-55W TORPEDOED." As the engine room flooded, steam escaped into the air and oil poured onto the surface of the sea. Within two minutes of the explosion, the depth of water in the engine room was thirty-five feet. The cold seawater washed against the still-hot boilers, and a minute later the boilers blew up.

During this time, and to the gagging odor of cordite, Lieutenant (jg) Arthur Weber led three of his men to the forward gun. Because of the elevation of the bow due to the settling stern, he could not bring this gun to bear on the now-surfaced U-boat. He rushed to the after gun; his men stuck by his side, loaded a shell, and prepared to fire. The gun jammed. While the men tried to free the shell, the *U-66* fired a second torpedo while cruising at high speed. This one hit the port side amidships, breaking the ship in two. With water lapping at the gun platform, Weber and his men leaped overboard and outswam the suction as the ship went down.

Markworth was still not content, so he fired a couple of shells at the disabled hulk before she slipped beneath the waves. He must not have been watching where he was going, because he rammed No. 1 lifeboat in the stern, raising it out of the water and spilling out several of its occupants. One man thudded onto the U-boat's gray hull and rolled off. All were able to climb back into the boat, none the worse for their dunking.

Five and a half hours later, the Navy blimp *K-52* spotted the survivors and directed rescue craft. First to arrive on the scene was *SC-1048*. She plucked Weber and his three gunners from the sea; they were in good shape after six hours of immersion. Then she rounded up the men in the lifeboats and took them to Charleston, South Carolina.

Where a year before, sinkings had been an almost daily event, now they were barely monthly; and U-boat commanders who had openly flaunted their prowess against unprepared U.S. Naval forces, now skulked silently through the ESF, fearing that they might be spotted and soundly beaten.

On the night of July 28–29, 1943, Kapitanleutnant Paul Siegmann of the *U-230* laid mines off the mouth of the Chesapeake Bay, then slunk quietly away. Inbound and outbound shipping went on as ever, in blissful ignorance. The next night, Oberleutnant zur See Hans Hornkohl of the *U-566* repeated the operation. Both U-boat commanders later reported that they had penetrated deep into Chesapeake Bay to lay their deadly explosives, but none of the mines was ever found. Either they were defective in some way, or they were dropped in accordance with instructions but in an area much more conducive to the U-boat's escape: possibly far at sea.

Hornkohl scuttled away from the coast like a cowering sand crab. Although he broke cover long enough to shoot and run, it was more of a defensive measure.

On August 5, the USS *Plymouth* was escorting a

southbound convoy when she picked up a target on her sound gear. The converted luxury yacht, once the *Alva* owned by W. K. Vanderbilt, veered off to investigate. Lieutenant Ormsby Mitchel ordered the depth charge watch and the gun watches to stand by. While still in her initial turn, a torpedo slammed into her port side forward of midships. The vessel reeled to starboard under the force of the explosion, while the entire port side erupted into flames as diesel oil in the port deep tank was ignited by the blast. The ship rocked back to port, taking on water by the head.

Lieutenant Mitchel was slammed against a bulkhead and sustained serious injuries. That he recovered quickly undoubtedly saved his life. The wheelhouse was a mass of flames, forcing Mitchel out onto the bridgewing. Because the ladder had been carried away by the explosion, he was forced to jump to the well deck, severely cutting his leg. Despite his injuries, he ordered a sailor to hold him up so he could supervise the abandonment of his ship. Possibly remembering the fate of the *Jacob Jones*, he ordered the depth charges put on "safe."

Many men and officers in the forward section were killed instantly. Those who survived the blast got away in lifeboats and life rafts. Lieutenant Mitchel stayed aboard the *Plymouth* until the vessel sank, two minutes later. He went down with his ship, but was brought back up by the buoyancy of his life preserver.

The Coast Guard cutter *Calypso* steamed into the melee of floating men. She launched a small rowboat that picked up those who were drifting down wind, while her ladders offered purchase for the rest. Lieutenant Mitchel at first refused to be picked up, instead directing rescue operations from the water. His injuries were so bad that his left leg eventually had to be amputated above the knee. A British tug helped pick up survivors. When the tally was completed, nearly half the one hundred eighty-three man crew were unaccounted for.

The last casualty of 1943 was the Cuban freighter *Libertad*. She ran independently from Cuba to Florida, carrying 8,000 tons of sugar, then joined northbound Convoy KN-280 on December 1. The convoy crept along the coast at the speed of the slowest vessel. At 0330 on the fourth, a torpedo slammed into the *Libertad*'s port side at No. 4 hold. Men on watch reported "a terrific vibration, followed immediately by a flash of red light," and the sulphurous odor of gunpowder.

There was no time to transmit a distress call, or to launch lifeboats. The vessel listed rapidly to thirty-five degrees, and settled by the stern. The men managed to cut free some of the life rafts as the ship sank. Within minutes the *Libertad* was gone, taking with her nearly half her complement. Twelve men found refuge on two rafts, four others clung to an overturned lifeboat that had torn free, nine found drifting planks.

Twelve hours later, the blimp *K-82* spotted two men on planks: during the day the others had been washed off by heavy seas and drowned. A call for help went out over the airwaves. The two men were picked up by the USS *Natchez*. At 1726, the blimp *K-72* located the two rafts and directed the *Natchez* toward the spot. It was not until the next day, however, that the blimp *K-76* found the four men who had spent the night stuck like limpets to the bottom of the capsized lifeboat. Again, the *Natchez* made the rescue. The value of the fleet of blimps could not possibly be contested, especially by the eighteen survivors of the *Libertad*.

The culprit that sank the *Libertad* was the *U-129*, this time under the command of Kapitanleutnant Richard von Harpe.

The ESF enjoyed a winter devoid of the baying of the undersea wolves. With spring came the aggressors, and more death. Convoy CU-21, consisting of twenty-eight merchant ships and six escorts, departed New York for England on April 15, 1944. Instead of continuing out of the swept channel for the Hudson Canyon as planned, the convoy was steered due east in order to avoid an inbound convoy. Thick fog caused quite a bit of confusion, resulting in a collision between the *Aztec* and the *Sag Harbor*. As these vessels dropped out, the rest headed for the grouping area south of Nantucket.

The *Pan Pennsylvania*, making fourteen knots, jockeyed for position among the local group. Around midnight, without warning, a torpedo struck the port side aft, blowing a fifty foot hole in the side of No. 8 tank, ripping up the main deck, knocking out the steering mechanism, and destroying No. 4 lifeboat. No one was injured by the blast.

The ship settled slightly, and there was fire in the boiler room as some of the cargo of eighty octane gasoline seeped into the bilges, but the vessel was not in immediate danger of sinking. Nevertheless, a group of panicked crewmen and armed guard personnel jumped into a lifeboat and lowered away. Captain Delmar Leidy was unable to stop them. Because the tanker still had considerable way on, the lifeboat swamped when it hit the water, and all the men drowned.

Captain Leidy kept the rest of the men aboard, lest the flames in the boiler room ignite the gasoline-covered sea like a giant torch. Destroyer escorts converged on the burning tanker like moths on a flame. The *Joyce* drove in to pick up survivors while the *Peterson* covered her.

The *Gandy* swung in a wide arc at flank speed and began a sonar sweep. A torpedo passed by the *Gandy* on a parallel course, missing the warship by seventy-five yards. The DE then stood erratically down the course for three miles, but failed to establish contact. Worse yet, her No. 4 engine blew her crankcase because of overheating cylinders; she was forced to a reduced and unbalanced speed.

The *Gandy* swept back toward the scene of the rescue operation then in progress. The *Pan Pennsylvania* was definitely sinking by the stern, so Captain Leidy gave the order to abandon ship. Three men were crushed between No. 2 lifeboat and the tanker's hull. There were too many survivors for the *Joyce* to handle, so the *Peterson* was ordered to assist. Thirty-one survivors, including Captain Leidy, clambered aboard the *Joyce*; another twenty were picked up by the *Peterson*. As the *Gandy* circled close to cover them, another torpedo track passed by her.

The wily U-boat was hiding under and close alongside the sinking tanker, masking it from sonar gear.

With the last of the survivors safely on her deck, the

*Joyce* got up speed and raced toward a target picked up by her astute sound man. She dropped a pattern of thirteen depth charges on shallow settings. The bow of the *U-550*, Kapitanleutnant Klaus Hanert, was blown to the surface by the force of the underwater detonations.

From the bridge of the *Gandy*, Lieutenant Commander W. A. Sessions shouted, "Right full rudder, come to 320, open fire, and stand by to ram." The U-boat's forward momentum was more than Commander Sessions anticipated, so he quickly ordered the rudder thrown back to port. Germans poured out of the conning tower hatch and rushed for the guns. At the last moment, with collision imminent, Lieutenant H. W. Perkerson ordered the sound head hoisted.

Commander Sessions was aiming the *Gandy* at the after antiaircraft gun mount, but missed by twenty-five feet. The bow of the destroyer escort sliced through the U-boat just aft of the deadly armament. The rudder was kept at "left full" in order to throw the propellers clear. Accompanying the awful, grinding scrape of steel on steel was the cacophony of gunfire directed at the men on the U-boat. Several Germans fell under the hail of machine gun bullets, but others rushed to take their places.

Now the *Gandy* and the *U-550* ran along a parallel course. Guns from the destroyer continued to rake the conning tower and gun positions of the U-boat until Commander Sessions heard a voice "on one of our voice radios shouting something in a Germanic accent. Supposing it an offer to surrender, I ordered 'cease firing' which, after a few seconds delay, got through to the guns. Almost immediately the sub manned a machine gun battery and commenced firing on us. We swung left to bring guns to bear."

The deck of the U-boat was littered with the dead and dying. Aboard the *Gandy*, four men lay wounded. Tracer shells from the running gun battle hit the *Pan Pennsylvania*, igniting the growing pool of gasoline that surrounded her. The sea erupted in a sheet of flames.

The *Peterson* cornered the U-boat from the other side of the *Gandy* and fired two shallow-set depth charges from her starboard K-guns. Severely holed and damaged, the *U-550* became unmanageable. Hanert ordered abandon ship and scuttling charges set. An explosion ripped open her pressure hull aft. The U-boat sank by the stern, leaving only thirteen of her crew on the surface. The *Joyce* picked up the survivors.

The *Gandy* suffered the loss of four feet of her reinforced bow strake, had several antennas shot away, and numerous .50 caliber and shrapnel holes. For a warship only eight days out of shakedown, her crew had performed their duties well under her baptism of fire.

The *Pan Pennsylvania* capsized and sank. Her bow protruded from the water, a hazard to navigation, so the next day a salvage vessel was dispatched to the site. Salvage proved impossible because of the depth of water (some two-hundred seventy feet). Instead, the salvage crew tried for some time to sink the still burning and still buoyant derelict by gunfire. When this failed, Allied planes made a run on the obnoxious bow on the eighteenth, and bombed it into submersion.

Of the thirteen survivors from the *U-550*, one died of his injuries and was buried at sea the following day. Hanert and the other eleven were imprisoned aboard the *Joyce*. All three escort vessels rejoined the convoy and made the transatlantic crossing. The German prisoners were then turned over to authorities at Londonderry, Northern Ireland.

On May 5, fully nineteen days after the double tragedy, the Coastal Picket Patrol Boat *CGR-3082* came across a body at sea: that of a German sailor wearing an escape lung. An autopsy report indicated no injuries except burns on the head and face, probably from diesel oil; that the sailor had died prior to submersion, as though he had been on a raft; and that he had died only five days previously. The conclusion was that he had escaped from the submerged *U-550*, and died on the surface.

Two other bodies were later found in the vicinity of the sunken U-boat. The one picked up by the *SC-630* had been in the water for more than eighteen days. The one recovered by the *CGR-1989* on May 11 was not only wearing an escape lung and a life jacket, but was still on a rubber raft: he was Wilhelm Flade, last of the *U-550*'s casualties.

On May 27, at 1140, the tanker *Bulkoil* was struck by a torpedo that failed to explode. Sharp-eyed lookouts spotted the U-boat half a mile away. The gun crew opened fire with such accuracy that the U-boat was forced to submerge while the tanker made good her escape.

The next U-boat attack was made on June 13. The line trawler *Lark* was returning to Boston from a successful eight day haul off the La Have Banks with a hold full of fish. Captain James Abbott was designated as a Confidential Fisherman Observer, so it was with more than passing interest that he watched an unknown vessel pass through the moon's silvery beam early that morning. What he thought was a patrolling corvette fired a shot through the *Lark*'s rigging. If that shot was intended as a message, the crew caught on quickly.

Captain Abbott had the engine secured. As the vessel began to lose way, the crew lowered the dories and prepared to escape. Only one dory got away on the starboard side before the U-boat circled and commenced firing at that side of the *Lark*. Four other dories put off from the now protected port side. Captain Abbott and Daniel Maloney, the seventy-four-year-old cook, and the *Lark*'s fourteen-year-old dog mascot Rex, remained aboard.

Then the U-boat began shelling in earnest, raking the decks and hull with twenty-mm and thirty-caliber machine gun fire. Said Captain Abbott: "It made a hell of a noise and I was damn well scared. I don't think the Nazis knew anyone was aboard the trawler. Some of the dories had started to come back, but they pulled away again when they saw the sub. I didn't have a chance to abandon ship after that, the shells and bullets were coming too fast for the next fifteen minutes.

"I ran out of the pilot house and beat it forward. As the sub circled, I hid behind the two nests of dories and the pilot house, trying to keep them between me and the shells and the bullets. Sometimes I lay flat on my face on the deck; others, I scurried along on my hands and knees. I said more than a few prayers, I'll tell you. I tried to comfort myself by thinking that I was no worse off than a lot of our boys who are fighting. I didn't expect to pull through, but I told myself I should be ready to take my medicine as well as the soldiers and sailors.

"After fifteen minutes the sub dove. I'm sure the only reason it left was because her skipper was sure the *Lark* would sink—was all done for. I went to the forecastle and found old Dan, the cook. I didn't know whether he would be dead or alive. But there he was, dressed in his best clothes, with a bundle of bread, molasses and water, and he greeted me as cool as you please. I don't think he was concerned at all about the shelling."

One of the dories returned, and the men were able to get the engine restarted. Captain Abbott then followed the course the other dories had taken. They and all the men were picked up. The bullet-riddled and shell-pocked trawler headed for home. She arrived under her own power on the morning of the fifteenth, none of her twenty-seven men the worse for wear.

Three months passed before another U-boat ventured to press home an attack within the borders of the ESF. While Oberleutnant zur See Hans Offermann, *U-518*, cannot be credited with the tonnage loss of the Liberty ship *George Ade*, he was the cause of a far more reaching chain of events.

By this time the coastal waters of the United States were so safe from attack that many ships were routed independently. They were kept under surveillance by blimps and airplanes, and patrol boats swarmed the seas like a horde of angry gnats. Thus the *George Ade* proceeded alone northward with her lend-lease cargo on her way to a New York rendezvous with a transatlantic convoy. About twenty minutes after midnight on September 12, while making fifteen knots in the Gulf Stream current off Frying Pan Shoals, a single torpedo hit aft and threw a sheet of water twenty-five feet into the air.

Captain Torlief Selness ordered the engines secured,

general quarters sounded, and a distress call sent. Two or three minutes later, lookouts watched helplessly as another torpedo sped toward the barely moving freighter. It passed under the counter stern from starboard to port without exploding.

The Submarine Tracking Office already had three baby flat-tops (the *Core*, the *Guadalcanal*, and the *Croatan*) searching for the *U-518*. It now dispatched an additional eight destroyer escorts, plus the HMNS *Van Kinsbergen* and three smaller patrol vessels organized as a killer group. In addition, the *Natchez* and the *Temptress* were ordered to the scene from New York, while the Coast Guard cutters *Bedloe* and *Jackson* charged out from Morehead City, the latter to protect the minesweeper *Project* and the tugs *Relief* and *Escape*. It was this awesome kind of mobilization that an encroaching U-boat had to face off the East Coast in 1944.

The after end of the *George Ade* was flooded, but the engine was still clear of the water. Still, the crew was unable to repair the damaged rudder. The Liberty ship floated helplessly. The U-boat was sighted in the darkness, and the *George Ade*'s gun crew fired upon it. Offermann hung around until dawn, but as soon as he stuck his periscope out of the water it was shot at. Offermann prudently retired from the action when the *Project* arrived and dropped depth charges.

The *George Ade* was taken in tow by the *Escape*. All through the day and night, they crept toward Cape Henry at four knots. Rising winds in advance of a hurricane reduced their speed until the night of the thirteenth, when the tow line parted off Wimble Shoals. The Liberty ship drifted out of control toward Bodie Island, North Carolina.

Captain Selness dropped his anchors. One carried away, but the other held with the engine going forward at slow revolutions. The *Escape* stood by, while the escort vessels shifted for themselves. On the *George Ade*, winds of more than a hundred miles per hour and seas over fifty feet high washed overboard two lifeboats and four life rafts. There were no personal injuries.

Those aboard the *Jackson* and *Bedloe* did not fare so

well. The *Jackson* was hit broadside by a mountainous wave, laid on her beam ends, and stayed there. In three minutes the crew was able to release four life rafts. Eleven men drowned as they abandoned ship in the fury of the storm. The *Jackson* stayed afloat for a half hour before being pounded under the sea.

The *Bedloe* rolled onto her side twice, each time coming back slowly like a weighted punching doll. The third time, she stayed on her side for three minutes before sinking. Her crew got away in three life rafts. One of these was never found. Ten men from one raft and two from the other were picked up by a whaleboat from the minesweeper *Inflict*.

The twenty-nine survivors of the *Jackson* were beat by tumultuous seas for two days and nights, continually being washed off by pounding waves. The captain and eight others succumbed to the forces of nature during the night of the twenty-fifth. Only nineteen lived through the forty-five hours of terror.

Meanwhile, as the storm abated, the *Escape* was able to take aboard another towing cable. The *George Ade* was towed into the safety of the Chesapeake Bay on the sixteenth. She was eventually repaired and returned to service.

On November 30, 1944, the *U-1230*, Kapitanleutnant Hans Hilbig, arrived not *off* the Maine coast, but *on* it. Hilbig's primary objective was to disembark two agents onto the deserted New England shore. This was not the first time spies had been dropped off on American shores by German submarines, but the story of infiltration, tracking, capturing, and execution of enemy agents is a book in itself.

Hilbig hung around in the Gulf of Maine for several days afterwards, looking for targets of opportunity. On December 3, he torpedoed and sank the Canadian freighter *Cornwallis*, en route from Barbados to St. John's. The vessel took such a strong starboard list that the lifeboats were smashed by the sea before they could be cast free. The few survivors jumped or were washed overboard as the ship sank beneath them; they climbed onto rafts that had floated free.

The radio operator, who went down with the ship, had time to make only a brief transmission: "SSSS—OFF DESERT." It was assumed this meant Mount Desert Rock or Mount Desert Island. Two planes were dispatched to the suspected area, but they found nothing. At 1134, five hours after the sinking, the fishing boat *Iva M* reported sighting bodies and barrels. Two destroyers and a Coast Guard cutter were diverted for the search. The only two survivors were picked up two hours later, by the fishing boat *Notre Dame*. Captain Emerson Robertson, thirty-five of the crew, and seven gunners were lost.

Once again, the winter months were devoid of U-boat activity. But with the spring, and with Germany's certain oncoming defeat, Doenitz made a last ditch attempt to wreak havoc off the East Coast of the United States. He sent four U-boats on a virtual suicide mission, from which none returned. For a brief time only, after a hiatus of nearly three years, more than one U-boat at a time dared operate inside the ESF.

On April 5, 1945, the *Atlantic States* was torpedoed by the *U-857*, Oberleutnant zur See Rudolf Premauer. The tanker was traveling alone and in ballast from Boston to Venezuela. As she passed Cape Cod, she was struck by a torpedo that blew in the boiler room bulkhead. Captain E. L. Lindemuth ordered abandon ship. Fifty-two crewmen and armed guard took to the boats, while the captain and four others stayed aboard. The USS *Guinivere* picked up all the men who had abandoned ship. Later, the Naval tug *ATR-14* towed the tanker back to Boston. The ship was duly repaired. There were no injuries.

While Premauer may have initially escaped, alerted antisubmarine units swarmed into action. The *Gustafson*, the *Eugene*, the *Knoxville*, and the *Micka* formed a scouting line with overlapping sound ranges, and swept the entire area north of Cape Cod. At 0212 on April 7, the *Gustafson* obtained a solid sonar contact. Like a well-oiled machine, the four ships split into a prearranged pattern, with the *Gustafson* making a dry run for evaluation while the other three vessels conducted a box search around the point of contact.

The Navy analysis of the action was succinct: "At 0227 *Gustafson* made a hedgehog attack with negative results. At 0248 *Gustafson* made her second hedgehog attack, and obtained one explosion approximately 11 seconds after firing. An oil slick was seen at 0315 about 900 yards from scene of second attack. Four more hedgehog attacks were made by *Gustafson* at 0409, 0427, 0452, and 0503, with negative results. Contact was held until 0600 and subsequent efforts to regain it were not successful."

Each hedgehog attack consisted of twenty-four launched charges. The depth recorder indicated that the target was moving at two hundred eighty feet. The eleven-second flight time of the second attack, from launching to detonation, equates to a depth of two hundred seventy-seven feet. Yet, plotting room opinions varied from "probably sunk" to "slightly damaged" to "insufficient data." By this time in the war, the Navy had gained an incredible amount of experience not only in conducting depth charge attacks, but in understanding how much of a pounding the German machine could take and still survive.

The final recommendation stated that "it is considered that although a submarine, known to have been in this area, may have been lost, it was not lost as a result of this action."

Despite this conclusion, the *U-857* was never heard from again. In all likelihood it was damaged beyond its ability to regain the surface, and slowly sank to the bottom at a depth of seven hundred fifty feet.

On April 14, Kapitanleutnant Erwin Manchen, *U-879*, made his sole foray into the ESF about a hundred miles off Cape Henry. He cornered the *Belgian Airman* running independently from Houston to New York, there to join a transatlantic convoy. Her cargo holds were filled with sorghum in bulk and dairy feed in bags.

The U-boat's torpedo struck the Belgian freighter on the starboard side opposite No. 5 hatch, blowing a gaping hole in her hull and damaging the main antenna and signal mast. The ship lingered on for four hours, until 1600. The only casualty was a seaman who hit his head while jumping into the lifeboat, fell into the sea, and drowned. The remainder of the crew were picked up by the *Harold A. Jordan*.

The *U-879* did not make it home. Four days later it was trounced some two hundred miles east of Cape Cod by the U.S. destroyer escorts *Buckley* and *Reuben James*. There were no survivors.

Two U-boats remained in the ESF, but only because they had so far failed to reveal themselves. Now they took turns sniping and hiding. First of this pair to attack was the *U-548*, Kapitanleutnant Erich Krempl, on April 18. The target was the *Swiftscout*, then about one hundred fifty miles off Cape Henry.

The *Swiftscout* was traveling independently from the Delaware Capes to Puerta La Cruz, Venezuela, in ballast. At 0925, a torpedo hit low in No. 6 tank, port, and broke the ship's back. The bow and stern pointed upward as the midship section slowly collapsed. No one was injured by the blast. Both bow and stern gun crews fired at what they thought was a U-boat, keeping it submerged. Twenty minutes later, however, a second torpedo followed the path of the first and completed the destruction of the midship area. The ship buckled and sank. Chief Engineer Alfred Brennan drowned during abandon ship.

Captain Peter Katsares sent a distress call using the emergency transmitter with which the lifeboats were equipped. The *Chancellorsville* intercepted the message and soon had all the survivors safely aboard.

Five days later the USS *Eagle 56* (which, among other actions during a long and glorious career, had rescued the survivors of the *Jacob Jones*) met with catastrophe just off Portland, Maine. Lieutenant John Scagnelli was lying in his bunk about noon when "there was an explosion and I was thrown against the bulkhead." Only semiconscious, and with blood pouring from a head wound, he opened his eyes to find his room a shambles. He climbed through a porthole and gained a corridor that was "filled with smoke, steam, glass and debris." As the forward part of the *Eagle 56* listed to starboard, he fought his way through the tangle of wreckage, noticing on the way that the magazine was intact. The bow was just about to go under when he crawled through a now-horizontal hatchway and "just walked off" into the 42 degree water.

The blast had occurred amidships, and had torn the vessel in two. The stern sank in two minutes. The bow rolled over, with its jagged after end flooding, and sank stem upward.

Men on the USS *Selfridge*, only three miles away, said the geyser of water accompanying the blast rose a hundred feet in the air and lasted as long as twenty seconds. The destroyer reversed course and steamed at high speed for the tragic scene, followed by the *Portland* lightship. When they arrived they found men without life jackets bobbing in the water or clinging to pieces of wreckage. Both ships lowered lifeboats to rescue survivors.

While her boats were in the water, the *Selfridge* picked up a firm contact on her sound gear. She left the rescue operation in progress and took off to retaliate against the submerged U-boat. She dropped nine depth charges without result, then lost contact. When she got back to the scene of the sinking, she found that her boats had picked up ten men, the lightship three. Only one body was recovered, leaving fifty-three missing and presumed lost in the cataclysmic explosion. All thirteen survivors were seriously wounded, requiring morphine and plasma, so the *Selfridge* rushed them to port for hospitalization.

The U-boat that slunk off into the safety of deep water was the *U-853*, Oberleutnant zur See Helmut Fromsdorf.

Five hours later, and five hundred miles to the south, the *U-548* attacked the Norwegian tanker *Katy*. The tanker was en route from New York to Houston, in ballast, when a torpedo slammed into her No. 1 tank. A distress call went out immediately. Fearing a follow-up attack, the master ordered his merchant crew to abandon ship. He stayed aboard with his officers and the armed guard.

Although the *Katy* was so far down by the bow that

her propeller was out of the water, those still aboard managed to shift enough water ballast to right the ship. Three lifeboats returned. The *Katy* proceeded unassisted at six knots to Lynnhaven Roads, Virginia, arriving early on the twenty-fourth. The men in the other lifeboat were brought in by a Coast Guard cutter. There were no casualties.

The *U-548* escaped undetected that time, but a week later it met its nemesis. On April 30, the U-boat poked its periscope out of the water directly in the path of Convoy KN-382: thirty-six ships in nine columns headed north at eight and a half knots. Before the *U-548* could get off a shot, it was detected by the U.S. patrol escort *Natchez*.

The *Natchez* homed in on the sonar contact. Almost immediately she spotted the high wake of a schnorchel tube and the clearly discernible feather of a periscope. *Natchez* altered course to ram, but did not realize how quickly the schnorchel boat was moving. The *U-548* charged ahead on its diesels, feeding them air sucked in through the schnorchel tube. The *Natchez* overshot the U-boat, which passed in the opposite direction just off the port side. *Natchez* released an "embarrassing pattern of hydrostatically set Mark 8 charges," and reversed her course to pursue.

By this time the entire convoy was bearing down on them. The *Natchez* was forced to take evasive maneuvers in order to avoid being run down by her own ships. The convoy executed an emergency turn to starboard, clearing the area where the U-boat had submerged. Three destroyer escorts turned back to hold the U-boat at bay.

As the *Natchez* cleared the rear of the convoy she regained sound contact. The U-boat was dead ahead. *Natchez* backed down on her engines and made an ahead thrown attack with her forward hedgehogs. Contact was temporarily lost in the noise of the underwater detonations. When it was regained, the *Natchez* drove in and delivered a depth charge attack.

By this time, the destroyer escorts had arrived. The *Natchez* stood off while the *Thomas*, the *Coffman*, and the *Bostwick* took turns crisscrossing the position triangulated by the coordinated sonar scans. The U-boat "maneuvered radically during entire period of contact, turning in circles, fishtailing, changing speeds, backing down, and on two occasions firing pillenwerfers."

These concerted attacks went on for eight hours, until after dawn. Large amounts of oil were then seen on the surface. Breaking-up noises were detected on the sonar gear during the final attack. Eighteen minutes after the last set of depth charges had been dropped, a loud underwater explosion was heard. Then, there was silence. The *U-548* was no more.

By this time, Germany was beaten. Only a few days remained before Doenitz, Hitler's successor, officially declared the cessation of hostilities. Still, many U-boats remained on patrol, and continued to fight aggressively for the cause of the Fatherland. The *U-853* was one of these. On the evening of May 5, with the westering sun still above the horizon, Fromsdorf tracked the collier *Black Point* along the crosshairs of his raised periscope. He fired what was to be the last shot against the merchant marine in the long battle of the Atlantic.

The collier was bound from Norfolk, Virginia, to Boston, Massachusetts, with 7,595 tons of coal, and had only recently separated from a northbound convoy at New York. From there she threaded the circuitous East River until she made open water in the Long Island Sound. She was proceeding independently along the coastal waterway between Block Island and Point Judith, Rhode Island, when, at 1730, a torpedo exploded aft and tore away forty feet of her stern. Twelve men who were below decks were killed instantly. Stephen Svetz, a Naval armed guard, was on duty by the stern gun when the blast catapulted him into the air. He landed amid fallen debris. Henry Barryhill, another member of the gun crew, dragged him from the wreckage and took him to a lifeboat.

Said Captain Charles Prior: "I was lighting a cigarette when a thunderous explosion rocked the ship. Everything in the wheel house came apart . . . even the glass face on the clock smashed on the deck . . . To this day, I can't remember if I lit the cigarette or swallowed it."

# TRACK OF THE GRAY WOLF

A passing Yugoslavian ship, the *Kamen*, witnessed the blast, and immediately transmitted an SOS. The thirty-four survivors made good their escape in two lifeboats, and within the hour were picked up by the Coast Guard cutters *Hornbeam* and *Hibiscus*. The *Black Point* rolled over slowly, settling by the stern, but did not go under completely until three and a half hours after the attack.

Meanwhile, a task force operating thirty miles to the south intercepted the transmission. The destroyer escorts *Atherton* and *Amick*, and the Coast Guard frigate *Moberly*, took off at flank speed for the scene of the attack. They fanned out as they approached the east side of Block Island with the intent of boxing in the escaping U-boat. The destroyer escort *Ericsson*, having already entered Cape Cod Canal to the north, turned around and raced back toward the scene. Lieutenant Commander Tollaksen of the *Moberly* was senior officer of the three vessels closest to the scene, and was designated Officer in Tactical Command.

The three warships ran abreast, sweeping the darkened seas with their sonar. The *Atherton* had on board the best sound team and the latest equipment, so she took the position most likely to be used by an escaping U-boat. Two miles to the west ran the *Amick*, and two miles farther west ran the *Moberly*. With a precision borne of experience, the *Atherton*'s course ran right over the skulking U-boat. The screws of the *U-853* were clearly discernible as Fromsdorf cruised slowly along the bottom at a depth of one hundred twenty-five feet, desperately seeking the safety of deep water.

The *Atherton* drove in for the attack, dropping thirteen magnetic depth charges. Only one exploded, and it could not be determined if the U-boat's hull had triggered the charge, or whether it had been dropped on a shipwreck known to be in the area. With the U-boat definitely pinned down, the *Amick* was called off to escort another merchantman through the Block Island-Cape Judith narrows.

The *Atherton* made another run and launched a full load of hedgehogs. The geysers had just splashed down when a secondary explosion occurred a hundred feet off the edge of the pattern. This was evaluated as a depth charge from the first run detonated by the hedgehogs. The *Atherton* worked over the area with another hedgehog attack. After that, because of the disturbance of the water, she lost contact and was unable to regain it.

Not knowing whether the original contact was U-boat or wreck, the *Atherton* left a lighted marker buoy at the site. The two warships then resumed the sonar search. By this time the *Ericsson* had arrived, and tactical control was passed to that vessel and Commander McCune. By 2200 the area was surrounded by three more destroyers and four other escort vessels. The Navy was leaving nothing to chance.

It was nearly midnight before the *Atherton*'s sonar man heard pinging from a stationary object. No propeller noise was heard. The U-boat appeared to be sitting silently on the bottom. At this stage in the technology of sound navigation and ranging, a good listener could just about pinpoint a target. The *Atherton* fired a pattern of hedgehogs which quickly brought to the surface bubbles of air, oil, and pieces of freshly broken wood. The *Atherton* circled the spot. The sound contact was excellent, and unmoving.

The *Ericsson* did not join the attack, but McCune ordered the *Atherton* to make yet another run on the supposed U-boat in order to split the pressure hull and ensure that the enemy did not escape. The *Atherton* trounced the target again, with depth charges. Air and oil continued to rise to the surface. Searchlight beams from the *Atherton* and *Moberly* fell on water thick with oil and covered with cork and dead fish. The *Atherton* recovered a pillow, a life jacket, and a wooden flagstaff.

The *Atherton*'s gear had been temporarily disabled by the last set of depth charges, due to the shallow setting because of water depth. So the *Moberly* was ordered in for another attack. If McCune thought the enemy was done for, the report from the *Moberly*'s sound man that the target was again on the move soon dispelled that notion. The *Moberly* attacked at high speed, in order to get away from the blast of her own depth charges. Even so, the concussion damaged her steering gear.

While she was recovering, the *Atherton* got her sound gear working again, and discovered that the target was still on the move at two to three knots. The *Moberly* laid down a pattern of hedgehogs. After this, contact was lost due to reflections from the sandy bottom. The U-boat was soon detected by the presence of pools of oil coagulating on the surface. For the next four hours the two ships drove back and forth over the site, constantly re-establishing sonar contact. The U-boat finally had come to rest.

As the sun rose over the smooth Atlantic swells, the stark yellow glow highlighted a huge debris field filled with emergency life rafts, escape lungs, life jackets, even an officer's cap. McCune had boats lowered to recover the material. Then, still with the idea of cracking the U-boat's pressure hull, he had all three warships run depth charge attacks in a cloverleaf pattern: each took her turn from a different angle while the others stood by. In between the depth charging, a boat would go in to pick up any loose items that floated up from the bottom.

Blimps flying over the area assisted by dropping marker buoys and sonar transponders over the sunken U-boat. Finally convinced that the U-boat had been completely destroyed, McCune had a buoy dropped on the site. That afternoon, a diver from the *Penguin* descended through the cold water using the buoy line as a guide. He landed right on the conning tower. He saw gaping holes blown in the pressure hull, and observed bodies inside. Fromsdorf and the entire crew of the *U-853* were dead.

The next day, Karl Doenitz, former admiral and now President of the Reich, met with Allied commanders at Reims, France and capitulated for Germany. The U-boat war was officially over.

# AFTERWORD

"The American people have reason to be proud of the heroism and patriotism of the officers and seamen of their Victory fleet. During these dangerous days and nights on the sea lanes of the world, with danger lurking above, below and on the surface, they do not falter in the performance of their duty. Hundreds of them render service far beyond the call of duty. It is gratifying that the Congress has recognized such heroism and authorized the bestowal of proper awards to these men of the sea, who are just as vital to our ultimate victory as the men in the armed forces."

President Franklin Roosevelt
May 22, 1942

The sinking of the *Black Point* ended the U-boat devastations in the Eastern Sea Frontier just sixty miles from where they had all begun three years and four months earlier with the torpedoing of the *Norness*.

The British Admiralty Report of 1942 had proven with great prescience that "history is repeating itself and, as in 1914–1918, so in 1939–1942, although we shall not win the war by defeating the U-boats, we shall assuredly lose the war if we do not defeat them."

As part of Germany's capitulation, all U-boats still on operational patrol were ordered to surrender to the nearest Allied forces. While no U-boats or their crews had survived the East Coast onslaught of the previous month, five others made their presence known in mid Atlantic, and were escorted to U.S. ports. In order of surrender—not arrival—the *U-805*, the *U-1228*, the *U-873*, and the *U-234* were brought into Portsmouth, New Hampshire; the *U-858* was brought into Cape May, New Jersey. All were soon sunk in deep water in the North Atlantic as part of the British "Operation Deadlight."

What remained was an offshore grave of sunken merchant ships, and the shattered families of those who had manned them. For those who had survived, however, the battle was not yet over. Although before his untimely death President Roosevelt granted veteran status to all wartime members of the merchant marine service, making them eligible for medical treatment at Veterans Administration hospitals and burial in national cemeteries, no benefits were forthcoming.

Decades passed. On November 23, 1977, a public law was passed that reiterated the previous Presidential dictate that "the service of any person in any other similarly situated group the members of which rendered service to the Armed Forces of the United States in a capacity considered civilian employment or contractual service at the time such service was rendered, shall be considered active duty for the purposes of all laws administered by the Veterans Administration."

One would think that a law passed twice should accrue to those indicated the benefits they so admirably earned. But such was not the case. It then took a Federal lawsuit to make the Department of Defense give the merchant marine what was owed to them.

The final decision was rendered on July 15, 1987, pursuant to Civil Action No. 86-2015-LFO. Even then, it was not until January 20, 1988, that Edward Aldridge, Jr., Secretary of the Air Force, "acting under a court order to review a previous denial, agreed to award veterans status to any seamen who sailed on a U.S. flag ocean going merchant ship between December 7, 1941, and August 15, 1945."

Walter Jones, Chairman of the House Merchant Marine & Fisheries Committee, summed up the long, drawn-out triumph: "This marks an extremely important and long overdue breakthrough for our heroic seamen. Years of effort have now managed to turn the tide forever and close a dark chapter in our country's military history.

"The only down side to this victory is that it took 43 years, a federal court case, countless hearings and bills introduced by Members of Congress, and untold thousands of letters written by and on behalf of the seamen, to do something that was promised by the Roosevelt Administration to a group that lost a higher percentage of its ranks in the war than any other except the Marines.

"My only hope is that we are able, as a nation, to help these men before it is too late."

Even among civilized nations, reason is sometimes slow in coming.

# APPENDICES

Lloyd's of London, that time-honored chronicler of ships, has adopted a rather cumbersome method of alphabetization for their Register, and unfortunately this system has been carried on by museums and other organizations in modern cataloguing. For example, all ships beginning with initials are found at the beginning of the listing for that letter, instead of in their appropriate place according to customary order. Likewise, double word names stop being alphabetized when the first word reaches its alphabetical location; at that point, all ships with the same first name are listed before a similar name consisting of only one word.

For example, *R.P. Resor* would come before *Rio Tercero*, *Gulf of Mexico* before *Gulfamerica*. To complicate matters, *John R. Williams* would come before *John Rettig* because the take off point becomes the "R" after "John." This system of alphabets within alphabets based on punctuation and spacing between words is unnecessary and ridiculous.

Therefore, in order to make it easy for the reader unfamiliar with such unruly rules, in this book I have arranged all words, places, names (place and people's names as well as ship names), in the simple order of dictionary usage with which everyone is familiar. The only thing to remember is that ships' names are treated contiguously, not in reverse order as people's names. For example, *John D. Gill* will not be listed as *Gill, John D.*

As to what ships or actions are included both in this volume and in the following appendices, there must of necessity be a certain amount of selective license. The evolution of the Eastern Sea Frontier began in 1923 as a defense strategy inspired by the U-boat incursion of World War One. The concept of coastal frontiers developed over the years through many permutations of administrative, organizational, and operational resolutions. In September of 1940, with the exchange of fifty outdated, flush deck, four stack destroyers for defensive base rights in England, the home fleet depletion created a serious gap in U.S. coastal protection.

Therefore, by December, the Naval Coastal Frontier Operating Plan was put into action, with boundaries extending seaward as far as necessary to include "coastal sea lanes and the focal points of shipping routes." Protective authority of this expanse of ocean fell to the adjacent Naval Districts. The boundaries and overall administration did not become formalized until February 6, 1942, when the North Atlantic Naval Coastal Frontier officially became the Eastern Sea Frontier.

Command of the ESF was bestowed upon Admiral Adolphus Andrews, who was also Commandant of the Third Naval District. He was separated from this dual role on March 26, 1942. Rear Admiral Marquart moved into the top slot of the Third Naval District, relieving Andrews of the burden of wearing two hats.

Generally, the ESF covered the coast from Maine to Georgia, running offshore at first to about one hundred miles, later extended halfway to Bermuda. The specific boundaries started at the southern coastal extreme of Duval County, Florida, just below the Georgia border at Jacksonville Beach. A southeasterly line was drawn from there to a point at 25° north, 72° west, somewhat paralleling the Bahamas. The offshore limit was defined as then heading northerly to 40° north, 69° west; thence due north along the 69th parallel to 43° north; thence to Lucher Shoal Lightship; thence to land along the International Boundary Line between the U.S. and Canada.

However, it was always maintained that the tactical area of responsibility of the ESF be flexible in order to meet the demands of shipping, and in order to effectively succor vessels in distress and effect the rescue of survivors of stricken vessels. "This force will attack and destroy the enemy; protect shipping and sea communications of the Associated Powers; defend the Eastern Sea Frontier; provide adequate Air/Sea Rescue; and Support the U.S. Atlantic Fleet, the U.S. Army, Eastern Defense Command, and other friendly forces.''

On December 1, 1944, the boundaries were altered. Starting at the International Boundary, the line went south to 43° north, 67° west; thence southeasterly to 42° north, 65° west; thence southwesterly to the boundary of the Gulf Sea Frontier at 27° north, 75° 30' west; thence back to the Jacksonville Beach area now defined as 30° 15' north, 81° 20' west.

This means that a ship sunk within the boundaries of the ESF in 1945 might not have been included had she sunk in the same position in 1942.

Bearing these flowing and somewhat nebulous demarcations in mind, it is left up to the historian to establish his own criteria for inclusion of specific incidents and events. With such an arbitrary set of standards, the statistics of the East Coast war are therefore meaningless. Within the artificial parameters set by this volume, I have tried to tell a story of war, of suffering, of callousness, of heroism, of the life and death struggle of the men of the merchant marine.

Tonnage losses and casualties are for the purpose of overview only, and are not intended to be the last word on the sinkings and fatalities within an artificial arena. U-boats might have sunk ships on previous patrols, on the way to or from the States, and on subsequent patrols; the totals mentioned here do not reflect on success or failure: they are merely guidelines.

Ships sunk on the borders of the Canadian Coastal Zone, the Bermuda Area, or the Gulf Sea Frontier can technically be included in either of those regions. No compartmentalization makes sense. Vessels lost off the coast of Maine might not be mentioned here because of their proximity to Nova Scotia, while those that went down off the coast of northern Florida, if they were far enough offshore, are covered.

What is important is not the number of notches on a submarine commander's torpedo head, but the true narrative of those seamen who, in the name of war, were represented by those notches.

# APPENDIX 1

## Allied Shipping Action Chronology

### 1942

| Date of Attack/ Position | Ship | Gross Registered Tonnage | Type of Ship | Nation- ality | U-Boat/ Commander | How Attacked* | Result |
|---|---|---|---|---|---|---|---|
| 1/11/42 41-51N/63-48W | Cyclops | 9076 | liner | Br | U-123 Hardegen | T | sunk |
| 1/14/42 40-28N/70-50W | Norness | 9577 | tanker | Pan | U-123 Hardegen | T | sunk |
| 1/15/42 40-25N/72-21W | Coimbra | 6768 | tanker | Br | U-123 Hardegen | T | sunk |
| 1/17/42 39-15N/74-09W | San Jose | 1932 | freighter | US | | N | sunk |
| 1/18/42 35-57N/74-20W | Allan Jackson | 6635 | tanker | US | U-66 Zapp | T | sunk |

*How Attacked:    T: torpedoed    S: shelled    M: mined    N: not caused by enemy action

| Date of Attack/Position | Ship | Gross Registered Tonnage | Type of Ship | Nationality | U-Boat/Commander | How Attacked* | Result |
|---|---|---|---|---|---|---|---|
| 1/19/42 35-00N/72-30W | Lady Hawkins | 7988 | liner | Can | U-66 Zapp | T | sunk |
| 1/19/42 35-42N/75-21W | City of Atlanta | 5269 | freighter | US | U-123 Hardegen | T | sunk |
| 1/19/42 35-40N/75-20W | Malay | 8207 | tanker | US | U-123 Hardegen | TS | attacked not sunk |
| 1/19/42 35-25N/75-23W | Ciltvaira | 3779 | freighter | Lat | U-123 Hardegen | T | sunk |
| 1/19/42 34-30N/75-30W | Brazos | 4497 | freighter | US | | N | sunk |
| 1/22/42 North Carolina | Norvana | 2677 | freighter | US | U-66 Zapp | T | sunk |
| 1/22/42 36-01N/75-30W | Olympic | 5335 | tanker | Pan | U-130 Kals | T | sunk |
| 1/23/42 35-06N/74-58W | Empire Gem | 8139 | tanker | Br | U-66 Zapp | T | sunk |
| 1/23/42 34-50N/75-20W | Venore | 8017 | freighter | US | U-66 Zapp | T | sunk |
| 1/25/42 37-55N/74-56W | Olney | 6836 | tanker | US | U-125 Folkers | T | attacked not sunk |
| 1/25/42 38-58N/74-06W | Varanger | 9305 | tanker | Nor | U-130 Kals | T | sunk |

| Date / Position | Ship | Tonnage | Type | Flag | U-boat / Commander | How Attacked* | Result |
|---|---|---|---|---|---|---|---|
| 1/27/42 38-05N/74-53W | Francis E. Powell | 7096 | tanker | US | U-130 Kals | T | sunk |
| 1/29/42 Diamond Shoal | Halo | 6986 | tanker | US | U-130 Kals | S | attacked not sunk |
| 1/30/42 37-10N/73-58W | Rochester | 6836 | tanker | US | U-106 Rasch | TS | sunk |
| 1/31/42 37-33N/69-21W | Tacoma Star | 7924 | liner | Br | U-109 Bleichrodt | T | sunk |
| 2/01/42 36-36N/74-10W | Amerikaland | 15355 | freighter | Swe | U-106 Rasch | T | sunk |
| 2/02/42 38-25N/73-00W | W.L. Steed | 6182 | tanker | US | U-103 Winter | T | sunk |
| 2/03/42 38-05N/74-40W | San Gil | 3598 | freighter | US | U-103 Winter | T | sunk |
| 2/04/42 38-45N/73-50W | India Arrow | 8327 | tanker | US | U-103 Winter | T | sunk |
| 2/05/42 37-44N/73-18W | China Arrow | 8403 | tanker | US | U-103 Winter | T | sunk |
| 2/08/42 37-05N/74-46W | Ocean Venture | 7174 | freighter | Br | U-108 Scholtz | T | sunk |
| 2/11/42 35-00N/72-27W | Blink | 2701 | freighter | Nor | U-108 Scholtz | T | sunk |
| 2/11/42 38-20N/74-50W | Hagan | 6401 | tanker | US | | T | attacked not sunk |
| 2/15/42 36-35N/75-20W | Buarque | 5152 | freighter | Bra | U-432 Schultze | T | sunk |

*How Attacked:    T: torpedoed    S: shelled    M: mined    N: not caused by enemy action

| Date of Attack/ Position | Ship | Gross Registered Tonnage | Type of Ship | Nation- ality | U-Boat/ Commander | How Attacked* | Result |
|---|---|---|---|---|---|---|---|
| 2/16/42 36-57N/75-52W | E.H. Blum | 11615 | tanker | US | | N | sank/ salvaged |
| 2/18/42 37-30N/75-00W | Olinda | 4053 | freighter | Bra | U-432 Schultze | TS | sunk |
| 2/19/42 34-37N/76-10W | Oklahoma | 9264 | tanker | US | | T | attacked not sunk |
| 2/20/42 43-14N/64-45W | Lake Osweya | 2398 | freighter | US | U-96 Lehmann-Willenbrock | T | sunk |
| 2/21/42 38-00N/73-00W | Azalea City | 5976 | freighter | US | U-432 Schultze | T | sunk |
| 2/24/42 35-05N/75-20W | Norlavore | 2713 | freighter | US | U-432 Schultze | T | sunk |
| 2/26/42 35-33N/74-58W | Marore | 8215 | tanker | US | U-432 Schultze | T | sunk |
| 2/26/42 39-47N/73-26W | R.P. Resor | 7451 | tanker | US | U-578 Rehwinkel | T | sunk |
| 2/28/42 38-37N/74-32W | USS Jacob Jones | 1090 | destroyer | US | U-578 Rehwinkel | T | sunk |
| 3/07/42 35-15N/73-55W | Arabutan | 7874 | freighter | Bra | U-155 Piening | T | sunk |

268

| Date | Position | Ship | Tonnage | Type | Nat. | U-boat / Commander | How* | Result |
|---|---|---|---|---|---|---|---|---|
| 3/08/42 | 39-10N/72-02W | Cayru | 5152 | freighter | Bra | U-94 / Ites | T | sunk |
| 3/10/42 | 39-50N/73-52W | Gulftrade | 6667 | tanker | US | U-588 / Vogel | T | sunk |
| 3/10/42 | 38-27N/74-54W | Hvoslef | 1630 | freighter | Nor | U-94 / Ites | T | sunk |
| 3/11/42 | 34-40N/76-10W | Caribsea | 2609 | freighter | US | U-158 / Rostin | T | sunk |
| 3/12/42 | 33-55N/77-39W | John D. Gill | 11641 | tanker | US | U-158 / Rostin | T | sunk |
| 3/13/42 | 40-10N/73-50W | Tolten | 1858 | freighter | Chi | U-404 / von Bulow | T | sunk |
| 3/13/42 | 37-00N/73-25W | Trepca | 5042 | freighter | Jug | U-332 / Liebe | T | sunk |
| 3/14/42 | 39-21N/74-33W | Lemuel Burrows | 7610 | freighter | US | U-404 / von Bulow | T | sunk |
| 3/15/42 | 34-37N/76-20W | Ario | 6952 | tanker | US | U-158 / Rostin | T | sunk |
| 3/15/42 | 34-22N/76-29W | Olean | 7118 | tanker | US | U-158 / Rostin | T | sunk/ salvaged |
| 3/16/42 | 35-43N/75-22W | Australia | 11628 | tanker | US | U-332 / Liebe | T | sunk |
| 3/16/42 | 35-43N/73-49W | Ceiba | 1698 | freighter | Hon | U-124 / Mohr | T | sunk |
| 3/17/42 | 37-03N/73-50W | San Demetrio | 8073 | tanker | Br | U-404 / von Bulow | T | sunk |

*How Attacked:     T: torpedoed     S: shelled     M: mined     N: not caused by enemy action

| Date of Attack/ Position | Ship | Gross Registered Tonnage | Type of Ship | Nationality | U-Boat/ Commander | How Attacked* | Result |
|---|---|---|---|---|---|---|---|
| 3/17/42 35-05N/75-20W | Acme | 6878 | tanker | US | U-124 Mohr | T | sunk/ salvaged |
| 3/17/42 35-05N/75-25W | Kassandra Louloudis | 5106 | freighter | Gr | U-124 Mohr | T | sunk |
| 3/18/42 34-50N/75-35W | E. M. Clark | 9647 | tanker | US | U-124 Mohr | T | sunk |
| 3/18/42 34-17N/76-39W | Papoose | 5939 | tanker | US | U-124 Mohr | T | sunk |
| 3/19/42 Cape Lookout | Gulf of Mexico | 7807 | tanker | US | | S | attacked not sunk |
| 3/19/42 34-35N/76-32W | Mercury Sun | 8893 | tanker | US | | S | attacked not sunk |
| 3/19/42 34-25N/76-50W | W. E. Hutton | 7076 | tanker | US | U-124 Mohr | T | sunk |
| 3/19/42 35-05N/75-30W | Liberator | 7720 | freighter | US | U-332 Liebe | T | sunk |
| 3/20/42 36-22N/68-50W | Oakmar | 5766 | freighter | US | U-71 Flachsenberg | S | sunk |
| 3/21/42 33-35N/77-22W | Esso Nashville | 7943 | tanker | US | U-124 Mohr | T | sunk/ salvaged |

| Date | Location | Ship | Tonnage | Type | Nat. | U-boat / Cmdr | How | Result |
|---|---|---|---|---|---|---|---|---|
| 3/21/42 | 33-34N/77-25W | *Atlantic Sun* | 11615 | tanker | US | *U-124* Mohr | T | attacked not sunk |
| 3/23/42 | 33-59N/76-40W | *Naeco* | 5373 | tanker | US | *U-124* Mohr | T | sunk |
| 3/26/42 | 34-55N/75-02W | *Dixie Arrow* | 8046 | tanker | US | *U-71* Flachsenberg | T | sunk |
| 3/27/42 | 36-00N/70-00W | USS Atik (Carolyn) | 3209 | Q-ship | US | *U-123* Hardegen | TS | sunk |
| 3/27/42 | 36-36N/74-45W | *Equipoise* | 6210 | freighter | Pan | *U-160* Lassen | T | sunk |
| 3/29/42 | 35-16N/74-25W | *City of New York* | 8272 | passenger/fr | US | *U-160* Lassen | T | sunk |
| 3/31/42 | 37-34N/75-25W | *Allegheny* | 914 | barge | US | *U-754* Oestermann | S | sunk |
| 3/31/42 | 37-34N/75-25W | *Barnegat* | 914 | barge | US | *U-754* Oestermann | S | sunk |
| 3/31/42 | 37-34N/75-25W | *Menominee* | 441 | tug | US | *U-754* Oestermann | S | sunk |
| 3/31/42 | 37-34N/75-25W | *Ontario* | 490 | barge | US | *U-754* Oestermann | S | attacked not sunk |
| 4/01/42 | 35-16N/75-18W | *Rio Blanco* | 4086 | freighter | Br | *U-160* Lassen | T | sunk |
| 4/01/42 | 36-50N/74-18W | *Tiger* | 5992 | tanker | US | *U-754* Oestermann | T | sunk |
| 4/02/42 | 34-11N/76-08W | *Liebre* | 7057 | tanker | US | *U-123* Hardegen | S | attacked not sunk |

*How Attacked:   T: torpedoed   S: shelled   M: mined   N: not caused by enemy action

| Date of Attack/ Position | Ship | Gross Registered Tonnage | Type of Ship | Nation- ality | U-Boat/ Commander | How Attacked* | Result |
|---|---|---|---|---|---|---|---|
| 4/03/42 37-57N/75-10W | David H. Atwater | 2438 | freighter | US | U-552 Topp | S | sunk |
| 4/03/42 36-25N/72-22W | Otho | 4839 | passenger/fr | US | U-754 Oestermann | T | sunk |
| 4/04/42 36-08N/75-32W | Byron D. Benson | 7953 | tanker | US | U-552 Topp | T | sunk |
| 4/06/42 34-25N/75-57W | Bidwell | 6837 | tanker | US | U-160 Lassen | T | attacked not sunk |
| 4/07/42 35-07N/75-19W | British Splendour | 7138 | tanker | Br | U-552 Topp | T | sunk |
| 4/07/42 35-08N/75-22W | Lansing | 7866 | whaling factory | Nor | U-552 Topp | T | sunk |
| 4/08/42 31-02N/80-53W | Esso Baton Rouge | 7989 | tanker | US | U-123 Hardegen | T | sunk/ salvaged |
| 4/08/42 31-18N/80-59W | Oklahoma | 9264 | tanker | US | U-123 Hardegen | T | sunk/ salvaged |
| 4/09/42 30-46N/81-11W | Esparta | 3366 | freighter | US | U-123 Hardegen | T | sunk |
| 4/09/42 34-28N/75-56W | Malchace | 3516 | freighter | US | U-160 Lassen | T | sunk |

| Date / Location | Ship | Tonnage | Type | Flag | U-boat / Commander | How Attacked* | Result |
|---|---|---|---|---|---|---|---|
| 4/09/42 34-27N/76-16W | Atlas | 7137 | tanker | US | U-552 Topp | T | sunk |
| 4/09/42 35-35N/75-06W | San Delfino | 8079 | tanker | Br | U-203 Muzelburg | T | sunk |
| 4/09/42 34-25N/76-00W | Tamaulipas | 6943 | tanker | US | U-552 Topp | T | sunk |
| 4/10/42 30-10N/81-15W | Gulfamerica | 8081 | tanker | US | U-123 Hardegen | TS | sunk |
| 4/11/42 34-25N/76-30W | Harry F. Sinclair, Jr. | 6151 | tanker | US | U-203 Muzelburg | T | sunk/salvaged |
| 4/11/42 34-23N/75-35W | Ulysses | 14647 | liner | Br | U-160 Lassen | T | sunk |
| 4/12/42 33-53N/77-29W | Stanvac Melbourne | 10013 | tanker | Pan | U-203 Muzelburg | T | attacked not sunk |
| 4/14/42 35-08N/75-18W | Empire Thrush | 6160 | freighter | Br | U-203 Muzelburg | T | sunk |
| 4/14/42 US East Coast | Margaret | 3352 | freighter | US | U-571 Mohlmann | T | sunk |
| 4/16/42 35-35N/72-48W | Desert Light | 2368 | freighter | Pan | U-572 Hirsacker | T | sunk |
| 4/16/42 35-34N/70-08W | Alcoa Guide | 4834 | freighter | US | U-123 Hardegen | S | sunk |
| 4/18/42 35-32N/75-19W | Axtell J. Byles | 8955 | tanker | US | U-136 Zimmerman | T | sunk/salvaged |

*How Attacked:    T: torpedoed    S: shelled    M: mined    N: not caused by enemy action

| Date of Attack/ Position | Ship | Gross Registered Tonnage | Type of Ship | Nation- ality | U-Boat/ Commander | How Attacked* | Result |
|---|---|---|---|---|---|---|---|
| 4/20/42 36-25N/74-55W | Chenango | 3014 | freighter | Pan | U-84 Uphoff | T | sunk |
| 4/20/42 41-14N/65-55W | West Imboden | 5751 | freighter | US | U-752 Schroeter | TS | sunk |
| 4/22/42 31-10N/70-45W | San Jacinto | 6069 | passenger/fr | US | U-201 Schnee | TS | sunk |
| 4/23/42 39-10N/72-00W | Reinholt | 4799 | freighter | Nor | U-752 Schroeter | S | attacked not sunk |
| 4/24/42 40-50N/68-42W | Tropic Star | 5088 | freighter | Nor | U-576 Heinicke | T | attacked not sunk |
| 4/24/42 37-00N/69-15W | Empire Drum | 7244 | freighter | Br | U-136 Zimmerman | T | sunk |
| 4/28/42 40-10N/73-44W | Arundo | 5163 | freighter | Dut | U-136 Zimmerman | T | sunk |
| 4/29/42 34-19N/76-31W | Ashkhabad | 5284 | tanker | Rus | U-402 von Forstner | T | sunk |
| 4/30/42 41-52N/67-43W | Taborfjell | 1339 | freighter | Nor | U-576 Heinicke | T | sunk |
| 4/30/42 40-13N/73-46W | Bidevind | 4956 | freighter | Nor | U-752 Schroeter | T | sunk |

274

| Date / Position | Ship | Tonnage | Type | Nat. | U-boat / Commander | How* | Result |
|---|---|---|---|---|---|---|---|
| 5/04/42 35-46N/69-35W | *Fredden* | 1172 | freighter | Swe | *U-558* Krech | T | attacked not sunk |
| 5/12/42 34-10N/76-41W | *HMS Bedfordshire* | 913 | A/S trawler | Br | | T | sunk |
| 5/14/42 39-45N/72-35W | *Stavros* | 4853 | freighter | Gr | *U-593* Kelbling | T | attacked not sunk |
| 5/17/42 43-07N/67-18W | *Skotland* | 2117 | freighter | Nor | *U-588* Vogel | T | sunk |
| 5/18/42 43-01N/63-07W | *Fort Binger* | 5250 | freighter | Br | *U-588* Vogel | T | attacked not sunk |
| 5/21/42 38-53N/69-57W | *Plow City* | 3282 | freighter | US | *U-588* Vogel | T | sunk |
| 5/22/42 39-00N/68-00W | *Margot* | 4545 | freighter | Br | *U-588* Vogel | T | sunk |
| 5/25/42 39-44N/73-53W | *Persephone* | 8426 | tanker | Pan | *U-593* Kelbling | T | sunk/ salvaged |
| 6/01/42 34-10N/68-20W | *West Notus* | 5492 | freighter | US | *U-404* von Bulow | S | sunk |
| 6/02/42 39-22N/70-00W | *Berganger* | 6826 | freighter | Nor | *U-578* Rehwinkel | T | sunk |
| 6/03/42 43-50N/67-00W | *Ben and Josephine* | 102 | fishing boat | US | *U-432* Schultze | S | sunk |
| 6/03/42 43-50N/67-00W | *Aeolus* | 41 | fishing boat | US | *U-432* Schultze | S | sunk |
| 6/09/42 42-53N/67-11W | *Kronprinsen* | 7073 | freighter | Nor | *U-432* Schultze | T | attacked not sunk |

*How Attacked:    T: torpedoed    S: shelled    M: mined    N: not caused by enemy action

| Date of Attack/ Position | Ship | Gross Registered Tonnage | Type of Ship | Nation- ality | U-Boat/ Commander | How Attacked* | Result |
|---|---|---|---|---|---|---|---|
| 6/11/42 34-57N/75-56W | F. W. Abrams | 9310 | tanker | US | U-701 | N | sunk |
| 6/15/42 36-52N/75-51W | Robert C. Tuttle | 11615 | tanker | US | Degen U-701 | M | sunk/ salvaged |
| 6/15/42 36-52N/75-51W | Esso Augusta | 11237 | tanker | US | Degen U-701 | M | sunk/ salvaged |
| 6/15/42 36-52N/75-51W | HMS Kingston Ceylonite | 448 | A/S trawler | Br | Degen U-701 | M | sunk |
| 6/15/42 42-11N/69-25W | Port Nicholson | 8402 | freighter | Br | Degen U-87 | T | sunk |
| 6/15/42 | Cherokee | 5896 | liner | US | Berger U-87 | T | sunk |
| 6/17/42 36-52N/75-51W | Sanore | 7117 | freighter | US | Berger U-701 | M | sunk |
| 6/19/42 34-53N/75-31W | USS YP-389 | 165 | patrol craft | US | Degen U-701 | S | sunk |
| 6/22/42 39-15N/72-32W | Rio Tercero | 4864 | freighter | Arg | Degen U-202 | T | sunk |
| 6/24/42 34-30N/75-40W | Ljubica Matkovic | 3289 | freighter | Yug | Linder U-404 von Bulow | T | sunk |

| Position | Date | Ship | Type | Tons | Flag | Submarine / Commander | How* | Result |
|---|---|---|---|---|---|---|---|---|
| 38-45N/74-50W | | | | | | Loeser | | |
| 34-30N/75-40W | 6/24/42 | Manuela | freighter | 4772 | US | U-404 / von Bulow | T | sunk |
| 34-30N/75-40W | 6/24/42 | Nordal | freighter | 3845 | Pan | U-404 / von Bulow | T | sunk |
| 34-59N/75-41W | 6/25/42 | Tamesis | passenger/fr | 7256 | Nor | | N | attacked not sunk |
| 34-45N/75-22W | 6/27/42 | British Freedom | tanker | 6985 | Br | U-701 / Degen | T | attacked not sunk |
| 38-03N/70-52W | 6/27/42 | Moldanger | freighter | 6827 | Nor | U-404 / von Bulow | T | sunk |
| 35-07N/75-07W | 6/28/42 | Wm. Rockefeller | tanker | 14054 | US | U-701 / Degen | T | sunk |
| 35-10N/70-53W | 6/30/42 | City of Birmingham | liner | 5861 | US | U-202 / Linder | T | sunk |
| 41-48N/66-35W | 7/03/42 | Alexander Macomb | freighter | 7191 | US | U-215 / Hoeckner | T | sunk |
| 34-47N/75-22W | 7/15/42 | Chilore | freighter | 8310 | US | U-576 / Heinicke | T | sunk |
| 34-46N/75-42W | 7/15/42 | J.A. Mowinckel | tanker | 11147 | Pan | U-576 / Heinicke | T | sunk/ salvaged |
| 34-46N/75-22W | 7/15/42 | Bluefields | freighter | 2063 | Nic | U-576 / Heinicke | T | sunk |
| 40-32N/69-00W | 7/24/42 | USS Captor | Q-ship | 520 | US | | T | attacked not sunk |
| 42-02N/65-38W | 7/25/42 | Lucille M. | schooner | 54 | Can | U-89 / Lohmann | S | sunk |

*How Attacked:   T: torpedoed   S: shelled   M: mined   N: not caused by enemy action

## 1943–1945

| Date of Attack/ Position | Ship | Gross Registered Tonnage | Type of Ship | Nation- ality | U-Boat/ Commander | How Attacked* | Result |
|---|---|---|---|---|---|---|---|
| 5/05/43 34-11N/76-12W | Panam | 7277 | freighter | Pan | U-129 Witt | T | sunk |
| 6/10/43 31-02N/79-17W | Esso Gettysburg | 10173 | tanker | US | U-66 Markworth | T | sunk |
| 7/02/43 31-33N/78-57W | Bloody Marsh | 10195 | tanker | US | U-66 Markworth | TS | sunk |
| 8/05/43 36-17N/74-29W | Plymouth | 2265 | gunboat | US | U-566 Hornkohl | T | sunk |
| 12/04/43 34-12N/75-20W | Libertad | 5441 | freighter | Cub | U-129 von Harpe | T | sunk |
| 4/16/44 40-07N/69-24W | Pan Pennsylvania | 11017 | tanker | US | U-550 Hanert | T | sunk |
| 5/22/44 US East Coast | Bulkoil | | tanker | US | | T | attacked not sunk |
| 6/13/44 La Have Banks | Lark | 148 | trawler | US | | S | attacked not sunk |

| Date | Position | Ship | Tonnage | Type | Nationality | Submarine/Commander | How* | Result |
|---|---|---|---|---|---|---|---|---|
| 9/12/44 | 33-30N/75-40W | George Ade | 7176 | freighter | US | U-518 Offermann | T | attacked not sunk |
| 12/03/44 | 43-59N/68-20W | Cornwallis | 5458 | freighter | Can | U-1230 Hilbig | T | sunk |
| 4/05/45 | 42-07N/70-00W | Atlantic States | 8537 | tanker | US | U-857 Premauer | T | attacked not sunk |
| 4/14/45 | 36-09N/74-05W | Belgian Airman | 6959 | freighter | Bel | U-879 Manchen | T | sunk |
| 4/18/45 | 37-30N/73-03W | Swiftscout | 8300 | tanker | US | U-548 Krempl | T | sunk |
| 4/23/45 | Portland, Maine | Eagle 56 | 615 | A/S patrol | US | U-853 Fromsdorf | T | sunk |
| 4/23/45 | 35-56N/74-52W | Katy | 6825 | tanker | Nor | U-548 Krempl | T | attacked not sunk |
| 5/05/45 | 41-19N/71-23W | Black Point | 5353 | collier | US | U-853 Fromsdorf | T | sunk |

*How Attacked:   T: torpedoed   S: shelled   M: mined   N: not caused by enemy action

# APPENDIX 2

# U-Boat Successes (by submarine)

| U-Boat and Type/Captain | Ships Sunk |
| --- | --- |
| *U-66* (Type IX-C) Korvettenkapitan Richard Zapp | *Allan Jackson, Empire Gem, Lady Hawkins, Norvana, Venore* |
| *U-66* (Type IX-C) Kapitanleutnant Friedrich Markworth | *Bloody Marsh, Esso Gettysburg* |
| *U-71* (Type VII-C) Kapitanleutnant Walter Flachsenberg | *Dixie Arrow, Oakmar* |
| *U-84* (Type VII-B) Oberleutnant zur See Horst Uphoff | *Chenango* |
| *U-87* (Type VII-B) Kapitanleutnant Joachim Berger | *Cherokee, Port Nicholson* |
| *U-89* (Type VII-C) Kapitanleutnant Dietrich Lohmann | *Lucille M.* |
| *U-94* (Type VII-C) Oberleutnant zur See Otto Ites | *Cayru, Hvoslef* |
| *U-96* (Type VII-C) Kapitanleutnant Heinrich Lehmann-Willenbrock | *Lake Osweya* |
| *U-103* (Type IX-B) Kapitanleutnant Werner Winter | *China Arrow, India Arrow, San Gil, W.L. Steed* |
| *U-106* (Type IX-B) Oberleutnant zur See Herman Rasch | *Amerikaland, Rochester* |
| *U-108* (Type IX-B) Kapitanleutnant Klaus Scholtz | *Blink, Ocean Venture* |
| *U-109* (Type IX-B) Kapitanleutnant Heinrich Bleichrodt | *Tacoma Star* |
| *U-123* (Type VII-B) Kapitanleutnant Reinhard Hardegen | *Alcoa Guide, Carolyn (USS Atik), Ciltvaira, City of Atlanta, Coimbra, Esparta, Gulfamerica, Norness* |

# Appendix 2

| U-Boat and Type/Captain | Ships Sunk |
|---|---|
| *U-124* (Type IX-B)<br>Kapitanleutnant Johann Mohr | *Ceiba, E.M. Clark, Esso Nashville* (1/3), *Kassandra Louloudis, Naeco, Papoose, W.E. Hutton* |
| *U-129* (Type IX-C)<br>Kapitanleutnant Hans Witt | *Panam* |
| *U-129* (Type IX-C)<br>Kapitanleutnant Richard von Harpe | *Libertad* |
| *U-130* (Type IX-C)<br>Korvettenkapitan Ernst Kals | *Francis E. Powell, Olympic, Varanger* |
| *U-136* (Type VII-C)<br>Kapitanleutnant Heinrich Zimmerman | *Arundo, Empire Drum* |
| *U-155* (Type IX-C)<br>Kapitanleutnant Adolf Piening | *Arabutan* |
| *U-158* (Type IX-C)<br>Kapitanleutnant Erich Rostin | *Ario, Caribsea, John D. Gill* |
| *U-160* (Type IX-C)<br>Oberleutnant zur See Georg Lassen | *City of New York, Equipoise, Malchace, Rio Blanco, Ulysses* |
| *U-201* (Type VII-C)<br>Oberleutnant zur See Adalbert Schnee | *San Jacinto* |
| *U-202* (Type VII-C)<br>Kapitanleutnant Hans-Heinz Linder | *City of Birmingham, Rio Tercero* |
| *U-203* (Type VII-C)<br>Kapitanleutnant Rolf Mutzelberg | *Empire Thrush, San Delfino* |
| *U-215* (Type VII-D)<br>Kapitanleutnant Fritz Hoeckner | *Alexander Macomb* |
| *U-332* (Type VII-C)<br>Kapitanleutnant Johannes Liebe | *Australia, Liberator, Trepca* |
| *U-373* (Type VII-C)<br>Oberleutnant zur See Paul-Karl Loeser | *John R. Williams* |
| *U-402* (Type VII-C)<br>Kapitanleutnant Siegfried von Forstner | *Ashkhabad* |
| *U-404* (Type VII-C)<br>Kapitanleutnant Otto von Bulow | *Lemuel Burrows, Ljubica Matkovic, Manuela, Moldanger, Nordal, San Demetrio, Tolten, West Notus* |
| *U-432* (Type VII-C)<br>Kapitanleutnant Heinz-Otto Schultze | *Aeolus, Azalea City, Ben and Josephine, Buarque, Marore, Norlavore, Olinda* |

# TRACK OF THE GRAY WOLF

| U-Boat and Type/Captain | Ships Sunk |
|---|---|
| *U-548* (Type IX-C) Kapitanleutnant Erich Krempl | *Swiftscout* |
| *U-550* (Type IX-C) Kapitanleutnant Klaus Hanert | *Pan Pennsylvania* |
| *U-552* (Type VII-C) Oberleutnant zur See Erich Topp | *Atlas, British Splendour, Byron D. Benson, David H. Atwater, Lansing, Tamaulipas* |
| *U-558* (Type VII-C) Kapitanleutnant Gunther Krech | HMS *Bedfordshire* |
| *U-566* (Type VII-C) Oberleutnant zur See Hans Hornkohl | USS *Plymouth* |
| *U-572* (Type VII-C) Kapitanleutnant Heinz Hirsacker | *Desert Light* |
| *U-576* (Type VII-C) Kapitanleutnant Hans-Dieter Heinicke | *Bluefields, Chilore, Taborfjell* |
| *U-578* (Type VII-C) Korvettenkapitan Ernst-August Rehwinkel | *Berganger, R.P. Resor*, USS *Jacob Jones* |
| *U-588* (Type VII-C) Kapitanleutnant Viktor Vogel | *Gulftrade, Margot, Plow City, Skottland* |
| *U-593* (Type VII-C) Kapitanleutnant Gerd Kelbling | *Persephone* (1/3) |
| *U-701* (Type VII-C) Kapitanleutnant Horst Degen | *British Freedom*, HMS *Kingston Ceylonite, Santore*, USS *YP-389, Wm. Rockefeller* |
| *U-752* (Type VII-C) Oberleutnant zur See Karl-Ernst Schroeter | *Bidevind, West Imboden* |
| *U-754* (Type VII-C) Kapitanleutnant Johannes Oestermann | *Allegheny, Barnegat, Menominee, Otho, Tiger* |
| *U-853* (Type IX-C) Oberleutnant zur See Helmut Fromsdorf | *Black Point*, USS *Eagle 56* |
| *U-879* (Type IX-C) Kapitanleutnant Erwin Manchen | *Belgian Airman* |
| *U-1230* (Type IX-C) Kapitanleutnant Hans Hilbig | *Cornwallis* |
| Total: | 120 ships sunk |

# APPENDIX 3

## U-Boats Lost

| Date of Sinking/ Position | U-Boat/ Type | Commander | Sunk by |
|---|---|---|---|
| 4/14/42 35-55N/75-13W | U-85 VII-B | Oberleutnant zur See Greger | USS Roper, (DD-147) |
| 5/09/42 34-14N/76-35W | U-352 VII-C | Kapitanleutnant Rathke | USCGC Icarus, (WPC-110) |
| 7/03/42 41-48N/66-38W | U-215 VII-D | Kapitanleutnant Hockner | HMS Le Tigre, (armed yacht) |
| 7/07/42 34-50N/74-55W | U-701 VII-C | Kapitanleutnant Degen | US Army Bomber Squadron 396, Captain Kane |
| 7/15/42 34-51N/75-22W | U-576 VII-C | Kapitanleutnant Heinicke | Two US Navy planes, Ensigns Lewis & Webb; SS Unicoi |
| 6/02/43 37-43N/73-16W | U-521 IX-C | Kapitanleutnant Bargsten | PC-565 |
| 4/16/44 40-09N/69-44W | U-550 IX-C | Kapitanleutnant Hanert | USS Gandy, (DE-764); USS Joyce, (DE-317); USS Peterson, (DE-152) |
| 4/07/45 42-22N/69-46W | U-857 IX-C | Oberleutnant zur See Premauer | USS Gustafson, (DE-182) |
| 4/19/45 42-19N/61-45W | U-879 IX-C | Kapitanleutnant Manchen | USS Buckley, (DE-51); USS Reuben James, (DE-153) |

| Date of Sinking/ Position | U-Boat/ Type | Commander | Sunk by |
|---|---|---|---|
| 4/30/45 36-34N/74-00W | *U-548* IX-C | Kapitanleutnant Krempl | USS *Natchez*, (PF-2); USS *Coffman*, (DE-191); USS *Bostwick*, (DE-103); USS *Thomas*, (DE-102) |
| 5/06/45 41-13N/71-27W | *U-853* IX-C | Oberleutnant zur See Fromsdorf | USS *Atherton*, (DE-169); USS *Moberly*, (PF-63) |

# APPENDIX 4

# Tonnage Losses and Fatalities
## (In which there was either loss of vessel or loss of life)

| Ship | Tonnage | Survivors | Fatalities |
|---|---|---|---|
| **January** | | | |
| Norness | 9577 | 38 | 2 |
| Coimbra | 6768 | 6 | 36 |
| Allan Jackson | 6635 | 13 | 22 |
| Lady Hawkins | 7988 | 71 | 250 |
| City of Atlanta | 5269 | 3 | 44 |
| Malay | | 29 | 5 |
| Ciltvaira | 3779 | 30 | 2 |
| Norvana | 2677 | 0 | 29 |
| Olympic | 5335 | 0 | 31 |
| Empire Gem | 8139 | 2 | 55 |
| Venore | 8017 | 21 | 21 |
| Varanger | 9305 | 40 | 0 |
| Francis E. Powell | 7096 | 28 | 4 |
| Rochester | 6836 | 30 | 3 |
| Tacoma Star | 7924 | 0 | 92 |
| Total: | | | |
| 14 ships sunk | 95,345 | 311 | 596 |
| **February** | | | |
| W.L. Steed | 6182 | 4 | 34 |
| Amerikaland | 15355 | 34 | 5 |
| San Gil | 3598 | 39 | 2 |
| India Arrow | 8327 | 12 | 26 |
| China Arrow | 8404 | 37 | 0 |
| Ocean Venture | 7174 | 13 | 32 |
| Blink | 2701 | | 24 |
| Buarque | 5152 | 84 | 1 |
| Olinda | 4053 | 46 | 0 |
| Azalea City | 5976 | 0 | 39 |
| Lake Osweya | 2398 | 0 | 30 |
| Norlavore | 2713 | 0 | 28 |

# TRACK OF THE GRAY WOLF

| Ship | Tonnage | Survivors | Fatalities |
|------|---------|-----------|------------|
| | **February** | | |
| *Marore* | 8215 | 39 | 0 |
| *R.P. Resor* | 7451 | 2 | 48 |
| *Jacob Jones* | <u>1090</u> | <u>11</u> | <u>134</u> |
| Total: | | | |
| 15 ships sunk | 88,789 | 321 | 403 |
| | **March** | | |
| *Arabutan* | 7874 | 54 | 1 |
| *Cayru* | 5152 | 32 | 43 |
| *Gulftrade* | 6667 | 16 | 18 |
| *Hvoslef* | 1630 | 14 | 6 |
| *Caribsea* | 2609 | 7 | 21 |
| *John D. Gill* | 11641 | 26 | 31 |
| *Tolten* | 1858 | 1 | 27 |
| *Trepca* | 5042 | 34 | 4 |
| *Lemuel Burrows* | 7610 | 14 | 20 |
| *Ario* | 6952 | 28 | 8 |
| *Olean* | | 36 | 6 |
| *Australia* | 11628 | 37 | 4 |
| *Ceiba* | 1698 | 6 | 44 |
| *San Demetrio* | 8073 | 34 | 19 |
| *Acme* | | 20 | 11 |
| *Kassandra Louloudis* | 5106 | 35 | 0 |
| *E.M. Clark* | 9647 | 40 | 1 |
| *Papoose* | 5939 | 32 | 2 |
| *W.E. Hutton* | 7076 | 23 | 13 |
| *Liberator* | 7720 | 31 | 5 |
| *Oakmar* | 5766 | 30 | 6 |
| *Esso Nashville* | 7943 | 38 | 0 |
| *Naeco* | 5373 | 14 | 24 |
| *Dixie Arrow* | 8046 | 22 | 11 |
| *Atik (Carolyn)* | 3209 | 0 | 141 |
| *Equipoise* | 6210 | 13 | 40 |
| *City of New York* | 8272 | 100 | 24 |
| *Menominee* | 441 | 2 | 16 |
| *Allegheny* | 914 | 3 | 0 |
| *Barnegat* | <u>914</u> | <u>3</u> | <u>0</u> |
| Total: | | | |
| 28 ships sunk | 161,010 | 745 | 546 |

# Appendix 4

| Ship | Tonnage | Survivors | Fatalities |
|------|---------|-----------|------------|
| | **April** | | |
| *Rio Blanco* | 4086 | 21 | 19 |
| *Tiger* | 5992 | 41 | 1 |
| *Liebre* | | 25 | 9 |
| *David H. Atwater* | 2438 | 3 | 24 |
| *Otho* | 4839 | 16 | 37 |
| *Byron D. Benson* | 7953 | 28 | 9 |
| *Bidwell* | | 32 | 1 |
| *British Splendour* | 7138 | 41 | 12 |
| *Lansing* | 7866 | 49 | 1 |
| *Esso Baton Rouge* | | 36 | 3 |
| *Oklahoma* | | 18 | 19 |
| *Esparta* | 3366 | | |
| *Malchace* | 3516 | 28 | 1 |
| *Atlas* | 7137 | 32 | 2 |
| *San Delfino* | 8079 | 21 | 28 |
| *Tamaulipas* | 6943 | 35 | 2 |
| *Gulfamerica* | 8081 | 29 | 19 |
| *Harry F. Sinclair, Jr.* | | 26 | 10 |
| *Ulysses* | 14,647 | 290 | 0 |
| *Stanvac Melbourne* | | 45 | 3 |
| *Empire Thrush* | 6160 | 55 | 0 |
| *Margaret* | 3352 | 0 | 29 |
| *Desert Light* | 2368 | 30 | 1 |
| *Alcoa Guide* | 4834 | 27 | 6 |
| *Chenango* | 3014 | 1 | 32 |
| *West Imboden* | 5751 | 35 | 0 |
| *San Jacinto* | 6069 | 169 | 14 |
| *Reinholt* | | 33 | 1 |
| *Empire Drum* | 7244 | 41 | 0 |
| *Arundo* | 5163 | 37 | 6 |
| *Ashkhabad* | 5284 | 47 | 0 |
| *Taborfjell* | 1339 | 3 | 17 |
| *Bidevind* | <u>4956</u> | <u>36</u> | <u>0</u> |
| Total: | | | |
| 26 ships sunk | 147,615 | 1,369 | 307 |
| | **May** | | |
| *Bedfordshire* | 913 | 0 | 37 |
| *Skottland* | 4853 | 24 | 1 |
| *Plow City* | 3282 | 30 | 1 |
| *Margot* | 4545 | 39 | 1 |
| *Persephone* | <u>8426</u> | <u>28</u> | <u>9</u> |
| Total: | | | |
| 5 ships sunk | 22,019 | 121 | 49 |

# TRACK OF THE GRAY WOLF

| Ship | Tonnage | Survivors | Fatalities |
|---|---|---|---|
| **June** | | | |
| West Notus | 5492 | 36 | 4 |
| Berganger | 6826 | 43 | 4 |
| Ben and Josephine | 102 | 8 | 0 |
| Aeolus | 41 | 6 | 0 |
| Kronprinsen | | 39 | 1 |
| Robert C. Tuttle | | 46 | 1 |
| Kingston Ceylonite | 448 | 15 | 17 |
| Port Nicholson | 8402 | | 8 |
| Cherokee | 5896 | 83 | 86 |
| Santore | 7117 | 43 | 3 |
| YP-389 | 165 | 18 | 6 |
| Rio Tercero | 4864 | | 1 |
| Ljubica Matkovic | 3289 | 32 | 0 |
| John R. Williams | 396 | 4 | 14 |
| Manuela | 4772 | 38 | 3 |
| Nordal | 3845 | 31 | 0 |
| Moldanger | 6827 | 21 | 23 |
| Wm. Rockefeller | 14054 | 50 | 0 |
| City of Birmingham | 5861 | 372 | 9 |
| Total: | | | |
| 17 ships sunk | 78,397 | 885 | 180 |
| **July** | | | |
| Alexander Macomb | 7191 | 56 | 10 |
| Chilore | 8310 | 54 | 2 |
| J.A. Mowinckel | | 57 | 2 |
| Bluefields | 2063 | | 0 |
| Lucille M. | 54 | 11 | 0 |
| Total: | | | |
| 4 ships sunk | 17,618 | 178 | 14 |

# 1943–1945

| Ship | Tonnage | Survivors | Fatalities |
|---|---|---|---|
| Panam | 7277 | 49 | 2 |
| Esso Gettysburg | 10,173 | 15 | 57 |
| Bloody Marsh | 10,195 | 75 | 3 |
| Plymouth | 2265 | 92 | 91 |
| Libertad | 5441 | 18 | 25 |
| Pan Pennsylvania | 11,017 | 56 | 25 |
| Cornwallis | 5458 | 2 | 43 |
| Belgian Airman | 6959 | 46 | 1 |

| Ship | Tonnage | Survivors | Fatalities |
|---|---|---|---|
| *Swiftscout* | 8300 | 46 | 1 |
| *Eagle 56* | 615 | 13 | 54 |
| *Blackpoint* | 5353 | 34 | 12 |
| Total: | | | |
| 11 ships sunk | 73,053 | 446 | 314 |

| | Totals | | |
|---|---|---|---|
| January | 95,345 | 311 | 596 |
| February | 88,789 | 321 | 403 |
| March | 161,010 | 745 | 546 |
| April | 147,615 | 1,369 | 307 |
| May | 22,019 | 121 | 49 |
| June | 78,397 | 885 | 180 |
| July | 17,618 | 178 | 14 |
| Rest: | 73,053 | 446 | 314 |
| 120 ships sunk | 683,846 | 4,376 | 2,409 |

# APPENDIX 5

# Comparative Ranks

| German Navy | U.S. Navy |
| --- | --- |
| **Offiziere mit Patent** | **Commissioned Officers** |
| Grossadmiral | Commander in Chief, Admiral of the Fleet |
| Generaladmiral | Admiral, Commander of a Fleet |
| Admiral | Admiral |
| Vizeadmiral | Vice Admiral |
| Kapitan zur See | Captain |
| Kommodore | Commodore, Courtesy Title (senior captain) |
| Fregattenkapitan | Commander (junior captain) |
| Korvettenkapitan | Lieutenant Commander |
| Kapitanleutnant | Lieutenant (senior grade) |
| Oberleutnant zur See | Lieutenant (junior grade) |
| Oberleutnant (Ing.) | Lieutenant (junior grade) (Engineer) |
| Leutnant zur See | Ensign |
| **Offiziersnachwuchs** | **Officer Candidates** |
| Oberfahnrich zur See | Senior Midshipman |
| Fahnrich zur See | Midshipman |
| Fahnrich (Ing.) | Ensign (engineering duties only) |
| Seekadett | Naval Cadet |
| Matrose (Seeoffiziersanwarter) | Seaman (officer's apprentice) |
| **Offiziere ohne Patent** | **Noncommissioned Officers** |
| Obersteuermann | Quartermaster of Warrant rank |
| Obermaschinist | Warrant machinist |
| Oberbootsmann | Chief Petty Officer, Chief Boatswain's Mate |
| Bootsmann | Petty Officer, first class Boatswain's Mate, first class |
| Mechaniker | Artificer's Mate, first class Torpedoman's Mate, first class |
| Oberbootsmannsmaat | Petty Officer, second class, Boatswain's Mate, second class |
| Obermechanikersmaat | Artificer's Mate, second class Torpedoman's Mate, second class |
| Oberfunkmaat | Radioman, second class |

# Appendix 5

| German Navy | U.S. Navy |
| --- | --- |
| Bootsmannsmaat | Petty Officer, third class<br>    Coxswain |
| Maschinistenmaat | Fireman, first class |
| Mechanikersmaat | Artificer's Mate, third class<br>    Torpedoman's Mate, third class |
| Funkmaat | Radioman, third class |
| **Mannschaften** | **Enlisted Personnel** |
| Stabsmatrose,<br>    Matrosenobergefreiter,<br>    Mechanikerobergefreiter,<br>    Funkobergefreiter | Seaman, first class |
| Maschinenobergefreiter | Fireman, second class |
| Obermatrose,<br>    Matrosengefreiter,<br>    Mechanikergefreiter,<br>    Funkgefreiter | Seaman, second class |
| Maschinengefreiter | Fireman, third class |
| Matrose | Seaman, Recruit (apprentice) |

# INDEX

# Index

# TRACK OF THE GRAY WOLF

294

# Index

# Index